Labor and Industrial Relations

Labor and Industrial Relations

Terms, Laws,
Court Decisions,
and Arbitration Standards

Matthew A. Kelly

The Johns Hopkins University Press
Baltimore and London

The Johns Hopkins University Press
701 West 40th Street
Baltimore, Maryland 21211
The Johns Hopkins Press Ltd., London

∞ The paper used in this publication meets the minimum requirements
of American National Standard for Information Services — Permanence of
Paper for Printed Library Materials, ANSI Z39.48-1984.

Library of Congress Cataloging-in-Publication Data

Kelly, Matthew A., 1913–
Labor and industrial relations.

Includes index.
1. Labor laws and legislation — United States.   2. Collective labor
agreements — United States.   I. Title.
KF3319.K43   1987   344.73′0189   86-21353
347.304189
ISBN 0-8018-3310-8 (alk. paper)
ISBN 0-8018-3311-6 (pbk. : alk. paper)

Contents

Acknowledgments

In the preparation of this text I am indebted to the many colleagues and students with whom I have been associated over the years for their observations and comments; that association has ever been a learning experience for me. I am indebted, too, to my son Randall M. Kelly, Esq., for his help in the preparation of terms and analyses of labor relations law generally and the National Labor Relations Act in particular, and to my daughter, Deborah P. Kelly, Ph.D., who was especially helpful in the finalizing of those sections of the text which deal with court decisions and legislation governing the public regulation of wages, hours, and working conditions. I am also grateful to Professor Andrew R. Banks, Center for Labor Research and Studies, Florida International University; Professor Isadore Goldberg, University of the District of Columbia; Professor Emeritus Al Nash, former Director, Labor Studies, Credit and Certificate Program, New York State School of Industrial and Labor Relations, Cornell University; James McFadden, President and Executive Director, Manpower Education Institute, New York City; and Professor Roger Keeran, present Director, Labor Studies, Credit and Certificate Program, New York State School of Industrial and Labor Relations, Cornell University, all of whom read the manuscript and made many helpful suggestions. I am especially indebted to Persis, my wife, for her interest, understanding, and everlasting encouragement.

Introduction

The labor relations terms, laws, court decisions, and arbitration standards identified and summarized in this text have been selected with a twofold purpose in mind. Basically, as with all glossaries and dictionaries of industrial relations terms, a principal objective has been to provide a source book for labor-management practitioners as well as scholars. Of equal import, however, has been the desire to provide an instructional aid for the teaching of courses in labor and industrial relations. To this end, the definition or identification of each labor relations term, law, and court decision has, where possible, been expanded to include a brief description and analysis as well. Thus the text also points up the historical significance of certain terms in the annals of labor, and the legislative history of laws that have played a prominent role in the evolution of the public regulation of labor and industrial relations.

From my initial teaching of courses in "labor problems" and economics at Princeton University to my recent courses in collective bargaining, arbitration, and industrial dispute settlement at Cornell University's New York State School of Industrial and Labor Relations, and my work as Co-Director of the Cornell/Baruch MSILR Joint Graduate Degree Program, I have found it a helpful learning experience for students to "identify and define with examples wherever possible" the terms, laws, and court decisions that have special relevance to the subject matter being taught. In a sense, then, this text has been "decades in the making" for it embodies labor terms and laws assembled for teaching purposes in courses going back as far as the 1940s and 1950s and continuing to date. Even in the close to fifteen years I was away from university teaching, becoming instead a labor relations practitioner "at the bargaining table," I continued the practice of compiling industrial relations terms of special use and significance by labor and industry generally. It is my hope that the present compilation of these terms will prove as useful to others as it has been to me over the years as student, teacher, and practitioner.

The text is divided into three parts. Part I is a glossary of terms; Part II is a compendium of labor legislation; and Part III sets forth major court decisions and standards in arbitration. The glossary, which is arranged alphabetically, includes terms that have been selected for their importance to subject areas that are generally the principal focus of industrial relations courses such as collective bargaining, labor history, labor law, arbitration, and industrial dispute settlement. Thus, in addition to being a ready reference for labor lawyers and labor-management practitioners, Part I is of use to students and teachers in basic labor relations courses. In fact, the terms and analyses readily lend themselves to subject area groupings for use in the classroom. Care has been taken to ensure that the selection and analysis of labor relations terms is current, and such recent legal concepts and collective bargaining innovations as comparable worth, cafeteria-style benefits, double-breasting, employment at will, health care cost containment contract provisions, lump-sum wage payment provisions, and two-tier wage plans are included.

Part II, a compendium of labor legislation, is divided into two chapters: "Labor Relations Laws" and "Protective Labor Legislation." The section on labor relations laws summarizes and analyzes legislation and major court decisions affecting union status, collective bargaining, and labor dispute settlement in the private and public sectors. Included are analyses of the Conspiracy Doctrine, its application by the courts to prohibit the formation of labor organizations in the early 1800s, and the reversal of that decision in *Commonwealth v. Hunt,* 1842. Also covered is the legislation governing railway labor relations from the 1888 act to the 1926 Railway Labor Act, as amended, with analyses of major railway court decisions and such railway dispute settlement bodies as the National Mediation Board, the National Railroad Adjustment Board, the Special Adjustment Boards, and the Presidential Emergency Board. Included in this section as well are summaries and analyses of the following laws, along with pertinent court decisions pertaining to their application to labor unions: the 1890 Sherman Antitrust Act and the 1914 Clayton Antitrust Act; the Federal Anti-injunction Act (Norris-LaGuardia Act), 1932; Section 7(a) of the National Industrial Recovery Act (NIRA), 1933; the National Labor Relations Act (Wagner Act), 1935; the Labor-Management Relations Act (Taft-Hartley Act), 1947; and the Labor-Management Reporting and Disclosure Act (Landrum-Griffin Act),

1959. Attention is also given to the Postal Reorganization Act, 1970, and its provisions on the scope of bargaining and procedures for dealing with impasse; the 1974 amendments to the Labor-Management Relations Act, which set forth impasse procedures and define the status of the health care industry under the act; bankruptcy law as it affects the labor contract, with a summary of the Supreme Court's 1985 *Bildisco* decision. This section of Part II concludes with an overview of federal employee labor relations law under Executive Orders 10988 and 10987, 1962; Executive Order 11491, 1969; and the Civil Service Reform Act, Title VII, Federal Service Labor-Management Relations, 1978. Also analyzed are the federal agencies covered by Title VII, the scope of bargaining, the Federal Labor Relations Authority, unfair labor practices, impasse procedures, and the Federal Service Impasses Panel.

The section on protective labor legislation covers maximum hours, minimum wages, child and women's labor, workers' compensation, and social insurance. Hours laws are summarized from the early "shop hours" for federal employees in 1836 and President Van Buren's executive order establishing the 10-hour day in 1840, to subsequent 8-hour laws and adoption of the 40-hour week in the Walsh-Healy Public Contracts Act, 1936, and the Fair Labor Standards Act (Federal Wage-Hour Law), 1938. Pertinent court decisions are analyzed, including the 1985 decision in *Garcia v. San Antonio Metropolitan Transit Authority* extending coverage of the Fair Labor Standards Act to state employees. The overview of minimum-wage legislation includes the "prevailing wage" provisions of the Davis-Bacon Act of 1931 covering employees on Federal construction jobs, and the wage provisions of the codes of fair competition, NIRA, the Walsh-Healy Public Contracts Act, and the Fair Labor Standards Act. Also summarized in this section of Part II are the Welfare and Pension Disclosure Act, 1958; the Equal Pay Act, 1963; the Civil Rights Act, Title VII, Equal Employment Opportunity (EEO), 1964; the Occupational Safety and Health Act (OSHA), 1970; and the Employment Retirement Income Security Act (ERISA), 1974.

Part II will be of special interest to labor lawyers and labor-management practitioners who want a quick summary and reference to specific labor laws, their legislative history, and their place in the public regulation of labor. For students and teachers, this unit of the text is especially helpful as an overview of labor law and as an essential background for courses in labor relations, labor history, and collective bargaining.

Part III, on arbitration, summarizes the status of arbitration under federal law and the landmark court decisions that provide the legal basis for industrial jurisprudence and the role of arbitration in labor contract dispute settlement. Sections 201(b), 203(d), and 301 of the Labor-Management Relations Act are analyzed with respect to their provisions establishing arbitration as the preferred way of settling labor disputes. The landmark decisions of the United States Supreme Court enunciating the preeminence of arbitration in the resolution of labor disputes are reviewed and analyzed. These decisions include *Textile Workers Union v. Lincoln Mills,* 1957; *Boys Markets v. Retail Clerks,* 1970; and the *Steelworkers Trilogy,* 1960. The status of arbitration proceedings and awards and the deferral policy of the National Labor Relations Board are reviewed in an analysis of the *Spielberg Mfg. Co.* case, 1955, and the *Collyer Insulated Wire* case, 1971. Arbitration and the legal obligation of a union's duty of fair representation are reviewed in light of the Supreme Court's decisions in *Vaca v. Sipes,* 1967; *Hines v. Anchor Motor Freight, Inc.,* 1976; and *Bowen v. United States Postal Service,* 1983. Arbitration and employee rights under Title VII of the Equal Employment Opportunity Law, the Fair Labor Standards Act, and the Occupational Safety and Health Act are analyzed in a summary of the Supreme Court's decisions in *Alexander v. Gardner-Denver Co.,* 1974; *Barrentine v. Arkansas-Best Freight System, Inc.,* 1981; and *Marshall v. N. L. Industries, Inc.,* 1980. The bases for vacating arbitration awards are set forth in a summary of the United States Arbitration Act, 1947, and the United States Supreme Court's decisions in *Southland Corp. v. Keating,* 1984, and *United Steelworkers v. Enterprise Wheel & Car Corp.,* 1960.

Also included in Part III is an analysis of the standards or "tenets" of arbitration for both discipline and contract interpretation disputes. There are no absolute standards of decision-making in arbitration, for each dispute tends to be "a case unto itself." Over the years, however, certain tenets or standards have evolved in arbitration awards which are "more generally followed than not" and these are reviewed in this concluding section of the text. Part III will be of special interest to labor lawyers and labor-management practitioners who are involved in collective bargaining, contract administration, and labor arbitration, and to students and teachers in courses in arbitration and collective bargaining.

A bibliography follows Part III. It is not intended to be definitive or all-inclusive, but lists a select group of glossaries and dictionaries of labor and industrial relations terms as well as a few of the principal texts in labor relations, collective bargaining, labor law, and arbitration.

The book ends with an index of terms and an index of court decisions.

Notes on Usage

Type Styles

Within each entry of the glossary, alternative or closely related terms are set in **boldface** type; terms that appear as separate entries are set in SMALL CAPS or CAPS AND SMALL CAPS; and cross-references to other entries are given in SMALL CAPS or CAPS AND SMALL CAPS. In Parts II and III, some terms are set in **boldface** for emphasis. Throughout the text, the names of court cases, as well as words that are followed by their definition, are set in *italic* type.

Abbreviations

AAA	American Arbitration Association
AFL-CIO	American Federation of Labor and Congress of Industrial Organizations
BNA	Bureau of National Affairs, Inc.
COLA	Cost of Living Adjustment
CPI	Consumer Price Index
CWA	Communications Workers of America
DFR	Duty of Fair Representation
EEO	Equal Employment Opportunity Law
ERISA	Employee Retirement Income Security Act
FLRA	Federal Labor Relations Authority
FLRC	Federal Labor Relations Council
FLSA	Fair Labor Standards Act
FMCS	Federal Mediation and Conciliation Service
FOTLU	Federation of Organized Trade and Labor Unions of the United States and Canada
FSIP	Federal Service Impasses Panel

GAW	Guaranteed Annual Wage
GHI	Group Health Insurance
HIP	Health Insurance Plan (of Greater New York)
HMO	Health Maintenance Organization
ITU	International Typographical Union
LMRA	Labor-Management Relations Act
NLRA	National Labor Relations Act
NLRB	National Labor Relations Board
NRA	National Industrial Recovery Act
OSHA	Occupational Safety and Health Act
PBGC	Pension Benefit Guaranty Corporation
QWL	Quality of Work Life
SUB	Supplemental Unemployment Benefit
UAW	United Automobile, Aerospace, and Agricultural Implement Workers of America
USWA	United Steelworkers of America

PART I

Glossary of
Collective Bargaining and
Labor-Related Terms

Ad Hoc Arbitration   The arbitrator is selected by the parties for the particular case in dispute and may or may not be selected for succeeding cases. The vast amount of arbitration is done on an ad hoc basis.

Administrative Organizers   See LABOR ORGANIZER.

Advisory Arbitration   A procedures almost exclusively in the public sector. In fact, the term is incongruous to traditionalists and to labor and management generally in the private sector, where arbitration is intended and expected to provide finality in the settlement of a dispute. However, at the outset of collective bargaining in the public sector, when managerial rights were intertwined with the doctrine of the sovereignty of the state, there were many questions as to an arbitrator's legal authority to "bind the state." In any event, whenever public sector unions were unsuccessful in attaining "final and binding" arbitration at the bargaining table, they settled for advisory arbitration as "the next best thing to it." In advisory arbitration the parties are not bound by the ARBITRATOR'S AWARD, and this award is not enforceable in the courts. Use of advisory arbitration is currently on the decline, although it still persists, especially in certain sections of the country and predominantly in the negotiation of teacher contracts, in which boards of education insist on retaining final authority in adjudging whether an arbitrator's award is consistent with their policies.

Affidavit   A written statement made under oath usually, as presented in arbitration, before a notary public, although it can be made before an officer of the court. In an affidavit, the notary

3

public attests to the authenticity of the statement but not to its veracity, and its evidential worth is thus limited.

Afternoon Shift   See SHIFT DIFFERENTIALS.

Agency Plan   See AGENCY SHOP.

Agency Shop   A unionized shop in which nonunion employees in the bargaining unit are not required to join the union but must pay the union an "agency fee" traditionally equal to the union's regular fees and dues. Historically, such a contractual provision was often referred to as the **agency plan** and was adopted in the private sector when UNION SHOP proposals met strong employer resistance. The rationale for paying the union a service or representation fee was based on the fact that the law requires the union to represent all employees in the bargaining unit, and nonunion employees along with union members benefit from the terms and conditions of the labor agreement, including the processing of grievances through to arbitration. The agency shop is labor's protection against the **free rider**, a nonunion employee in the bargaining unit. In the construction industry, the Building Trades Union refers to a free rider as a **straight.**

An agency shop provision in which it is stipulated that the agency fee required of nonunion members be less than full union dues is often referred to as a **fair share agreement.** There has been much litigation over the years as to the legal status of the agency shop and, especially in the public sector, as to what constitutes a "fair share" of union dues to be paid to the union as a service or agency fee. In general, the United States Supreme Court has upheld the legality of agency shop provisions so long as the agency fees or service charges are used to finance expenditures by the union for collective bargaining, contract administration, and grievance handling, but not for such union expenditures as political action, death benefits for the families of deceased members of the union, and the like (see *Abood v. Detroit Board of Education* 431 U.S. 209 (1977)).

American Arbitration Association   A nongovernmental and nonprofit agency that promotes the peaceful and nonjudicial settlement of disputes by arbitration. Nationwide in its activities, its main office is in New York City and it has regional and branch offices throughout the country. The AAA maintains panels of impartial arbitrators for the use of the parties in each of its offices and appoints arbitrators in given disputes upon request. The parties often conduct their hearings in rooms made available by the AAA at a modest service fee. While the service of labor arbitration has been the AAA's primary focus over the years, it is by no means its sole activity. Commercial arbitrations, for example, in the AAA's large New York City offices frequently exceed labor arbitrations in number.

American Federation of Labor and Congress of Industrial Organizations (AFL–CIO)   The **American Federation of Labor (AFL),** an association of autonomous national and international unions, merged with the **Congress of Industrial Organizations (CIO)** in 1955 and is now known as the **AFL–CIO.** The CIO was initially formed in 1935 as the AFL's **Committee for Industrial Organization** for the primary purpose of organizing employees in the mass production industries. The unions were structured as industrial organizations as distinct from craft organizations. In 1937 the industrial unions formed by the Committee of Industrial Organizations were expelled from the AFL. Under the leadership of John L. Lewis, then president of the United Mine Workers national union, the Committee of Industrial Organizations formed an independent federation and changed its name to Congress of Industrial Organizations. The AFL–CIO, as merged in 1955, is largely a federation of craft and industrial unions. It is not a primary labor organization; workers generally belong not to it but, rather to local and national or international unions that are affiliated with the federation. The AFL–CIO does not negotiate collective bargaining agreements and is not directly a bargaining agent of any designated group of employees. It promotes the interests of organized labor and, in particular, the interests of the autonomous local, national, and international unions that are associated with it.

Annual Bonus or Lump-Sum Wage Payments   Lump-sum wage or annual bonus payments were negotiated by the auto industry in 1984 as a replacement for their annual 3% productivity improvement factor increase. As noted with the adoption of the TWO-TIER WAGE PLANS, the lump-sum wage or annual bonus payment represents an innovative effort on management's part to keep what is deemed to be an already high level of wage scale from escalating. The bonus, which is paid in a lump sum, is not factored into the base contract hourly rate. In this sense, the annual bonus payment is modeled after the auto industry's cost-of-living adjustments, which also are made in a lump sum and do not automatically affect the base contract hourly rate but need to be "negotiated in." The lump-sum wage or annual bonus payment is generally based on an employee's overall earnings. This is an additional advantage to management because it provides a built-in incentive for workers to hold down their absenteeism rate. Although lump-sum wage or annual bonus payments are not a substitute for, or a necessary alternative to, two-tier wage plans, many employers view the need to reduce absenteeism as paramount in their preference for the former. A further advantage of the lump-sum wage or annual bonus payment is that it avoids costly roll-up in employee benefits.

Apprentice   An employee who is a beginner and is taught a skilled trade or craft usually in a prescribed on-the-job training program for a designated period of time and often supplemented with classroom and "book" instruction. Apprenticeship training ranges from two years for operating engineers to from four to six years for linotype operators, compositors, printing pressmen, and tool- and die-makers. In the case of a union which has an **apprenticeship contract** establishing the length and type of training, including compensation (usually at varying percentages of the journeyman's rate at progressive stages of the training), the training is called an **indentured apprenticeship.** Often apprentice training program are state assisted and supervised. In contract negotiations with craft unions, employers have traditionally focused hard bargaining on such apprenticeship matters as the ratio of apprentices of journeymen, the nature and extent of training, the rates of pay for apprentices, and the like.

Apprenticeship Contract   See APPRENTICE.

Arbitrability   The state of being subject to arbitration. The questions raised, and disputes arising, over whether a particular matter is arbitrable are basically of two types; namely, (1) whether the issue in dispute falls within the scope of arbitration as provided in the contract, and (2) whether the matter at issue is timely and/or has been properly processed. When a question of arbitrability is raised before an arbitrator at an arbitration hearing, arguments as to arbitrability are heard, and then usually, but not always, the substantive issue in dispute is argued and heard without prejudice, the understanding being that if the arbitrator rules the matter is not arbitrable, the grievance is denied and the arbitrator does not adjudge and rule on the merits. It is for this reason that the question of arbitrability is generally referred to as the **threshold issue.**

Arbitration   A dispute resolution procedure in which an impartial person, generally called the **arbitrator,** adjudges the merits of a dispute and renders a decision which the parties have agreed to accept as binding. In some industries — for example, the railroads and airlines — arbitrators are frequently called **neutral referees;** in certain other industries they are referred to as umpires; and in still others they are known as **impartial chairmen**; in the last two instances they are said to hold an **umpireship** or **impartial chairmanship**. There are basically two major categories of labor arbitration: (1) that which covers labor-management disputes arising under a given contract, referred to as RIGHTS ARBITRATION; and (2) that which arises at impasse in the negotiation of the terms of a new contract, called INTEREST ARBITRATION.

Arbitration Panel List   A list of qualified arbitrators usually maintained by a governmental or impartial body such as the Federal Mediation and Conciliation Service (FMCS), the American Arbitration Association (AAA), or a state mediation board or public employment relations board for the use of the parties. In the event labor and management are unable to agree on the selection of an arbitrator from the panel lists forwarded to them, the FMCS, AAA, or other appropriate agency designates an arbitrator from among those who were not rejected by either party.

Arbitrator   See ARBITRATION.

Arbitrator's Award   This is the arbitrator's decision, and unless specifically stated otherwise, it is final and binding on the parties. The status of arbitration under the law, the arbitrator's authority, and the scope of judicial review of the arbitrator's award has been set forth for the private sector, at least, in several landmark court decisions. Foremost of these is the *Steelworkers Trilogy,* a trio of Supreme Court decisions in 1960 involving the United Steelworkers of America and arbitrations with American Manufacturing Company, Warrior and Gulf Navigation Company, and Enterprise Wheel and Car Corporation. The Supreme Court has held in the *Trilogy* and elsewhere that if a claim on its face is governed by the contract, it must be arbitrated, and that the court should not inquire into the merits of a dispute, and may not review a case on its merits, "under the guise of interpreting the agreement which is the exclusive function of the arbitrator." Doubts as to the scope of arbitration, as ruled by the Supreme Court, should be resolved in favor of coverage; all labor-management disputes should go to arbitration unless expressly excluded; and rulings on whether or not a question is arbitrable are to be left to the courts, although the parties may, and often do, refer them to the arbitrator. The Court held, further, that it should enforce an arbitrator's award so long as it draws its essence from the contract and the arbitrator has not exceeded his authority or "dispensed his own brand of industrial justice." The arbitrator, too, must address the evidential material presented and may not be discriminatory or in collusion with either party. Noted exceptions to the Supreme Court's rulings on the finality of the arbitrator's award in the private sector have been made in DUTY OF FAIR REPRESENTATION cases (see *Hines v. Anchor Motor Freight, Inc.* (1976) and *Vaca et al. v. Sipes* (1967) and discrimination cases under Title VII of the Civil Rights Act of 1964 as amended in 1972 and 1978 (see *Alexander v. Gardner Denver Co.* (1974)).

Arbitrator's Fee   The arbitrator's fee is generally set at a per diem rate and is made known to the parties prior to selection. Usually an arbitrator has an established per diem and does not vary it case by case, although special fee arrangements are often made for umpireships and impartial chairmanships as distinct from ad hoc cases. The arbitrator's total fee — per diem for hearing day(s), per diem for study and preparation of OPINION AND AWARD, and expenses — is customarily shared equally by the parties, although some labor contracts provide that the losing party pays the arbitrator's fee. "Loser pay" provisions were somewhat prevalent in the early years of labor arbitration. Experience has shown, however, that there is not always a "winner" and a "loser" in an arbitration award, and this has made it difficult to assess which party is to pay the arbitrator's fee under such provisions. Currently, it is a rare exception when the labor contract does not provide for an equal sharing of the arbitrator's fee. Expenses for counsel and advocates, of course, are paid individually by the parties.

Arbitrator's Oath   An oath taken by an arbitrator upon acceptance of appointment pledging to faithfully and fairly hear, examine, and adjudge the matter at issue. The arbitrator's oath is not required in most states, but even when it is, the parties may waive the requirement and usually do so. It is the obligation of the arbitrator to disclose pertinent relationships with either party whether or not the oath is taken.

Area-Wide Bargaining   Bargaining in which MULTIEMPLOYER BARGAINING covers all, or a predominant number, of an industry's employers in a locality or area.

Arsenal of Weapons   The variety of strike controls or preventives that may be invoked at impasse. The arsenal-of-weapons approach is sometimes called the **choice-of-procedures** approach, and in national emergency strikes it would empower the President to choose the type of approach to be followed in each dispute. In addition to the standard impasse procedures of MEDIATION, FACT-FINDING, and VOLUNTARY ARBITRATION, the arsenal of weapons available for use by the President include, among others, a "hands off" or "do nothing" approach, INJUNCTION, plant (governmental) seizure, COMPULSORY ARBITRATION, and STATUTORY STRIKE.

Assignability Clause   See SUCCESSOR CLAUSE.

Assimilated Craft Union   See CRAFT UNION.

Association Bargaining   See MULTIEMPLOYER BARGAINING.

Attitudinal Structuring   In negotiations, following procedures that are designed to change attitudes and to structure or conduce a greater receptivity of one's proposals by those on the other side of the bargaining table. While the primary focus of attitudinal structuring in labor negotiations is on one's current contract goals, it is often utilized to further the goals of future contracts as well, the view being that if one persists long enough, the desired change will in time be held to be inevitable. See also DISTRIBUTIVE BARGAINING, INTEGRATIVE BARGAINING, and INTRAORGANIZATIONAL BARGAINING.

Automatic Contract Renewal Clause   The duration provision of a labor contract which stipulates that in the event neither party serves notice at the specified time prior to the contract's termination of intent to modify, amend, or change its terms, the contract shall be extended and automatically renewed for one year, after which clause will once again become operative. Sometimes referred to as the **self-perpetuating provision.**

Automation   Mechanization in which the substitution of machines for manual labor is carried to the point of being in large part self-regulating; is accompanied by **feedback,** performing to set, requirements; predetermined and is a continuous process, integrating separate elements of production. Automation has been especially widespread in recent decades, occasioning extensive displacement of workers in certain production, clerical, and electronic fields. Examples of the several types of automation in industry are the assembly line in the automobile industry; the computerization of typesetting in the printing and newspaper industry and of many office and business operations; and the use of complex electronic processing equipment and controls in the manufacturing, refining, and public utilities industries. The most sophisticated automotive approaches currently entail the use of robots in one or more phases of production.

Back-Loaded Contract   A multiyear contract in which the larger wage increases and/or improvements in employee benefits are in the last or later years of the contract: for example, a 3-year contract with a 3% wage increase in the first year, a 4% increase in the second year, and a 5% increase in the third year.

Back-to-Work Movement   An action in which strikers return to work before the strike's end and without the union approval.

Bargaining a Benefit   Bargaining to obtain a specific benefit for employees — for example, Blue Cross, Blue Shield, Major Medical, a $100-a-month pension for eligible retirees, and the like. The employer is obligated to provide the benefit, whatever the cost increments might be over the life of the contract; in inflationary times, such a benefit could prove to be considerable in a multiyear contract of two or three years duration. Sometimes called a **defined benefit plan.**

Bargaining a Cost   Bargaining for a sum to provide employee benefits such as Blue Cross, Blue Shield, and the like. Usually the amount negotiated for providing the employee benefit is stated in cents per hour or dollars per shift worked, although sometimes, especially in public employee contracts, it is stated in terms of a percentage of salary earned or given as a lump-sum annual payment. Whatever the method used, the cost of the benefit is fixed for the employer for the duration of the contract and, hence, if carrier charges and costs rise, the nature of the benefit may have to be varied and trimmed, or employees may have to contribute. Sometimes called a **defined contribution plan.**

Bargaining Agent   The union or association of employees recognized or designated as the exclusive representative of employees in a bargaining unit. The bargaining agent is obligated by law to represent all employees, both union members and nonunion workers, in the bargaining unit. The union may be voluntarily recognized by an employer as the bargaining agent or it may be designated (certified) in a **representation election** conducted by the NLRB or by the appropriate state or public sector agency.

Bargaining in Good Faith   The National Labor Relations Act, Section 8 (d), requires that bargaining be carried on in "good faith." In the determination of the NLRB and the courts, "good faith" bargaining has frequently been defined in a negative fashion as, for example, "not bargaining in bad faith" or "the failure of either party to fulfill its bargaining obligations." Failing to meet at reasonable and convenient times; failing to meet with minds open to persuasion and a view toward reaching agreement; "surface" bargaining with repeated withdrawal of previous concessions; taking actions deliberately designed to weaken the union's status as the bargaining representative; and presenting proposals on a "take it or leave it" basis—all are examples of bad faith bargaining or, rather, lack of good faith bargaining.

Bargaining Pattern   The settlement reached in the initial, lead, or key bargaining unit, plant, or industry. When used in reference to a bargaining pattern in an area or industry, it is usually defined in terms of a wage or "package" settlement, as, for example, a 5% wage pattern or a 6% "package."

Bargaining Ploy   A tactic or strategem of bargaining in which a party's strong position for, or in opposition to, a particular proposal is a negotiating artifice or trick designed to hide its true position. As practiced most frequently, a party's proposal that is not a high-priority item but is known to be particularly distasteful to the other side is strongly argued for with the design that later when the "time is right" it will be "traded off." Generally, the trade-off is for a less strongly urged but high-priority proposal of one's own or, as an alternative, such a proposal will be "dropped" in a trade-off that gets "off the table" a proposal of the other party that is viewed as being especially onerous.

Bargaining Structure   *Bargaining structure* is a term used by analysts of the collective bargaining process when describing the way in which the parties are organized to bargain with one another. It is an economic, not a legal, term and is to be differentiated from the BARGAINING UNIT, which merely records the legal party of record to the bargaining. The nature of the bargaining unit is a vital consideration in any analysis of the structure of bargaining, but it is only one of many considerations, such as how the parties are organized to bargain with one another, "who bargains with whom," where the locus of power and decision-making is, and the like. In earlier years, economists often called such analyses of collective bargaining **patterns of bargaining** and **bargaining systems.**

Bargaining Systems   See BARGAINING STRUCTURE.

Bargaining Unit   The group of employees in jobs constituting the appropriate unit for representation by a union. In a sense, the employees in the bargaining unit are the electorate that determines which representative is to be chosen for collective bargaining. Historically, prior to the NLRA and the majority rule in determining the bargaining agent, the unit for collective bargaining was whatever the union was able to make it by exerting economic pressure on the employer. As provided by law, the bargaining unit is "the employer unit, craft unit, plant unit, or subdivision thereof," and essentially it consists of those employees who share a "community of interest." The employee bargaining unit embraces all employees, whether or not they are members of the union, and is basically of two types, namely, craft and industrial. The bargaining unit is separate and distinct from the union, and it is incorrect to refer to the union as the bargaining unit.

Base Contract Hourly Rate   Also called **contract rate,** the **scale,** and **straight-time rate,** this is the basic wage stipulated in a contract for specified jobs or classifications of work and is generally given in hourly terms; hence, the base contract hourly rate. In craft union contracts the base contract hourly rate is a minimum rate and it is a violation of the contract for the employer to pay less. In industrial union contracts the base contract hourly rate is generally both a minimum and a maximum rate; it is as much a violation of the contract for the employer to pay above the stipulated contract rate as it is to pay less.

Base Contract Hours   The hours stipulated by contract as constituting the basic or normal hours of work beyond which overtime rates are to be paid. Base contract hours are often called **straight-time hours** and are generally given per day and/or per week as an 8-hour **basic workday** and a 40-hour **basic workweek.** Also, and especially in cases where there is no labor contract, these increments of time are called the **normal workday** and **normal workweek,** or the **standard workday** and **standard workweek.**

Basic Hours   See BASE CONTRACT HOURS.

Basic Workday   See BASE CONTRACT HOURS.

Basic Workweek   See BASE CONTRACT HOURS.

Bench Decision   An oral decision requested of the arbitrator at the close of the hearing by the parties to a dispute. This is frequently done in EXPEDITED ARBITRATION, and the arbitrator is advised of the procedure beforehand.

Benevolent and Fraternal Societies   See LABOR ORGANIZATION.

Best-Evidence Rule   A rule of evidence usually applied in ruling on the most persuasive or best evidence made available as proof of the existence of a written document. Arbitrators generally follow this rule in requiring that the original document be produced unless unavailable for some valid reason.

Blacklist   An employer list of "troublesome" workers. Historically, the list was largely made up of allegedly militant union members, was circulated among employers, and workers on the list were not hired in new jobs or were fired if employed. The preparation and use of a blacklist by employers was made an unfair labor practice in 1935 under the Wagner Act (NLRA).

Blue-Collar Worker   See PRODUCTION WORKER.

Blue Flu   A job action by patrolmen and employees of law enforcement agencies who call in sick in large numbers to pressure the employer for concessions.

Board of Arbitration   A group of arbitrators (as opposed to a sole arbitrator) before whom arbitration is conducted. Usually the board of arbitration consists of three members, but occasionally it is larger. Where boards of arbitration are designated by statute, they are often composed of public or impartial members only. However, when boards of arbitration rather than sole arbitrators are provided for in a collective bargaining agreement, they are generally, **tripartite boards of arbitration;** namely, there is an employer designee, a union designee, and an impartial chairman chosen by both. Industries such as utilities, airlines, and railroads, which are complex and whose practices and operations differ from those usually encountered in manufacturing, tend to prefer tripartite boards of arbitration to arbitration before a sole arbitrator. Under the Railway Labor Act, the tripartite boards of arbitration in the airlines and railroad industries are called **system boards of adjustment.** Even-numbered **joint boards of arbitration** are composed solely of union and management representatives and are not utilized widely today except in the construction industry and in certain teamster contracts. Historically, however, most arbitration under the pre-1900 collective bargaining agreements was before a contract-named, even-numbered joint board of arbitration.

Bonus Pay Systems   Incentive pay systems that combine time payments and payments by output in myriad ways, such as extra pay for exceeding a given standard of level of daily output, or bonuses for completing a job in less than a specified standard time, or graduated increases in base pay in accordance with output or performance in excess of standard, and the like.

Boulwareism   The name given to an employer bargaining tactic formulated by Lemuel Boulware, a vice-president of the General Electric Company. As practiced by General Electric and other large corporations in the 1960s, it was a "hard nosed" type of bargaining that virtually ignored the union. The employer's offer was the result of extensive research and was supposed to be what the employees needed and wanted, with no room for "starting low and bargaining up." Thus, in effect, the employer's "first offer" at the bargaining table was its "whole and final offer," and hence it was often called "take it or leave it" bargaining. Its acceptance was promoted not through the union but directly by management to the employees as "meeting their needs" and being "in their best interest." Further, the employer would not agree to modify or change the terms of its offer unless the union could show that the facts and statistics on which the offer was based were in error. In 1969 the courts sustained the NLRB's determination that this type of bargaining was an unfair labor practice since it constituted a refusal to bargain in good faith.

Boycott   A concerted refusal by workers and their union to deal with an employer with whom they have a dispute. Also called a **simple boycott.** Pressure put on consumers not to buy the goods of an employer with whom the union has a dispute is called a **primary boycott.**

Broken Time   See SPLIT SHIFT.

Business Agent   Also referred to as the **business representative, business delegate, walking delegate,** and **business manager,** although the last term is generally reserved for the chief executive officer of a union. Business agents are local union representatives who are engaged fulltime in contract negotiations with employers and in contract administration or grievance handling, usually after the first step of the grievance procedure. The early craft unions sent out **trampers** to check on shops to enforce the wage scale negotiated by the union. Journeymen **tramping committees** were unpaid union representatives and were the forerunners of the paid union walking delegates and business agents.

Business Delegate   See BUSINESS AGENT.

Business Manager   See BUSINESS AGENT.

Business Representative   See BUSINESS AGENT.

Buttoning-Up Clause   See ZIPPER CLAUSE.

Call-Back Pay Provision   A contractual provision which requires that premium pay be provided to employees who have left the plant at the end of their shift and are called back to work. The amount paid is called **call-back pay** or **call-in pay.**

Cafeteria-Style Benefits   See FRINGE BENEFITS.

Call-In Pay   See CALL-BACK PAY PROVISION.

Call Pay   See REPORTING PAY.

Cause   See JUST CAUSE.

Central Hiring Hall   See HIRING HALL.

Certification   The designation of a union as exclusive representative or bargaining agent of a given unit or group of employees. Certification is made by the NLRB or appropriate state or public sector agency and the union so certified is the majority choice of the workers in a secret-ballot **representation election.** When two or more unions compete for the right of representation, only one of the unions can be legally certified as the exclusive representative. In return for this exclusive right, the union must represent every employee in the bargaining unit whether or not they are union members. Certification protects the union against rival unions for one year and requires the employer to bargain.

Chairman   See CHAPEL CHAIRMAN; SHOP COMMITTEE; SHOP STEWARD.

Chapel   See CHAPEL CHAIRMAN.

Chapel Chairman   A union steward in a print shop or newspaper plant. Printers were among the earliest crafts to unionize, and virtually from the outset the local union members employed in the plant were known as a **chapel.** To this day, the terms are used by the International Typographical Union, and the members of the chapel in a shop elect the chapel chairman.

Chartered Local   A local union chartered by a national or an international union granting it jurisdiction within a craft, industry, or geographical area.

Checkoff   A clause in the labor contract providing for the deduction of union dues, fees, or assessments from the pay of a union member. The monies deducted are turned over to the union by the employer. Historically there were two types of checkoff: **automatic checkoff,** also called **compulsory checkoff,** referred to the deduction of union dues, fees, or assessments in instances when under the terms of the collective bargaining agreement it was not necessary to secure the authorization of the individual employee to do so; **voluntary checkoff** was used when the employees voluntarily authorized the employer in writing to make the deductions. Since the enactment of the Taft-Hartley Act in 1947, all checkoff provisions have been of the voluntary type because the Act requires written permission by the individual employee for the sums to be deducted.

Chief Steward   See SHOP COMMITTEE; SHOP STEWARD.

Circumstantial Evidence   Indirect evidence based on appearances. For example, an employee is charged with violating the no-smoking rule because he was the only one who had been in the tool room and the foreman found cigar butts and the room filled with smoke after the employee returned to his machine.

Classification Rate   Categorization of wage rates by job classification. Often done by group classification of categories of related jobs or jobs requiring essentially the same level of responsibility and skill, ranging from the unskilled category of laborers, cleaners, sweep-up, and the like, to the most skilled groups of journeyman and unit leadmen, working foremen, and so on.

Clear and Convincing Proof   See QUANTUM OF PROOF.

Closed Items   Those contract clauses in any given negotiations in which neither party proposes a change. Presumably, and this is usually the case, the parties are in agreement that these provisions be carried forward in the new contract "as is" except for changes in pagination, section numbering, and dates resulting from agreements reached on OPEN ITEMS.

Closed Shop   A unionized shop in which it is stipulated that the employer may hire only union members and retain only union members. The closed shop is now unlawful under the Taft-Hartley Act.

Closed Union   See HIRING HALL.

Close-Ended Contract   A labor contract with a beginning and a termination date. In the interest of stability in the labor-management relationship and a definitive contract term, unions and companies in the United States generally negotiate and agree upon close-ended labor contracts, the major exception being the railroads. In England and some other European countries, however, labor contracts are often open-ended, having no termination date.

Closing Statement   See SUMMATION.

Coalition Bargaining   See COORDINATED BARGAINING.

COLA Adjustment Period   The contractual period at which cost-of-living adjustments are made. Ideally, if the employee's real wage is to be fully protected, COLA adjustments need to be made monthly, if not weekly. But because of the administrative difficulties involved and the costs to employers of such frequent adjustments, and because Consumer Price Index (CPI) figures are released quarterly, COLA adjustments are made quarterly (at the earliest), semiannually, or annually.

COLA Cap   A "ceiling" or "cutoff" placed on the amount of cost-of-living increases that can be provided. For example, COLA increases may not exceed ten cents per hour, or may not exceed 5% of total pay, in the life of the contract, even though the actual increase in the cost of living has exceeded this level.

COLA Corridor   A "floor" or "pass through" for increases in the cost of living that limits when the COLA provision becomes operative. For example, COLA increases are not to be made until the cost of living as measured from the start of the contract has risen 5% or until the CPI exceeds a given point figure.

COLA Formula   The formula used to adjust wages to changes in the cost of living. The simplest, and the most costly to employers, is the percentage formula in which base contract wages are increased by the same percentage as the increase in the cost of living. The most commonly used formula, however, provides a one-cent per-hour increase in the base contract hourly rate per stipulated point change in the cost-of-living index.

"Cold" Strike   The term used to refer to situations in which the union, in anticipation of an employer turn-down of its demands, uses public pressure and the media to publicize the reasonableness of its position and to pressure the employer into a settlement. In such situations, the union often pickets the plant as well, but it is strictly an informational picket publicizing the nature of the controversy; there is no work stoppage, and no attempt is made to prevent persons or materials from entering the establishment.

Collective Bargaining   The process by which labor and management establish wages, hours, and working conditions at the workplace. The legal definition of *collective bargaining* as set forth in the Taft-Hartley Act (Labor-Management Relations Act, 1947, as amended), Section 8(d), is as follows: "[T]o bargain collectively is the performance of the mutual obligation of the employer and the representative of the employees to meet at reasonable times and confer in good faith with respect to wages, hours, and other terms and conditions of employment . . . the negotiation of an agreement or any question arising thereunder, and the execution of a written contract incorporating any agreement reached if requested by either party . . . such obligation does not compel either party to agree to a proposal or require the making of a concession." Collective bargaining is also called **contract negotiations, labor negotiations,** and **collective negotiations,** although the last term is reserved by some to characterize public sector negotiations in which the right to pressure a settlement on wages, hours, and working conditions by the threat or use of strike is largely not legally available.

Collective Bargaining Agreement   The written terms of the agreement of labor and management on wages, hours, and working conditions. Also called **labor agreement** and **labor contract,** the collective bargaining agreement need not be in writing to be legally enforceable, but in virtually all instances labor and management customarily record the terms of their agreement in a written document.

Collective Negotiations   See COLLECTIVE BARGAINING.

Committee for Industrial Organizations   See AMERICAN FEDERATION OF LABOR AND CONGRESS OF INDUSTRIAL ORGANIZATIONS.

Common Laborer   See UNSKILLED WORKER.

Common Situs Picketing   Picketing that is conducted where two or more employers share a common work site but only one of the employers is involved in the labor dispute. This is a frequent situation in the construction industry. The picketing is restricted to the entrance used by the employees of the struck employer, called the **reserve gate,** in order to leave free the entrance(s) used by the employees of the neutral employer(s) and avoid a secondary boycott.

Company Exhibits and Union Exhibits   Exhibits that support the position of the company or the union. They are generally placed into evidence through witnesses during the arbitration hearing.

Company Store   A retail store owned by a company whose principal business is manufacturing or other than retailing. The store is operated for the use of the company's employees and their families. Historically, the company store was generally the only store in a COMPANY TOWN.

Company Town   A community whose inhabitants are employees of the company owning all or substantially all of the community's housing. Historically, workers in mines and steel and textile mills were often required to live in company towns.

Company Union   Historically, the term *company union* invariably meant a labor organization that had been formed, financed, or dominated by the company employing its members. Since the prohibition of the company-dominated union by law, the term has also been used to describe a union that is not affiliated with the AFL–CIO or any other federation, or with any national or international union, that consists solely of employees who work for a single company. Unaffiliated unions whose members are employed by one or several employers in one or more industries are also called **independent unions.** Rank-and-file union members often use the term *company union* broadly and derogatorily to describe any local union administration that appears to support management's needs over and against the workers' needs.

Company-wide Bargaining   See MULTIPLANT BARGAINING.

Comparable Worth   A pay concept and form of job evaluation that seeks to relate and equalize pay for workers whose jobs require a similar degree of training, skills, and responsibility. The concept of comparable worth goes beyond the "fairness" and "equity" standard of "equal pay for equal work" in which the traditional focus in the measurement and comparison of pay and job has been largely confined to the same or related job families. Assessing pay and job comparability is not an easy task. Clearly, there is no single, sure, scientific method, since there are many variables that are intangible, defy precise measurement, and entail much value judgment in assessment. Nonetheless, comparable worth has proven to be of more than academic interest, and several state and local governments have taken positive steps to ascertain comparable worth in public employment jobs. Acceptance of the concept of comparable worth inevitably results in the acceptance of a new standard and definition of pay discrimination. As such, comparable worth has become especially prominent recently in considerations of pay discrimination against women. It is argued that the pay of women relative to men would be more equitable if the comparable worth of jobs that are predominantly women's occupations — for example, secretaries and cleaning women — were measured against that of predominantly men's occupations — for example, truck drivers and janitors. Debates over the applicability of the concept of comparable worth have reached the political arena, and opponents have criticized the concept as being wholly impractical and unworkable: "a truly crazy idea . . . an idea whose time has passed . . . a medieval concept of the just price and the just wage." Such views may impede the enactment of legislation promoting comparable-worth pay standards in the private sector. However, while few federal courts presently recognize, let alone accept, the principle of comparable worth, it would appear that the courts in the future will need to pay increasing attention to the concept in litigations arising under the Equal Pay Act and Title VII (Equal Employment Opportunity) of the Civil Rights Act. Considerations of the DUTY OF FAIR REPRESENTATION and pressures from their female members may well prompt unions in both the public and private sectors to promote more overtly and forcibly the concept of comparable worth in wage bargaining.

Compulsory Arbitration   Negotiations in which the parties are required to arbitrate by statute or law. In the private sector, there is no compulsory arbitration, although from time to time special legislation has been enacted to require arbitration in certain industries and strike situations in which the public impact is deemed to be severe and of emergency proportions. However, in the public sector, where with few exceptions the right to strike is legally prohibited, compulsory arbitration is commonplace for many statutes provide impasse procedures to deal with terminal or new contract disputes that have finality in INTEREST ARBITRATION.

Compulsory Checkoff   See CHECKOFF.

Concession Bargaining   A term popularized in the early 1980s by the bargaining in the automotive industry in which the United Auto Workers of American gave major contract concessions first to Chrysler and then, successively, to Ford, General Motors, and American Motors. The term *concession bargaining* is now used to describe labor contract negotiations in any industry in which generally poor economic conditions, cutbacks, and layoffs make it imperative that the union make concessions to the employer that will improve productivity, reduce nonproductive time, decrease labor costs per unit of output, and the like.

Conciliator   A term currently used interchangeably with mediator. Historically, however, the conciliator was more constrained in his/her third-party efforts: more a go-between for the parties in their negotiations, and rarely, if ever, aggressively suggesting or proposing an alternative or compromise solution.

Congress of Industrial Organizations   See AMERICAN FEDERATION OF LABOR AND CONGRESS OF INDUSTRIAL ORGANIZATIONS.

Consent Award   An ARBITRATOR'S AWARD that has been fashioned with the consent of the parties to a dispute. Under the ethic of the profession, the arbitrator needs to be assured that the consent to the settlement specifically includes the consent of the grievant as well as that of the union and the company, and that the award will be clearly designated a consent award.

Consumer Price Index (CPI)   The measure of changes in cost of living computed nationally and released quarterly by the United States Bureau of Labor Standards. The most generally used index in labor contract COLA provisions.

Continuous Bargaining   Bargaining that continues during the life of a contract. It is generally "unfinished" or "follow-up" bargaining. An example is bargaining in which the parties to a contract agree that a given sum is be spent in providing employment benefits in health and welfare (or dental care, or legal services) and to that end set up a joint committee (usually chosen from among the members of the respective bargaining teams), charging it with the responsibility of working out the details of implementation during the life of the contract. Often there is a specified period of time for working out the details plus a provision that if agreement is not reached, either party may take the matter to arbitration. In complex issues such as pensions or incentive pay plans, the continuous bargaining on the part of the joint committee during the life of a contract is limited to reporting to the full negotiating committee for its considerations at the time of negotiating a successor contract.

Contract Administration   Taking steps to make certain that contract provisions are being complied with and that questions and disputes arising under the agreement are processed under the grievance procedure. Sometimes called **grievance administration** or **grievance handling.**

Contract Bar   The term used to describe the period designated by the NLRB or by the appropriate state or public sector agency as a bar to the displacement of a union as the exclusive representative and bargaining agent in a given contract. In the interest of balancing labor relations stability with the need to protect workers in their right to designate unions of their own choosing, the NLRB has held that a union's representational status may not be challenged for at least one year after certification, or during the existence of a valid COLLECTIVE BARGAINING AGREEMENT. Contracts of longer duration than one year are examined on an individual basis by the NLRB, but to date, at least, the Board has ruled a contract bar to union challenges for the duration of multiyear contracts of up to three years. This policy of the NLRB has had a positive influence on the receptivity of labor and management to multiyear contracts, and has led to the predominance of 3-year agreements.

Contract Duration   The precise time frame of a labor contract: usually not less than one year, and largely because of the NLRB's CONTRACT BAR policy, rarely longer than three years. Also called **contract term** and **contract length.**

Contract Extension Provision   See AUTOMATIC CONTRACT RENEWAL.

Contract Finality Clause   See ZIPPER CLAUSE.

Contracting-out Clause   A clause that deals with management's right to subcontract work. The clauses vary widely, ranging from prohibiting the SUBCONTRACTING of any work, to, in the other extreme, specifically providing management with unlimited contracting-out rights. Often, however, the clause specifically sets forth conditions under which subcontracting may be done, such as when no unit employees are on layoff or when none are capable of performing the work. Also called a **subcontracting clause.**

Contract Interpretation Arbitration   See RIGHTS ARBITRATION.

Contract Length   See CONTRACT DURATION.

Contract-Named Arbitrator   See PERMANENT ARBITRATOR.

Contract Negotiations   See COLLECTIVE BARGAINING.

Contract Rate   See BASIC CONTRACT HOURLY RATE.

Contract Term   See CONTRACT DURATION.

Contributory Joint Pension Fund   See JOINT PENSION FUND.

Contributory Joint Welfare Fund   See JOINT WELFARE FUND.

Coordinated Bargaining   Labor negotiations in which two or more unions "coalesce" or "coordinate" their bargaining in an effort to obtain common terms for individual unit contracts. When practiced by several large industrial unions in the 1960s, employers labeled all such bargaining "coalition bargaining" and denounced it as being "unilaterally imposed" and an expression of the "monopoly power" of unions. Unions, on the other hand, contended that they were coordinating mutual bargaining interests and referred to the practice as "coordinated bargaining." In the early stages of the use of such bargaining structures, the NLRB reserved the term *coalition bargaining* for situations that involved international as well as local unions. Practitioners, at least, do not make such a distinction, and by and large *coalition bargaining* and *coordinated bargaining* are currently used synonymously.

Core Time   See FLEXTIME.

Cost-of-Living Adjustment Clause   Often referred to as **COLA.** Contractual wage provisions which stipulate that adjustments are to be made in the base contract wage rate in accordance with fluctuations in the cost of living. The objective of such a clause is to protect the employee's real wage and to maintain the purchasing power of the employee's basic contract wage during the term of the contract.

Craftsman   A worker in a manual occupation requiring a high degree of skill and usually a period of apprenticeship training as well. Linotype operators, tool and die-makers, lithographers, carpenters, and masons are typical craftsmen.

Craft Union   Also called a **skilled union** since it is a union of workers possessing a specific skill or craft and working at a trade such as carpentry, die-making, or plumbing. Traditionally, this form of labor organization was described as **horizontal unionism.** The early trade unions were largely made up of workers in the same craft or trade. The term **pure craft union** has sometimes been used to distinguish the craft union, whose membership base is confined to a single craft, from the **assimilated craft union,** whose membership base has been broadened to include two or more associated crafts and even their helpers and auxiliary workers as well. There are few pure craft unions left, and most craft unions today have widened their jurisdiction beyond the skills of the originally designated craft. This has often been made necessary by technological change and the desire of the union to include in its membership all workers associated with the craft in order to maintain its bargaining position with the employer. The craft union was the backbone of the **American Federation of Labor** when it was formed in 1886.

Craft Unit   A bargaining unit composed of employees in a skilled trade or sharing common craft skills: for example, tool and die-makers in a plant; pressmen, compositors, and photo engravers in a printing plant or newspaper; bricklayers, plumbers, masons, and carpenters in construction; and pilots and machinists working for an airline.

Creative Bargaining   Bargaining that is innovative and creatively, if not uniquely, designed to meet individualistic problems at the bargaining table. Creative bargaining is not necessarily mutually beneficial, or ideal, or model bargaining in a general labor relations or public interest sense. For example, BOULWAREISM, was categorized as creative bargaining when first designed and practiced by General Electric, but while innovative, it was by no means ideal from a labor relations standpoint, and, indeed, it was ultimately held by the NLRB to be a failure to bargain in good faith. The terms *creative bargaining* and **innovative bargaining** have often been used synonymously.

Crisis   See IMPASSE.

Crisis Bargaining   See ELEVENTH-HOUR BARGAINING.

Day Shift   See SHIFT DIFFERENTIALS.

Deadlock   See IMPASSE.

Decertification   The procedures by which the employees in a bargaining unit change the union designated as their representative and bargaining agent to another union or to a nonunion status. The NLRB and the appropriate state or public sector agency usually limit decertification while a contract is in place to a period between 60 and 30 days prior to the contract's end. To date, the union's exclusive representational status has continued until decertification; currently, however, this matter is before the NLRB for reconsideration. The NLRB will conduct a decertification election if 30% of the employees in a given bargaining unit sign a petition indicating dissatisfaction with their representative. If the election shows that the majority status of the union no longer exists, the union is decertified and the Board issues a certificate to that effect.

Defense Fund   See STRIKE FUND.

Defined Benefit Plan   See BARGAINING A BENEFIT.

Defined Contribution Plan   See BARGAINING A COST.

De Minimis   A legal doctrine to the effect that the law does not bother with trifles. Often used by arbitrators in the dismissal of a matter that is insignificant, frivolous, or minute. Even when the matter is of consequence on its face—take, for example, the use of an employee on out-of-title work—the *de minimis* rule would be applicable if the usage was for a very brief time, was a rarity (if not a first), and if there were sound reasons for having assigned the work to an out-of-title employee, such as it was essential that the work be done and in-title employees were not available to do it at the time.

Deposition   A statement of a witness taken under oath away from the place of trial or hearing. When done in a question-and-answer form, with an opportunity for opposing counsel to cross-examine the witness, the deposition has significant evidential worth. A deposition is especially useful when witnesses who are mentally competent are physically incapable of attending the arbitration hearing.

Dicta   See OPINION AND AWARD.

Dirty-Work Pay   A contract clause or clauses which provide premium pay for working on dangerous or hazardous jobs—for example, working with explosives or obnoxious gases, or working under particularly greasy, oily, and dirty conditions.

Discussion   See OPINION AND AWARD.

Distribution of Overtime   The way overtime is divided up among workers when available. Some labor contracts, especially craft union contracts, stipulate that the overtime goes to the journeyman or operator of the machine, press, or equipment that is being utilized on the job requiring the overtime work. Most contracts, however, provide that the overtime be distributed equally "insofar as possible" among workers qualified to do the work.

Distributive Bargaining   One of several terms used to depict attitude, posture, and behavior in labor contract negotiations (see Walton and McKersie 1965). *Distributive bargaining* is the term used to describe labor negotiations in which the parties behave in a "win-lose" fashion at the bargaining table: "your gain is my loss." The concept of distributive bargaining is not only useful in depicting overall attitudes and the behavior of the parties at the bargaining table. Practitioners also find the concept helpful when planning their bargaining approach on OPEN ITEMS in any given negotiating session. In the categorization of contract demands or proposals, economic items such as wages,hours, paid holidays, vacations, sick leave, and other such employee ("fringe") benefits tend to be "distributive prone" negotiating items. These items warrant a different approach, strategy, or tactic at the bargaining table from, for exam-

ple, integrative items. See also ATTITUDINAL STRUCTURING, INTE-
GRATIVE BARGAINING, and INTRAORGANIZATIONAL BARGAINING.

Double-breasting   A term used predominantly in the construction
industry to refer to a contractor with a union agreement who also
operates a nonunion firm or subsidiary. The prevalence of "double-
breasted" operations in construction is of relatively recent vintage.
It reflects both the increasingly large amount of construction being
done by nonunion shops and the fact that double-breasting has
been held not to be an unfair labor practice. The AFL–CIO Building and Construction Trades Department has charged that double-
breasting has enabled contractors "to avoid complying with union
agreements to which they are a party," and at both its 1985 national
legislative conference and convention it strongly urged congressional action on legislation to curb double-breasted contractor operations. A bill on construction industry contract security has been
introduced in the House of Representatives which would require
contractors to apply the provisions of a collective bargaining agreement to all of their operations. In brief, according to its sponsors
and proponents the bill "would clarify the Taft-Hartley Act's provision allowing a pre-hire union agreement in the construction industry because of the temporary and often short-term pattern of employment . . . [by making] such a union agreement binding on all
of an employer's operations unless worker's vote to decertify the
union as bargaining agent. . . . [The bill] is aimed at contractors
who sign standard pre-hire union agreements but then set up nonunion subsidiaries that pay lower wages, provide inferior benefits,
and disregard labor standards." While the bill has been approved by
a subcommittee of the House Education and Labor Committee, no
legislation curbing double-breasting in the construction industry
has been enacted to date. Double-breasting has spread into other
industries such as trucking, airlines, and tire manufacturing, but
the practice in these industries is by no means as prevalent as in the
construction industry.

Double Jeopardy   As provided in the Constitution of the United
States, Fifth Amendment, "No Person . . . shall . . . be subject
for the same offense to be twice put in jeopardy of life or limb."
The concept of double jeopardy is often applied in arbitration to
prevent a grievant from being disciplined twice for the same offense
and to prevent management from increasing the quantum of discipline once it has been imposed and accepted. The double jeopardy
concept is not applicable, however, in situations in which the grievant's actions at the workplace have been the cause for a jail sen-

tence or court fine as well as the basis of disciplinary action by management. The arbitrator will take this into account, but is not governed by the court's action and is not precluded from adjudging management's contention that it has just cause to discipline the employee. Similarly, the arbitrator is not obliged to absolve a grievant of wrongdoing even if he/she has been acquitted of criminal charges for the very acts that occasioned the disciplinary action by management.

Due Process   There is no uniform definition of the term *due process,* but as applied in arbitration, it pertains to the guarantee of procedural fairness to the grievant. For example, discharge and less severe disciplinary actions have been reversed on the basis of failure to provide due process in cases in which management did not conduct an inquiry and investigation before levying the penalty; or did not afford the employee an opportunity to give his/her side of what transpired; or did not provide the employee with an opportunity to have a union representative present at the disciplinary interview.

Duty of Fair Representation   As a quid pro quo for the right of EXCLUSIVITY, the union is required to represent all employees in the bargaining unit. As held by the United States Supreme Court, the union is obligated by the duty of fair representation to represent all unit employees in collective bargaining, grievance handling, and other aspects of contract administration fairly, in good faith, and without hostility or discriminatory or arbitrary conduct whether or not they are members of the union, of the political opposition in a union, or of a particular race or ethnic group, age group, sex, religion, and so on.

Early-Bird Mediation   The term used to describe mediation efforts in which the mediator gets involved early in the negotiations, before the parties have reached a point of impasse or deadlock. Early-bird mediation is not widely practiced since a major asset to the mediator in most bargaining situations, especially in the private sector, is the fact that there is a crisis in negotiations and the parties are well aware of the strike consequences of failure to settle in mediation. Nonetheless, early-bird mediation is valuable, especially when a complex series of issues is involved and the parties invite a mediator who is familiar with the problems of the industry and in whom they have mutual confidence to assist them virtually from the outset of negotiations.

Early Settlement   See PREACTIVITY.

Economic Items   The strictly "money items" discussed at the bargaining table, such as wages, hours, vacations, paid holidays, sick leave, bereavement leave, jury duty pay, pensions, health and welfare benefits, and the like.

Economic Package   The mix of improvements in wages and hours and in fringe benefits in a labor contract or the economic settlement *in toto*.

Economic Strike   See STRIKE.

Eleventh-Hour Bargaining   Bargaining against a strike deadline. Often, in fact, this occurs at the eleventh hour prior to the midnight end of an existing contract and in the face of a union's strong "no contract, no work" stance. Also referred to as **crisis bargaining** since failure to reach agreement at this late stage of negotiations often results in a strike crisis.

Emergency Fund   See STRIKE FUND.

Emergency Strike   See NATIONAL EMERGENCY STRIKE.

Employee Benefits   See FRINGE BENEFITS.

Employee Involvement   A form of JOB ENRICHMENT. In fact, as promoted and practiced recently by the Ford Motor Company, this process involves workers in determinations related to the nature and production procedures of given job assignments.

Employment-at-Will   A concept which holds that a worker's employment is "at the will of the employer" and that the employer is free to terminate an employee at any time. Conceived in early English laissez-faire economic doctrine, the "at will" rule has been the subject of controversy in varying degree over the years, but at no time has it been so strongly challenged as at present. The managerial right to discharge an employee at will has been largely curtailed through unionization and by the collective bargaining agreement, which states that the discharge of workers covered by contract must be for just cause. But coverage by collective bargaining agreements is largely limited to hourly rated employees, and employment for the vast majority of salaried employees, in the private sector at least, like that of all unorganized workers, is at the will of the employer. Title VII of the 1964 Civil Rights Act and state and local government and antidiscrimination laws prohibit discrimination against employees for reasons of sex, age, race, creed, national origin, or religion, and this statutorily limits employers in their application of the "at will" rule in dismissals. Direct legislation has been ardently urged by some, especially in academia, to extend the requirement of just cause for dismissal to all employees. To date, this has not been favorably received by federal or state legislators or by local government officials. Management generally has strongly resisted such legislation, and organized labor has viewed it as less than favorable and with concern that the extension of grievance and arbitration procedures in discharge to all employees would lessen the need for, and dependence upon, unions. Nonetheless, much progress has been made in the state courts in obtaining modifications of, and exceptions to, the employment-at-will rule. Some twenty states, for example, have adopted the "public policy" exception to the employer's right to discharge an employee. Employers have been held to have contravened public policy and thus to have wrongfully terminated an employee in cases in which the employee was dismissed for performing a public obligation such as serving on a jury; or for having exercised a protected right such as filing for unemployment insurance or workers' compensation; or for having refused to comply with an order to perform an unlawful act such as committing perjury at a trial. State courts have held, too, although far less widely, that the employment-at-will concept is modified by the implied fact that the employment relationship carries with it the managerial responsibility that termination will not be arbitrary, and by the implied in-law covenant of good faith and fair dealing in the employment relationship. One state, South Carolina, by interpretation of the broad powers given to its Commissioner of Labor or his agent in a 1976 statute to investigate industrial disputes and "remove as far as possible the causes . . . and induce an amicable settlement," has innovatively extended its state mediation services to disputes over "at will" dismissals. By and large these mediation efforts to curb and remedy the excesses and abuses of unjust discharges have been well received in South Carolina. Employers generally have been willing to cooperate in the mediation of "at will" discharges, and the fact that no imposed settlement or award is involved has seemingly met with union approval. In any event, it is presently held in many quarters that mediation rather than compulsory arbitration or litigation, which is often costly and time-consuming, is the preferred way to deal with disputes arising out of employment-at-will discharges.

End Run   The term applied to the tactic of going beyond the bargaining table to overcome opposition to a desired demand and achieve a goal elsewhere. The term is most generally used to describe a union that secures from a higher level of management or even the state legislature what it could not get from the employer; a frequent tactic, and achievement, by public employee unions.

Entrapment   Evidence obtained by trickery, inducement, enticement, or persuasion. When uncovered, such evidence is inadmissible in arbitration, as in the courts. Entrapment is especially difficult to ascertain in arbitration, for the line between the employer's legitimate right of investigation and surveillance to uncover wrong doing by his employees and entrapping an employee is thin at best. For example, in a hospital in which there has been a drinking problem among orderlies, it is not considered entrapment for the hospital to hire employees of an investigatory agency to observe and report on the deportment of orderlies during their supper break, and such testimony is admissible. But if the testimony reveals that the special observers suggested to the orderlies that they get "a six-pack" or "a bottle or two of vino" to go with supper and advised management when to "check in on the festivities," such action is labeled "entrapment." And if the report and testimony of such findings is admitted by the arbitrator, it is invariably held to be a mitigating factor in assessing the disciplinary action taken by management.

Escalator Clause   A cost-of-living adjustment clause that provides only for an upward adjustment in the base wage as the cost of living increases. When first negotiated in the 1950s, COLA clauses worked both "up and down," but as inflationary pressures rose and employers persisted in seeking the stability of long-term contracts, unions successfully demanded (by way of quid pro quo for agreeing to a multiyear contract) that there be a COLA clause and that it be an escalator clause.

Escape Clause   See MAINTENANCE-OF-MEMBERSHIP CLAUSE.

Estoppel   See LACHES.

Exclusivity   The lawful right of a union certified as a bargaining agent to be the sole representative of the employees in a bargaining unit.

Expedited Arbitration   A process whereby the parties to a dispute agree to procedures with the objective of speeding up the arbitration process and obtaining a quick decision. An early hearing date is scheduled and the parties sum orally, with the ARBITRATOR'S AWARD either being a BENCH DECISION or rendered within a stipulated short period of time such as a day or so after the close of the hearing but usually no longer than 7–10 days thereafter. Often, in expedited arbitration the parties advise the arbitrator that they do not require an OPINION AND AWARD, or, if they require one, that it be in the form of a brief statement of the bases for the award.

Fact-finder   A dispute resolution procedure in which an impartial third party, invariably called the fact-finder, assists the parties in ferreting out the essential facts, issues, and considerations in a dispute over the terms of a new contract. Fact-finding is widely used in the public sector and is generally the impasse-resolution step taken when the parties have not been able to reach a settlement in mediation. The fact-finder, like the arbitrator, holds hearings at which he/she receives the evidence, testimony, and oral and/or written arguments of the parties. Unlike the arbitrator, however, the fact-finder is not authorized to render a binding decision. In fact, in some instances the fact-finder's authority is expressly limited to **fact-finding without recommendation.** Recently, as evidenced in public employee relations statutes, the trend has been toward **fact-finding with recommendation,** in which case the fact-finder is required to assess the merits of the respective positions of the parties on the items in dispute and to render a report with recommendations on the terms of a new contract. The fact-finder's recommendations as to settlement, however, may be rejected by the parties severally or jointly, in whole or in part. As with mediation, there is no finality in fact-finding as an impasse procedure. Many statutes that provide for fact-finding, especially those in which recommendations are required and ultimately made public, set forth specific criteria that the fact-finder must consider. These include ability to pay, comparable wage settlements, the cost of living, and other such standards as would clearly need to be considered, evaluated, and adjudged in arbitration. Statutes providing for fact-finding frequently explicitly authorize the fact-finder to mediate wherever it appears that this may prove helpful.

Fact-finding   See FACT-FINDER.

Fact-finding without Recommendation   See FACT-FINDER.

Fact-finding with Recommendation   See FACT-FINDER.

Featherbedding   The term used to describe union practices that "make work," create nonessential jobs, require more workers than necessary to do the job, prevent adoption of labor-saving equipment, require payment for work not performed, and the like. Featherbedding is unlawful.

Federal Labor Relations Authority (FLRA)   The FLRA was established by Congress to "establish policies and guidance" and generally administer the labor-management provisions of Title VII of the Civil Service Reform Act of 1978. The Authority, which is "composed of three members, not more than two of whom may be adherents of the same political party," replaced the **Federal Labor Relations Council** that had virtually the same administrative responsibilities under Executive Orders 10988 and 11491. The duties of the Authority include determining the appropriate bargaining units; supervising or conducting representation elections; conducting hearings and resolving complaints of unfair labor practices; resolving issues related to the duty to bargain in good faith; and resolving appeals from arbitration awards.

Federal Labor Relations Council   See FEDERAL LABOR RELATIONS AUTHORITY.

Federal Labor Union   A local union that is directly chartered by and affiliated with the AFL–CIO. It is also referred to as a **federal local.** The AFL–CIO generally limits its chartering of federal locals to unions of workers in a industry or craft that are not affiliated with a national or international union and over whom no national or international union has claimed or exercised jurisdiction. Over the years, federal locals were the organizational structure used in the transition to, and formation of, a national union. As initially developed by Samuel Gompers, however, the federal union was the means by which the AFL at the turn of the century enrolled the unskilled. The affiliated national or international unions at the time viewed the federal locals as "feeder unions" since, as conceived, their skilled members were, in time, to be allocated to various craft unions in accordance with their respective jurisdictions.

Federal Local   See FEDERAL LABOR UNION.

Federal Mediation and Conciliation Service (FMCS)   Established under the Labor-Management Relations Act of 1947 as an independent federal agency to replace the United States Conciliation Service of the United States Department of Labor. Promotes the peaceful settlement of labor disputes in industries engaged in interstate commerce by providing mediation services upon its own initiative, or the request of the parties, and by maintaining a panel of impartial arbitrators for the use of labor and management in the voluntary arbitration of grievance disputes.

Federal Service Impasses Panel (FSIP)   Established under Title VII of the Civil Service Reform Act of 1978, which governs labor-management relations between federal agencies and employee associations or unions in the resolution of bargaining impasses. The FSIP becomes involved in a federal labor dispute in the event the FMCS or any other third-party mediation effort fails to resolve a negotiations impasse. The powers of the FSIP are broad, ranging from referral of the dispute back to the negotiating parties to fact-finding and arbitration.

Federation of Organized Trade and Labor Unions of the United States and Canada (FOTLU)   A federation of craft unions formed in 1881. In 1886 it changed its name to the **American Federation of Labor** (AFL) under the dynamic leadership of Samuel Gompers, then president of the **Cigar Makers International Union.**

Feedback   See AUTOMATION.

Final and Binding Arbitration   A term that is largely used in the public sector to clearly indicate that the arbitration that has been agreed to is not of the advisory type.

Final-Offer Arbitration   Also called **last-best-offer arbitration,** this form of INTEREST ARBITRATION limits the arbitrator's authority in adjudging and rendering an award to finding for the final position of either party. It is intended, as its advocates contend, to eliminate the alleged tendency of arbitrators to "compromise" and to "cut the melon in half." Statistics do not reveal that such compromise is commonplace in arbitrator's awards. Nonetheless, supporters of this type of arbitration believe that by restricting the arbitrator's freedom and range of alternatives in fashioning an award, one can prevent the parties themselves from "playing games"; rather, in the face of an "either/or" arbitration award, the parties will cease arguing and holding out for "extremes" and will narrow issues at the bargaining table to essential differences. Final-offer arbitration has been utilized both "issue by issue" and by the "package," in which case the arbitrator selects either the union's or the employer's final position on the disputed terms and conditions of the contract in their entirety. But the complexities of final-offer arbitration by the "package" are so great that "issue by issue" arbitration is used more often. Final-offer arbitration has been utilized predominantly in the public sector, but the best-known and most widely publicized use of it to date has been in the negotiation of professional baseball players' salaries.

Fink   A professional strikebreaker who makes a career of working at struck plants.

First Shift   See SHIFT DIFFERENTIALS.

Flexible Benefits   See FRINGE BENEFITS.

Flextime   The term given to the scheduling of hours to vary arrival and departure times at a plant. This is done at the mutual convenience of the workers and the employer, usually with the proviso that total hours worked in a day, but occasionally in a week or even a month, are equal to the number normally worked. **Core time** is the period of hours an employer designates and requires that an employee be present in the plant; the remainder of the required hours in a flextime program may be scheduled at the employee's discretion. Flextime scheduling is by no means practiced extensively, but it has been utilized, largely in nonunion shops, and recently some unions, especially in public utilities, have accepted it.

Fourth Shift   See SWING SHIFT.

Free Rider   See AGENCY SHOP.

Fringe Benefits   All nonwage economic benefits such as vacation, paid holidays, sick leave, and the like. Management prefers that these be termed **employee benefits.** It is estimated that 35–40% of the average employer's labor-cost dollar goes to nonwage economic benefits. When employee benefits are tailor-made to fit the choice of the individual employee, they are called **cafeteria-style** or **flexible benefits.** Married employees, for example, when entitled to a cafeteria-style selection of employee benefits, might prefer life insurance, or at least, a package of employee benefits with a larger amount of life insurance coverage than that selected by unmarried employees. Also, married employees with children might prefer employee benefits with educational insurance or "layaway" plans to cover the college education needs of their children. Since their initial use in the late 1960s and early 1970s, cafeteria-style employee benefits have increasingly been made available to, and become popular with, salaried and executive employees. Unions have also shown interest in obtaining one or another form of cafeteria-style benefits for their members, although such provisions are not yet prominent in collective bargaining agreements. In fact, some 30 years ago, long before the term *cafeteria-style benefits* was coined, "Big Six," the New York City local of the International Typographical Union, innovatively negotiated into its contracts with the newspaper publishers and book and job employers an employee package of health care benefits which permitted employees to make an annual choice as to the kind of health care they wanted. Under the health and welfare provisions of the contracts that have been continued to date, employees may individually elect health care coverage under HIP (Health Insurance Plan of Greater New York), or GHI (Group Health Insurance), or New York Life Insurance Company. The election that is made in October of each year becomes effective on January 1 of the following year, and the health care option selected by the employee may not be changed until the end of that calendar year. Young married employees with children tend to opt for HIP since visits to the doctors at HIP centers are unlimited and the health care coverage is broad. Employees who prefer being attended by their own personal physicians rather than by GHI-approved doctors or by HIP doctors have tended to select New York Life's health care package since it allows them a specified dollar amount per doctor visit regardless of who the physician visited may be or what he charges. The HIP, GHI, and New York Life health care packages are balanced so that the cost to the employer and the health and welfare fund is relatively the same whatever the individual employee's selection. In recent years, young workers have shown an increasing interest in cafeteria-style benefits, and this has prompted unions to be alert to ways they might attain greater individual employee choice in the utilization of employee benefits under the labor contract.

Front-Loaded Contract   A multiyear contract in which the parties agree to larger wage increases and/or employee benefit improvements in the early years of the contract. For example, a 3-year contract with a 5% wage increase, an additional paid holiday, and a fourth week of vacation in the first year; a 4% wage increase in the second year; and a 3% wage increase in the third year.

Full-Crew Rule   Rules that stipulate minimum crew size for a given operation. The full-crew rule has been promoted especially by railroad unions and has been enacted into state law in some areas as a safety precaution for the public and the railroad employees. Full-crew rules have drawn criticism in some management quarters as protecting the jobs of unessential workers and perpetuating featherbedding.

Full-time Steward   See SHOP STEWARD.

Full Union Shop Clause   When negotiating a UNION SHOP PROVISO, the parties need to address themselves both to present employees and to future, new employees. When the union shop proviso covers all existing employees and all new employees as well, it has historically been referred to as a full union shop clause. This term is used infrequently today since most union shop clauses currently being negotiated cover new hires as well as existing employees.

Gainsharing   A variation of profit sharing or production bargaining whereby employees receive bonuses or incentive pay based on production increases in the plant or department as measured by some standard other than profit — for example, the number of plant shipments, parts produced by the department, and the like. In the 1986 round of negotiations in the steel industry, gainsharing was agreed to by the parties involved.

General Labor Union   See KNIGHTS OF LABOR.

General Strike   A national or community-wide strike by unionized workers in all or mostly all industries. Historically, the general strike, which is often politically motivated, has been largely rejected and little used by organized labor in the United States.

Give-Backs   Concessions made by a union to the employer which involve the giving up of employee benefits and other contractual worker advantages gained in prior negotiations.

Goldfish Bowl Bargaining   Bargaining in which the industry, because of its predominance, or the parties, by design, conduct negotiations in the "public eye." In such bargaining, proposals, positions, and even concessions are thoroughly aired in the news media.

Good Cause   See JUST CAUSE.

Goon   A term used to describe a person who has been hired to instigate violence during a strike.

Grandfather Clause   An agreement in which the parties to a contract stipulate that employees as of a specified date will not be subject to changes in a new contract which are less beneficial to them. For example, if the parties agree that a certain machine will no longer carry a premium wage rate, workers receiving that rate will usually be "grandfathered" and will continue to receive the premium rate rather than a reduced wage.

Grass Roots   See RANK AND FILE.

Graveyard Shift   See SHIFT DIFFERENTIALS.

Grievance   A formal complaint alleging a violation, misapplication, or misinterpretation of the collective bargaining agreement. Usually a grievance is raised by an individual employee in a bargaining unit, with the SHOP STEWARD and various union representatives assisting the employee in carrying the grievance forward. Occasionally, depending on the nature of the grievance and the contractual provisions, the union or even the employer may bring a grievance.

Grievance Administration   See CONTRACT ADMINISTRATION.

Grievance Arbitration   See RIGHTS ARBITRATION.

Grievance Definition   A process in which the parties to a contract carefully define what may be grieved. When the contract limits a grievance to differences between the employee or union and management over the interpretation or application of a specific provision of the contract, the grievance definition is characterized as **narrow**. The definition is held to be **broad** if the contract permits any difference arising at the work place to be grieved. In the main, however, grievance definitions are of the narrow type.

Grievance Handling   See CONTRACT ADMINISTRATION.

Grievance Mediation   Mediation has been used primarily as an impasse procedure in the resolution of interest or new-contract disputes, and over the years it has rarely been utilized in the resolution of grievance or rights disputes arising under the contract. Recently, however, mediators have been used innovatively in the grievance procedure and in the resolution of rights disputes. This type of mediation has been applied with some success in certain establishments, especially in the steel and coal industries. As generally agreed, grievance mediation may be invoked in a given dispute under a contract only when mutually consented to by the parties and the grievant. Usually this is done at the step just prior to final and binding arbitration, and if the matter is not resolved in mediation, it automatically proceeds to arbitration. The mediator, however, may not serve as the arbitrator—a point of distinction from the process of MED-ARB or the efforts of impartial chairmen, widespread in the 1950s, to resolve all grievance disputes by mutual consent and to make an arbitration ruling only if the mediation efforts failed. Proponents of grievance mediation predict a growing use of the process (but not to the point of supplanting arbitration) because of the direct involvement of the grievant, the lessening of the likelihood that the union will be charged with failing to meet the DUTY OF FAIR REPRESENTATION, and the relatively low cost of settlement due to the avoidance of legal fees and the written OPINION AND AWARD. However, even strong supporters view the use of mediation in rights disputes as a supplement to, rather than a replacement for, arbitration.

Grievance Procedure   Also called **grievance steps,** this procedure consists of the successive steps or stages in processing a grievance. For example, the initial step is taking the matter up with the foreman; then, if denied or not acted upon within a specified time, presenting the grievance successively to the department head, the plan manager, and, ultimately in most instances if not resolved, to an arbitrator.

Grievance Steps   See GRIEVANCE PROCEDURE.

Guaranteed Annual Wage Plans   Commonly called **GAWs,** these agreements contractually provide employees a guaranteed minimum income or employment in a year.

Guaranteed Minimum Shift Pay   See REPORTING PAY.

Hard Bargaining   Bargaining in good faith but bargaining "tough" — for example, insisting on quid pro quos for concessions at the bargaining table.

Hazardous-Work Pay   See DIRTY-WORK PAY.

Head Steward   See SHOP COMMITTEE; SHOP STEWARD.

Health and Welfare Provisions   Any and all contractual clauses that provide such benefits as coverage by Blue Cross and Blue Shield; life, hospitalization, and medical insurance; Major Medical; prescription drug, dental, and optical insurance; and the like.

Health Care Cost-Containment Provisions   In the 1980s, the pressure on management to reduce labor costs has focused heavily on the cost of employee benefits generally and on health and welfare costs in particular. In recent years, the annual increase in the cost of employer-paid benefits has rarely been less than the increase in the average earnings of hourly rated employees, and the long-term cost trend in employee benefits, as reported by the BNA, seems to be in the direction of exceeding increases in average earnings. Benefits as a percentage of total payroll average between 35% and 40%, with such variations as 29% of payroll in wholesale and retail trades, and 47% of payroll in the primary metal industries. The total cost of employer-paid benefits for private employees, including both salaried and hourly rated workers, is upwards of $550 billion per annum. Drastic increases in the cost of health care coverage have prompted managemeant and labor to incorporate health care cost containment provisions in their collective bargaining agreements. As reported by the Bureau of National Affairs (BNA), about 15% of the nonconstruction contract settlements in 1984 made some provision for health care cost containment. Such provisions appeared most frequently in the transportation equipment, chemicals, machinery (nonelectric), utilities, and wholesale and retail trade industries. Over half of the health care cost-reducing measures provided for deductibles in some amount, $200 being a common figure. According to the BNA, the most frequently used deductible is that for basic medical coverage (cited in about two-thirds of the contracts with health care cost deductible provisions). About 10% of the 1984 contracts have deductibles for Major Medical, 9% have them for hospital admissions, and 5% require them for dental coverage, emergency room service, and prescription drug plans.

Health care cost containment is also evidenced in the provision for employee co-payment of, or increased contribution to, health care premiums and by the incorporation of provisions covering second surgical opinions. In over half of the latter provisions, second opinions are mandatory for certain types of surgery. Cost-saving measures of various types have also been provided for home health and hospice care, outpatient surgery, and preadmission testing. Protracted eligibility for new-hire coverage; penalties for admissions scheduled on Friday, Saturday, or Sunday; rewards for detecting hospital-bill errors; and establishment of individual health care reimbursement accounts are among the other innovative cost-reducing measures that have been included among the health care cost containment provisions of many collective bargaining agreements. In increasingly large numbers, labor and management are taking the cost-saving step of self-insuring certain of their health and welfare benefits, while others are abandoning traditional Blue Cross/Blue Shield coverage or are supplementing it with coverge at cost reductions by health maintenance organizations and preferred-provider organizations.

Health Maintenance Organization   A private health plan that provides a full range of medical services for a fixed fee paid by the employer and/or employee. By federal law, employers must offer an HMO option to their employees if they provide a medical plan and if the HMO certifies that it covers the geographical area in which the employees work. Employers are not required to pay any more for the HMO option than they pay for medical insurance. Among the well-known HMOs are the Kaiser Plan, GHI, HIP, the Family Health Plan, and the Blue Cross–Blue Shield Healthnet.

Hearsay Evidence   Evidence that is secondary in nature—for example, the testimony of an employee that he had heard it said in the locker room that the grievant charged with having struck his foreman "hated that guy and would take care of him." Hearsay evidence, which is not admissible in the courts (with certain exceptions), is often admitted in arbitration, but for the most part it is given little weight by the arbitrator.

Hiring Hall   A hiring place initially established by unions (especially in the skilled crafts, construction, and casual and seasonal trades) to provide workers with jobs and to meet the job needs of employers. Historically, the hiring hall was operated by the union for the benefit of its members only and was often coupled with a CLOSED SHOP contract agreement and a **closed union** membership policy—that is, the practice of restricting membership to the number set in a union-fixed quota. Such restrictions are now unlawful. In order to avoid discrimination and employer preference for one out-of-work member over another, referrals in response to job calls are usually assigned to workers in the **out-of-work room** in the order in which they have made their availability known by registering for work. Historically, hiring hall terms have often been differentiated: when the hiring hall is operated by both the union and the employer, it is called a **joint hiring hall;** when it is operated for the benefit of members of several unions in a trade, as, for example, the unions in the construction trades, it is called a **central hiring hall.**

Homework   See PIECEWORK.

Horizontal Job Enlargement   See JOB ENLARGEMENT.

Horizontal Parity   See PARITY.

Horizontal Unionism   See CRAFT UNION.

Illegal Strike   See UNAUTHORIZED STRIKE.

Impact Bargaining   Negotiations over the impact of exercising a managerial right provided by statue, appropriate administrative agency, or court. For example, in most states school districts (the boards of education) may freely determine class size and are not required to negotiate the size of classes with the teacher's union or association. But the effect of the district's decision on class size is a mandatory subject of bargaining.

Impartial Chairman   See ARBITRATION.

Impasse   A stage in the negotiations of a new contract in which the parties are unable to make further progress toward a settlement. *Impasse* is a legal term and its usage is relatively recent, coming into prominence with the rise of public sector unionism and bargaining. In the private sector, the terms **deadlock** and **crisis** are frequently used to describe that "point of no progress" or impasse in negotiations at which the parties frequently turn to an impartial mediation agency or dispute resolution professional for assistance in settling differences. In the public sector, industrial dispute resolution statutes often define *impasse* in terms of a specified number of days prior to the budget submission date. For example, if a new contract has not been agreed to 90 days prior to the budget date, an impasse is legally declared and mediation efforts are undertaken. In the private sector, the contract's termination date is the key in any assessment of deadlock or impasse in negotiations since beyond that date the parties are invariably legally free to strike or lock out, and the employer can implement the last contract offer.

Impasse Arbitration   See INTEREST ARBITRATION.

Implied Rights Theory of the Union's Contractual Rights   The theory which holds that in addition to the express rights provided to the union under the contract, the union has the right (implicit in the RECOGNITION CLAUSE) to perform the work and jobs of employees constituting the bargaining unit. Clearly, this theory of implied union rights stemming from the recognition clause of the contract countervails the RESERVED OR RESIDUAL RIGHTS THEORY OF MANAGEMENT'S CONTRACTUAL RIGHTS. The juxtaposition of the two theories is evidenced by their application in a contract that contains no clause on contracting-out. Under the reserved or residual management rights theory, management may have unit work performed by outside contractors since it is not prohibited from doing so by the contract. Under the implied union rights theory, management would be precluded from giving unit work to outside contractors since the recogniton clause gives the union, or more precisely, unit employees, the right to perform the work.

Improper Evidence   Evidence that has been obtained reprehensibly, surreptitiously, improperly, or unlawfully, as, for example, by breaking into an employee's locker. Generally an arbitrator will rule such evidence inadmissible. This is called the **exclusionary rule.**

Incentive Rate   See PIECE RATE.

Incentive Wage   See PIECE RATE.

Indentured Apprenticeship   See APPRENTICE.

Independent Union   See COMPANY UNION.

Individual Bargaining   Negotiations between an employer and an individual employee on the wages, hours, and other terms of the individual's employment.

Industrial Union   A union that represents all employees in a shop or industry regardless of the type of work they do (skilled or unskilled). This form of labor organization has been referred to as **vertical unionism** and, colloquially, as **wall-to-wall unionism.** Industrial unions were promoted by the **Knights of Labor** as early as 1869, and, while accepted in the AFL, they were definitely in the minority, both in number and in influence on AFL policy. The predominance of the craft unions was a major factor in the split of industrial unions from the AFL and their formation of a rival labor federation, the **Congress of Industrial Organizations (CIO),** in 1938. This schism in labor's ranks remained for close to two decades and was ended by the formation of the AFL–CIO in December 1955.

Industrial Unit   A bargaining unit composed of all production and maintenance employees in a particular plant or group of plants of a company or industry. The industrial unit covers employees of all levels of skill, with the unskilled and semiskilled generally being predominant in number.

Industry-wide Bargaining   See NATIONAL BARGAINING.

Industry-wide Strike   See NATIONAL STRIKE.

Informational Picketing   Picketing by a labor organization which is undertaken as an appeal to the public—for example, to inform the public that an employer pays below-standard wages (also called **area standards picketing**) or subcontracts to nonunion firms. Such picketing is a legal exception to the limitations on ORGANIZATIONAL PICKETING (Section 8(b)(7)) if it does not induce or encourage employees to refuse to work. It is sometimes called **consumer picketing.** Perhaps the most extensive use of this form of picketing in recent years has been by the United Farm Workers in the grape producing industry.

Injunction   A court order requiring individuals or groups to perform or not perform certain acts that the court has determined will do irreparable harm. When the acts involve a labor dispute and related matters, the court order is frequently referred to as a **labor**

injunction. An injunction that is issued for a limited period prior to a court hearing is called a **temporary restraining order.** An injunction that is issued by the court following a full hearing and that remains in force until the conditions that cause its issuance have been corrected is called a **permanent injunction.** Historically, until the Norris-LaGuardia Act of 1932, which vitually prohibited the court issuance of labor injunctions, employers were able to secure with relative ease court orders restraining unions from such acts as picketing, striking, threatening a strike, slow down, and the like. Under the Taft-Hartley Act of 1947, exceptions were made to the Norris-LaGuardia limitations on the use of the labor injunction and injunctions may now be issued to restrain unions from engaging in certain unfair labor practices and to prevent, for an 80-day cooling-off period, emergency disputes that imperil national health and welfare.

Innovative Bargaining   See CREATIVE BARGAINING.

Integrative Bargaining   The term used to describe the behavioral pattern of labor negotiations when the parties approach bargaining with the attitude that there is no winner or loser and that both parties will benefit from the negotiated settlement. Contract demands and proposals on such provisions as eligibility for holiday pay, sick leave, vacation time, shift preference, and the like, are generally viewed as "integrative prone" items. Practitioners reason that once the parties reach agreement, for example, on the number of paid holidays to be provided under the contract, both parties will want an eligibility provision that is fair and equitable to employees. Similarly, welfare or pension benefits provided under a cost-agreed or defined contribution plan, as distinct from a defined benefit plan, will tend to be approached in an integrative fashion. The negotiation of demands for reductions in the base contract hours of work, however, will more than likely tend to be "distributive prone" since, invariably, such demands are accompanied by the condition that there be no reduction in day or weekly base pay. On the other hand, negotiation of contract proposals for changes in the scheduling of base contract hours, including proposals for flextime, could well be "integrative prone." See also ATTITUDINAL STRUCTURING, DISTRIBUTIVE BARGAINING, and INTRAORGANIZATIONAL BARGAINING.

Interest Arbitration   The arbitration of disputes over the terms and conditions of a contract. Inasmuch as these issues involve the fundamental and basic interests of the parties in a new contract at the end of the old contract and at the time of impasse, interest arbitration is also referred to as **terminal arbitration, new-contract arbitration, major** or **primary dispute arbitration,** and **impasse arbitration.** Unlike RIGHTS ARBITRATION, which is provided in some 95% of existing labor contracts, interest arbitration is an exception and is estimated as being provided in less than 3% of the contracts in the private sector. In the early years of the use of interest arbitration its legal status was in contention and, in fact, the courts held that its provisions could not be enforced. These legal questions seem to have been laid to rest, however, and for more than a decade interest arbitration provisions, except for disputes over the renewal of the interest arbitration clause itself in a new contract, have been enforceable in the courts. Thus, once the parties to a contract enter into an interest arbitration agreement, they are legally bound to arbitrate disputes over wages, hours, and all other terms of employment in a successor contract except the interest arbitration clause itself, and the arbitrator's ruling on these disputed contractual terms is final and binding.

Interest arbitration is widely used in the public sector, however. Inasmuch as it is unlawful for federal employees and most state and local government employees to strike, interest arbitration is generally stipulated by statute as the final impasse step in negotiations involving public sector employees.

Interim Increases   Long-term contracts invariably provide for wage increases at the beginning of the contract and during the life of the contract as well. The wage increases provided during the life of a contract, usually at the anniversary date of a multiyear contract, are called interim increases. They are rarely provided in short-term or one-year contracts, although occasionally they have been given at 9-month or even 6-month intervals.

International Representative   See NATIONAL UNION.

International Union   See NATIONAL UNION.

Intraorganizational Bargaining   All bargaining is not done with one's adversaries at the negotiating table. The process of reconciling divergent interests, as between the negotiating team and one's constituents, or even among the members of one's negotiating team itself, involves a form of bargaining within one's organization that has been termed intraorganizational bargaining. Practitioners, especially the chief negotiators of a bargaining team, describe this bargaining within their respective organizations as frequently being as demanding, difficult, and intense as that which transpires with the other side at the bargaining table. See also ATTITUDINAL BARGAINING, DISTRIBUTIVE BARGAINING, and INTEGRATIVE BARGAINING.

Invoking the Rule   See SEQUESTERING.

Job Action   Any concerted action by workers — for example, a slowdown, work-to-rule, and the like — short of a work stoppage or strike.

Job Analysis   Scrutinizing all aspects of a job to determine its duties and responsibilities; the experience, training, and mental and physical requirements called for; the tools and equipment needed to perform the job; the working conditions under which the job is to be performed; its wage scale and promotional opportunities relative to other jobs; and the like.

Job Classification   The grade or level at which a job is classified according to such requirements as training, experience, skill, responsibility, effort, and the like, relative to other jobs in the plant. Also called **job grade** or **labor grade.**

Job Description   Generally the result of a JOB ANALYSIS. A written description of the key requirements and duties of a job, as well as a summary of the job's important features.

Job Enlargement   The term used to describe all employer actions in which the job is expanded to include more tasks. **Vertical job enlargement** is adding to the duties, responsibilities, and complexities of the worker's job assignment and is also often referred to as JOB ENRICHMENT. **Horizontal job enlargement** is the procedure of adding a number of somewhat similar tasks to a given job.

Job Enrichment   The term used to describe any procedure that broadens an employee's job tasks and duties and generally gives him/her greater responsibilities and autonomy at the workplace.

Job Evaluation   Measuring and evaluating jobs in terms of their relative worth for purposes of assigning appropriate wage rates to them. Also called **job rating.** Comparing, evaluating, and ranking all the jobs in a plant in order of importance is called **job ranking.**

Job Family   An umbrella term for jobs that are related in terms of skill, experience, or type of work performed. Such categorization is often helpful in developing promotional training, upgrading, and other manpower planning.

Job Grade   See JOB CLASSIFICATION.

Job Ranking   See JOB EVALUATION.

Job Rating   See JOB EVALUATION.

Job Specification   A written description of the requirements (training, skill, experience, physical and mental attributes, etc.) sought in individuals who are to be hired or promoted to a given job.

Job Study   See TIME-AND-MOTION STUDY.

Joint Boards of Arbitration   See BOARD OF ARBITRATION.

Joint Exhibits   Exhibits that the parties to a dispute jointly agree to submit to the arbitrator—for example, the contract, the written grievance, the replies at each grievance step, and the demand for arbitration. Joint exhibits are usually presented early in the hearing, following agreement on a submission or discussion of the issue in dispute before the arbitrator.

Joint Hiring Hall   See HIRING HALL.

Joint Pension Fund   A fund established and negotiated to provide pension benefits to covered employees. There are also **joint pension fund trustees** and **contributory joint pension funds** or **contributory joint pension plans.** See also JOINT WELFARE FUND.

Joint Pension Fund Trustees   See JOINT PENSION FUND.

Joint Welfare Fund   A fund established by contract to provide health and welfare benefits to covered employees. By law, it is jointly administered by an equal number of labor and management representatives designated as **joint welfare fund trustees.** Joint welfare funds are especially prevalent in multiemployer contracts and in contracts in which the parties negotiate payments into the fund—for instance, a specified dollar or cents amount per shift worked—for the provision of welfare benefits. Joint welfare funds are sometimes called **Taft-Hartley funds** because of the requirement for joint administration. When the employees as well as the employer are obligated by the contract to make payments into the fund, it is called a **contributory joint welfare fund.**

Joint Welfare Fund Trustees   See JOINT WELFARE FUND.

Journeyman   A skilled worker who has "served" his/her apprenticeship and has successfully completed all required training for admission to a craft, as, for example, a journeyman printer, a journeyman pressman, a journeyman carpenter. Often called a CRAFTSMAN.

Jurisdictional Strike   A strike which results from a dispute between two or more rival unions over the right to perform and exercise jurisdiction over specific work. Under the Taft-Hartley Act, an unfair labor practice. When an employer "caught in the middle" between the conflicting jurisdictional claims of rival unions takes the dispute to the NLRB for adjudication, the Board is obligated to make a ruling as to jurisdiction in what is called a **10-K case.** When the dispute between rival unions is over representation rights, the matter is generally resolved by the NLRB in a representation election. The AFL–CIO no-raiding pact seeks to eliminate jurisdictional strikes.

Just Cause   While the employer's right to hire, fire, and discipline employees is invariably set forth in the MANAGEMENT RIGHTS CLAUSE, most contracts in addition specifically state that management may not discipline or discharge an employee without **cause, just cause,** or as occasionally and variously stated, for **sufficient and reasonable cause,** for **good cause,** for **sufficient cause,** and the like. Whatever the qualifying term—*cause* or *just cause* or some other—the contractual obligation is clear: the managerial right to discipline and discharge an employee is not an absolute right, and the burden of proof as to the equity and propriety of the action, when challenged under the grievance procedure to the finality of arbitration, is management's.

Knights of Labor   A **general labor union,** now defunct, whose structure and prominence in its time are historically significant in the annals of American trade unionism. Formed in 1869 as the **Noble Order of Knights of Labor,** it was a general labor organization in the sense that it covered all crafts, occupations, and industries and was a primary organization as distinct from a federation of autonomous unions. At its peak fifteen years or so after its formation, the Knights of Labor was national in scope, with some three-quarters of a million members. The Knights of Labor under the leadership of Terence V. Powderly had broad social and political goals which at times superseded its economic objective of "improving the well-being of all working people." The Knights of Labor rapidly declined into oblivion in the 1890s with the emergence of the AFL and the predominance of rival autonomous national unions with a narrower craft or industry worker base and the primary economic goals of "bread and butter" trade unionism.

Labor Agreement   See COLLECTIVE BARGAINING AGREEMENT.

Labor Association   See LABOR ORGANIZATION.

Labor Contract   See COLLECTIVE BARGAINING AGREEMENT.

Labor Cost-Savings Bonus (Scanlon) Plan   The Scanlon Plan is named after the late Joseph Scanlon, who was the United Steelworkers research director and who became a member of the industrial relations research staff of the Massachusetts Institute of Technology in the 1950s. Scanlon first instituted his plan as a way to reduce labor costs in a steel mill where he was a union representative in the late 1930s. Unlike PROFIT-SHARING PLANS, the bonus or extra compensation to workers is geared to reductions in labor costs other than the base contract hourly rate; the greater the reduction in established "normal" labor costs, the greater the amount of worker bonus. To some workers, labor cost-savings bonus plans have been more attractive than profit-sharing plans. They have been variously described as "more tangible," something a worker "can do something about," and not subject to "accounting manipulations" or management decisions and administration in areas over which a worker has little or no control but which greatly affect a company's overall profitability picture. Nonetheless, labor cost-savings bonus plans have been resisted by unions in some quarters as a wage plan that requires workers to work harder. There are mechanical difficulties, too, in developing an appropriate labor cost-savings standard upon which to base the workers' wage bonus, and this has been a deterrent to its use.

Labor Federation   A federation of labor organizations formed for the purpose of promoting common interests. The **National Trades' Union,** founded in New York City in 1834, was the first national labor federation in the United States. It was dissolved in 1837; the AFL–CIO is its present-day successor.

Labor Grade   See JOB CLASSIFICATION.

Labor Injunction   See INJUNCTION.

Labor-Intensive Industry   An industry which by the nature of its operations affords little opportunity for the use of LABOR-SAVING DEVICES and requires much usage of, and reliance upon, individual manpower.

Labor-Management Cooperation   A term broadly used to cover any and all cooperative efforts between labor and management in their organized industrial relationship. This encompasses the achievement of peaceful and integrative bargaining with a high recognition of the mutuality of interest in dealing with the respective proposals on the negotiating table. It extends, too, to the day-today relationship of labor and management in the administration of the contract and thus to much problem-solving in grievance handling and reliance on labor-management committees for the administration of joint programs dealing with such subjects as safety, health and welfare, alcoholism, drug abuse, plant improvement, and, in some instances, productivity and quality of work life.

Labor Negotiations   See COLLECTIVE BARGAINING.

Labor Organization   Also referred to as a **union, trade union, labor union, labor association,** and **worker organization,** a labor organization is any association of workers having as its primary purpose the promotion of the economic interests of its members as wage earners. This definition distinguishes the labor organization from early workers' **benevolent and fraternal societies,** which were basically social, fraternal, cultural, and even spiritual in purpose and were only incidentally concerned with the economic betterment of their members. Virtually from the outset — carpenters, printers, and cordwainers (shoemakers) formed craft unions as early as 1791 — the primary focus of American unions was to organize for the purpose of bargaining collectively with the employer with respect to wages, hours, and other terms and conditions of employment. In effect, the National Labor Relations Act defines a labor organization as any organization freely chosen by the majority of employees in a bargaining unit to represent them in contract negotiations and contract administration, including grievance handling (see Section 9(a) of the NLRA). It makes unlawful the **company union,** in the sense of a company-dominated union, by stipulating that it is an unfair labor practice for an employer "to dominate or interfere in the affairs of the union" (see Section 8(a)(2) of the NLRA).

Labor Organizer   An employee of a union, usually a full-time worker, whose primary official responsibility is to organize the unorganized, solicit union membership, and help employees in a shop form or join a union. Such organizers were often referred to as **porkchoppers** in the early days of unionism. When their duties also include the servicing of employees in a shop or a group of shops under a multiemployer contract and representing them in the late steps of the grievance procedure, they are called **administrative organizers** by some unions.

Labor-saving Devices   Machinery and other equipment and methods of operation that reduce reliance on individual manpower in a given production procedure.

Labor Spies   Persons hired by an employer to get information about a union and its members. The use of labor spies is unlawful.

Labor Union   See LABOR ORGANIZATION.

Laches   A legal doctrine which holds that long-neglected rights cannot be enforced, that there has been negligence in the failure to exercise these rights promptly, and that conditions have so changed since the initial failure to act that it would be inequitable if the right were now exercised. In arbitration, as in law, where there is laches the matter is dismissed. This precludes a senior employee who in the past failed to bid for a posted opening from exercising his right a year later to displace the successful bidder, who is junior to him in terms of seniority. The legal term **estoppel** is often used to describe this bar to the senior employee's grievance under these conditions.

Last-Best-Offer Arbitration   See FINAL-OFFER ARBITRATION.

Laws Clause   A contractual clause which stipulates that in the event any provision of the contract is found to be in conflict with a federal, state, or local law and is invalidated, the remainder of the agreement shall not be affected. Also called a **separability clause** or a **savings clause.**

Leading Question   A question posed to a witness which suggests or leads the witness in his/her answer. Leading questions may be asked in cross-exmaination, but generally not on direct examination. While arbitration is quasi-judicial and often informal, court procedure in sustaining objections to a leading question on direct examination is generally followed by arbitrators when the examination that is being conducted touches on sensitive areas of the question at issue.

Lobster Shift   See SHIFT DIFFERENTIALS.

Local   See LOCAL UNION.

Local Union   The local union, frequently referred to as the local, is a labor organization chartered by and affiliated with a national or international union. The local union, along with its national or international union, is a **primary labor organization.** The local unions of an industrial national union such as textile workers and steelworkers are usually organized by plant. The local unions of a craft national union, such as typographical workers and carpenters, are usually organized by local area or region.

Lockout   A temporary shutdown of the plant and suspension of work by an employer involved in a labor dispute. The lockout is often said to be management's economic counterpart to the workers' strike.

Long- and Short-term Contracts   There is no firm or fast rule as to what is to be categorized as a short-term contract over and against a long-term contract. Inasmuch as, historically, labor contracts were entered into for one year and contracts were rarely, if ever, written for a shorter period, it has become commonplace to refer to a contract of one year or longer but less than two years in duration as a short-term contract. Multiyear contracts of two or more years duration are generally referred to as long-term contracts.

Maintenance-of-Benefits Clause   An agreement by an employer to maintain existing health, welfare, and pension benefits for the life of an agreement, whatever the cost. A form of BARGAINING A BENEFIT. The clause is most prevalent in multiemployer labor agreements.

Maintenance-of-Membership Clause   A provision in the labor contract requiring as a condition of employment that all employees who are or become union members remain members of the union in good standing for the duration of the contract. Often included in a maintenance-of-membership provision is an **escape clause,** which stipulates that during a given period of time, usually ten days or two weeks, employees who are union members may withdraw without being penalized by loss of employment.

Maintenance-of-Standards Clause   See PAST-PRACTICE CLAUSE.

Maintenance Worker   See PRODUCTION WORKER.

Major Disputes Arbitration   See INTEREST ARBITRATION.

Management Rights Clause   The clause which identifies, either generally or in detail, the employer's exclusive right to manage and conduct the business, and the right to direct the work force, including the right to hire, discipline, and discharge. Usually the clause is written to reserve to management all rights not expressly defined by, or in contravention of, the other provisions of the contract.

Mandatory Overtime Provision   A contractual provision which specifically requires that employees work overtime. While workers generally want, and freely volunteer for, the extra pay from overtime, industries in which overtime is essential and a frequent occurrence often find it necessary to include a mandatory overtime provision. Generally, the mandatory provision is qualified by the requirement that it be "a reasonable amount" of overtime and that advance notice be given usually some hours prior to or by noon of the shift on which the overtime is to be worked.

Mandatory Subjects of Bargaining   Subjects that by law must be negotiated by labor and management when insisted upon by either party. The NLRA refers to mandatory subjects broadly as "wages, hours, and other terms and conditions of employment." In the private sector, at least, there has been a persistent trend over the years, as determined by the Board and the courts, to broaden the scope of mandatory bargaining items.

Mass Picketing   The posting of large numbers of workers to patrol and picket in front of a struck plant. In many communities, there are local ordinances restricting the number of picketers, and mass picketing can be enjoined by state courts as an exercise of police powers.

Mechanical Employee   See PRODUCTION WORKER.

Mechanical Worker   See PRODUCTION WORKER.

Mechanization   The process of replacing human labor and skills with machines and mechanical operations. Usually a step toward AUTOMATION.

Med-Arb   A dispute resolution procedure in which the impartial third party's role is one of both mediator and arbitrator. As practiced, efforts are made to resolve any and all issues at impasse by mediation, but for those differences which cannot be mediated to settlement, the mediator-arbitrator is empowered to render a final and binding decision. There are strongly divergent views as to the desirability and effectiveness of "mixing" the impasse processes of mediation and arbitration. Proponents strongly contend that med-arb promotes settlements by providing the maximum inducement for the parties to work out their own differences with the help of the impartial third party. Opponents of med-arb, on the other hand, vigorously protest that the "mix" dilutes the impartial party's effectiveness and that the parties never benefit from the maximum values of either mediation or arbitration since the conciliator in whom one must have sufficient trust to divulge confidences about one's "bottom line" position, constituencies, internal political considerations, and the like, will also be one's "judge." Nevertheless, where selectively and adroitly utilized, med-arb has proven to be an effective "tool" for dispute resolution.

Mediation   A dispute resolution procedure in which a third party, often an impartial professional or trained mediator from a govern-

mental mediation and/or conciliation agency, endeavors to assist
the parties in narrowing their differences and reaching a settlement.
Generally, the mediator is called upon by the parties or appointed
by a governmental agency at the time of impasse or deadlock in the
negotiations of a contract. The mediator does not have the power
to decide and rule on the issues in dispute and cannot force the
parties to reach a settlement. Hence, there is no finality to a contract dispute in mediation except by the voluntary agreement of the
parties. Because of this and the fact that the mediator frequently
meets with the parties separately and jointly at the bargaining table, often suggesting but never compelling alternatives and compro-
mises in their respective positions, mediation as an impasse procedure is held to be an extension of the bargaining process.

Mediator   See CONCILIATOR; MEDIATION.

Mediator-Arbitrator   See MED-ARB.

Meet-and-Confer Laws   See MEET-AND-CONFER NEGOTIATIONS.

Meet-and-Confer Negotiations   A practice limited largely to the
public sector and to those states in which the public employee is
given the right to organize but not the right to bargain to impasse
with the public employer. In these instances the public employee is
provided the right to meet and confer on terms and conditions of
employment but the final decision is that of the public employer.
Meet-and-confer laws in some states stipulate that the final authority be the legislative body. In those cases the public employee union
or organization is given the right to make presentations and recommendations to the legislature for its determination. Exclusive representational rights and the right to written agreements, however, are
not provided.

Member-Only Contract   A contract in which the union is recognized by the employer as the bargaining representative for its members only. Now illegal, for by law the union must represent all
employees in the bargaining unit whether they are union members
or not.

Merit Shop   See OPEN SHOP.

"Me-Tooism" Clause   A contract negotiated by a union which assures it that if the employer in subsequent negotiations gives another union better terms, they will be extended to it as well. The
provision has been negotiated most frequently of late in the public
sector, where police, fire fighters, sanitation workers, and other
public employee unions hesitate to settle first for fear the city or

state will "soften up" and "give in" in the subsequent negotiation of wage increases, benefits, and terms of employment that were kept out of their contract. "Me tooism" is also used by nonmembers in multiemployer (association) bargaining. In order to stay open during a strike, the nonmember employer agrees to a "me too" contract which assures the union that it will accept whatever wages, hours, and conditions of employment are agreed to in the association contract.

Midnight Shift   See SHIFT DIFFERENTIALS.

Minor Disputes Arbitration   See RIGHTS ARBITRATION.

Modified Union Shop   In the initial negotiation of a UNION SHOP PROVISO, the parties may wish to make exception for existing employees who are not members of the union at the time When the union shop clause covers all new (future) employees, but only those existing employees who are members of the union at the date of signing, such a unionized shop is called a modified union shop.

Moonlighting   Holding more than one job. The second job, as implied by the term *moonlighting,* is generally an evening job. Initially, the term *moonlighting* had the derogatory connotation that the second job was held surreptitiously. While a number of employers still prohibit or frown on moonlighting, increasingly the practice has been accepted and is tolerated by the employer so long as it does not adversely affect the worker's job performance. Many workers — upwards of five million — engage in some moonlighting, although only a small percentage of these hold down two full-time jobs.

Morning Shift   See SHIFT DIFFERENTIALS.

"Most Favored Nation" Clause   A contract clause traditionally negotiated by an employer's association which requires the union to extend to the association's members any and all concessions and terms it has agreed to, or may agree to, that are more favorable to employers than those provided in the association contract. The clause seeks to preserve the association's bargaining primacy in an industry and to prevent the union from agreeing to a contract with nonmember employers which would adversely affect the competitive status of the association's affiliated member plants.

Motion Study   See TIME-AND-MOTION STUDY.

Multiemployer Bargaining   The employer unit for bargaining is predominantly the individual plant or company. When the bargaining covers several companies, it is called multiemployer bargaining and the resultant agreement is called a **multiemployer contract.** Generally, the companies form a trade association for purposes of collective bargaining, as, for example, the New York Printers League or the former Brewers Board of Trade; hence, multiemployer bargaining is often called **association bargaining.** It is significant that the NLRB insists on mutual consent for the approval of a multiemployer bargaining unit. Thus, association bargaining and multiemployer bargaining may not be entered into if the union objects.

Multiemployer Contract   See MULTIEMPLOYER BARGAINING.

Multiplant bargaining   Bargaining in which the ensuing contract covers several plants of a multiplant company. When the bargaining covers all of the plants of a multiplant company, wherever they are located, it is called **company-wide bargaining.**

Mutual Aid Pact   A form of employer strike protection. Unlike STRIKE INSURANCE, however, a mutual aid pact relies on mutual self-aid and help rather than on an insurance carrier. In its early bargaining history, a group of breweries in the metropolitan area of New York negotiated as a multiemployer unit and built up a strike fund for the use of its member companies from a self-imposed tax on each barrel brewed. The mutual aid pact that was set up in the airline industry, but that has since been discontinued, aided the struck carrier by providing funds obtained under a complicated formula designed especially to tax participating carriers that benefited from business increases on routes paralleling those of the struck airline.

Named Arbitrator   See PERMANENT ARBITRATOR.

National Bargaining   When multiemployer bargaining was extended to entire industries, regardless of where individual employers were located geographically throughout the nation, it was called national bargaining or **industry-wide bargaining,** as, for example, formerly in the case of steel.

National Emergency Strike   Under the Taft-Hartley Act, a strike affecting all or a substantial part of an industry which in the judgment of the President of the United States and the appropriate federal court imperils the nation's health or safety. Such strikes may be enjoined under the Act for an 80-day cooling-off period. Under the Railway Labor Act, a 90-day cooling-off period may be invoked by the President of the United States in emergency strikes affecting all or a substantial part of essential transportation. Also called an **emergency strike.**

National Representative   See NATIONAL UNION.

National Strike   A strike of all organized workers in an industry. Also called an **industry-wide strike.**

National Union   A national union is an organization that is nationwide or geographically wide spread enough to cover workers in its membership base wherever they are located in the United States. The many American unions that have extended their membership base to include Canada and Canadian locals are called **international unions.** Among other functions, the national or international union charters local unions, promotes union organization, sets jurisdictional boundaries, conducts research and educational programs, maintains political activities (including lobbying) to further its membership's interests, and aids local unions in collective bargaining and, often, in contract administration as well, especially in arbitration. Some national or international unions maintain tight control over their locals in contract negotiations. This is usually done by requiring national or international union authorization for strike, sending a **national** or **international representative** to assist in local contract negotiations, and not granting national or international union strike funds unless approved by the union's on-the-scene representative. In a number of instances, however, the locals have retained a high degree of autonomy over contract negotiations, and the role of the national or international union in collective bargaining is largely advisory. The first national labor union was the **National Association of Cordwainers,** which was formed in New York City in 1836 and lasted about a year. Printers, comb-makers, carpenters, and hand-loom weavers also formed early national unions. The Typographical Union, formed in 1852, was the first national union to continue through to the present day.

Neutral   An impartial person who is utilized by the parties at IM-PASSE to assist in dispute resolution efforts, usually by serving as a mediator, fact-finder, or arbitrator.

Neutral Referee   See ARBITRATION.

New-Contract Arbitration   See INTEREST ARBITRATION.

Night Shift   See SHIFT DIFFERENTIALS.

Noble Order of Knights of Labor   See KNIGHTS OF LABOR.

Nonaffiliated Shop   See OPEN SHOP.

Nondiscrimination Clause   A contractual provision which specifically prohibits discrimination on the basis of race, color, creed, sex, national origin, age, or union activity.

Noneconomic Items   All items of the labor contract other than the "money items." It is wrong to assume, however, that noneconomic items are not costly items or are less important than economic items. Some noneconomic items—for example, the management rights clause and the union shop or other union security clauses—often are "items of principle" to the parties and occasion some of the hardest and most intense bargaining. Other noneconomic items, such as a provision requiring employees to start and end a shift at the same time so as to eliminate the employer's use of split shifts, or prohibiting or limiting an employer's flexibility in contracting-out work, or stipulations on the manning of machines, can be, and generally are, very costly to management.

Nonskilled Worker   See UNSKILLED WORKER.

Nonstoppage Strike   See STATUTORY STRIKE.

Nonunion Shop   See OPEN SHOP.

No-Raiding Pact   An agreement between two or more unions, usually national or international unions, that they will not encroach on one another's jurisdiction. Specifically, there is agreement not to enroll workers in a plant who are members of another union that has been certified or has an established bargaining relationship. Several national unions and some local unions as well have entered into bilateral no-raiding agreements that extend to the organization of nonunionized plants and workers. The AFL–CIO has a general no-raiding pact to which affiliated national or international unions are signatory.

Normal Hours   See BASE CONTRACT HOURS.

Normal Workday   See BASE CONTRACT HOURS.

Normal Workweek   See BASE CONTRACT HOURS.

No Strike–No Lockout Clause   A contractual provision which states that the union will not strike and the employer will not resort to lockout during the life of the contract. As provided in 95% of the labor contracts in the United States, there is the quid pro quo that employee grievances and disputes over the interpretation of contractual provisions be submitted to a grievance procedure, with resolution, if necessary, in final and binding arbitration. Also, a no-strike promise is implied if there is an arbitration clause in the contract, whether or not there is an express no strike–no lockout clause.

Obnoxious-Work Pay   See DIRTY-WORK PAY.

Open-ended Contract   A labor contract that does not clearly specify a beginning and a termination date. The open-ended contract is commonplace in England and Europe, and because it lacks the definiteness of the contract duration of U.S. labor agreements, there is less stability in the contractual relationship. Open-ended contracts do not lend themselves to the application of "the law of contracts" or no strike–no lockout provisions with reliance on the impartial arbitration of grievance disputes as is prevalent in some 95% of U.S. labor contracts.

Opening Statement   The statement of the parties at the outset of an arbitration hearing as to their position and what it is they intend to prove in the proceedings. Opening statements have no probative value and are invariably presented by the parties to provide the arbitrator with an overview of their respective positions. There is no precise order for the parties to present their opening statement and argue their case. Usually, however, since the company has the burden of proof to justify its actions in a disciplinary matter, it goes first; in an interpretative question, where the burden of proof is reversed, it is up to the union to show that the company has violated the provisions of the contract.

Open Items   In any given negotiations, those contract clauses and items in which either party or both propose changes or inclusion in the contract are called the open items. While parties are generally not so legalistic in bargaining with one another as to preclude other items from being added, the initial list of open items as determined at the exchange of proposals at the table at the start of negotiations generally consists of close to all, if not all, the items the parties will negotiate on.

Open Shop   A place of work in which the employer does not recognize the union and there is no labor contract. Individual employees may be union members and are free to join a union, but the employer deals with them as individuals and not through a union or labor organization. The open shop has been referred to over the years as the **unorganized shop,** the **nonunion shop,** and the **nonaffiliated shop.** More recently, nonunion employers in the construction industry especially have referred to themselves as **merit shops.** This nomenclature is used to highlight the fact that in open shops, as they view it, wages, employee benefits, promotion, and job security are all based on an individual employee's skills, job performance, experience, and merit as distinct from the collective terms of a labor agreement.

Opinion and Award   An arbitrator's written determination. The **opinion,** or **discussion,** in an arbitration is analogous to the court's **dicta.** It contains the arbitrator's reasoning and considerations in reaching the conclusion set forth in the **award.** No matter how astute, learned, reasonable, or logical, however, the arbitrator's opinions are not enforceable; only the ARBITRATOR'S AWARD is enforceable in the courts.

Organizational Picketing   Picketing undertaken to obtain employer recognition of the union and to encourage unorganized workers to join the union. Also called **recognition picketing.**

Organizational Strike   A strike by workers seeking to organize a plant and gain employer recognition. Also called a **recognition strike.**

Organized Worker   An employee who is a **union member.** Also called a **unionized worker,** and, colloquially, a **union skate;** collectively, the RANK AND FILE.

Outlaw Strike   See UNAUTHORIZED STRIKE.

Out-of-Work Room   See HIRING HALL.

Outsourcing   A term that has recently surfaced among American workers in the automotive industry. It is used to describe the practice of U.S. motor companies shifting work from American plants to their foreign affiliates. From labor's standpoint, the practice impacts on job security and job opportunities in much the same way as subcontracting and it is met with similar resistance. In fact, in the fall of 1983 a group of UAW members and Ford employees staged an afternoon demonstration against "outsourcing" at the front of the company's headquarters in Dearborn, Michigan. The automotive companies, in contrast, view "outsourcing" as an essential cost-effective practice since the work transferred to the foreign affiliates has been on their small and low-priced cars. As management representatives reasoned, there is much economic justification in having a $12 an hour American worker putting in the glass windows of a $13,000 model rather than in one selling at $7,000.

Overscale   A term used in reference to craft union contracts primarily where the base contract rate is a minimum rate; the employer may not pay a journeyman less than the contract rate but may pay more. The rate paid journeymen in excess of the contract rate is called overscale. An overscale rate is considered to be the journeyman's base or straight-time rate and overtime is computed on it.

Overtime   Hours of work beyond the normal workday and/or workweek for which overtime rates must be paid either by contract or pertinent federal or state law. The **Fair Labor Standards Act** of 1938 is the federal wage-hour law which establishes minimum wages and maximum hours beyond which overtime rates are to be paid and sets restrictions on child labor. The federal minimum wage, initially set at 25¢ per hour in 1938, is currently $3.35 per hour, while the maximum hours are 40 hours per week. From time to time pressure has been exerted to lower the maximum-hours standard and especially to provide, as in the maximum hours of the Walsh-Healy Public Contracts Act, that overtime be paid for work beyond 8 hours a day as well as beyond 40 hours per week. To date, however, the maximum-hours standard of the FLSA remains unchanged.

Overtime Rates   Rates paid for work beyond the normal workday and/or workweek. The FLSA establishes the overtime rate at time and one-half the straight-time hourly rate and this is the rate generally paid for overtime work. Some labor contracts provide for a higher overtime rate, however, usually as overtime is extended in duration; for example, double time for overtime beyond 3 hours and triple time for overtime beyond 5 hours. Historically, and especially when the normal workday and workweek were of such duration as 10 hours per day and 48 hours or longer per week, overtime rates in the labor contract were know as **punitive overtime rates** since they were intended by the union to discourage employers from working their members long hours injurious to health. With the current, shortened workday and workweek, overtime rates have come to be thought of by many as **premium rates,** albeit this generalization is not wholly consistent with the traditional usage of the term.

Paper Local   A "pseudo" or "fictitious" union that is denounced by the AFL–CIO and is often formed by criminal elements for unlawful racketeering purposes such as extortion and obtaining payoffs from employers. More often than not, the paper local is a local union without members or one whose "token" members are largely ignored. The paper local operates under a charter that is usually self-initiated but occasionally is obtained from some national or international union.

Parity Equality or an established relationship (ratio) between the salary schedules of different categories of workers. Parity has been a major concern in public sector negotiations in particular, but especially in relation to the salary levels of fire fighters and police officers. Equality or an established ratio between the salaries for fire fighters and patrol officers is called **horizontal parity.** An established ratio between fire fighter and fire lieutenant, or fire lieutenant and captain, or patrolman and sergeant, or police sergeant and lieutenant, etc., is called **vertical parity.**

Parol Evidence Evidence by "word of mouth"—that is, evidence given verbally rather than in writing. In the courts the **parol evidence rule** stipulates that when there is an agreement in writing, evidence of oral discussion and agreement of a contrary nature is inadmissible. In arbitration, parol evidence is generally not excluded, but the substance and intent of the "rule" is complied with and the parol evidence is given little, if any, weight.

Partial Strike A strike in which the union permits the employer to operate partially. Usually the operation permitted to function in a partial strike is selected to meet urgent public needs—for example, the continuation of the emergency room and "life and death care" during a hospital strike, or the moving of defense or other nationally critical shipments during a longshore, maritime, airline, auto maker, or railroad strike.

Past-Practice Clause A contractual provision requiring that management continue practices, benefits, and standards of working conditions that were provided in the past but that are not otherwise contractually required. Also called a **maintenance-of-standards clause.**

Pattern Bargaining That structure of bargaining in which a settlement is reached in one bargaining unit and those terms are made the pattern for settlement with other, separate and distinct bargaining units. Historically, pattern bargaining has been an established bargaining structure at one time or another in the steel, automotive, meat packing, electrical equipment, and farm equipment industries.

Pattern Follower   A union or firm that traditionally "hangs back" in negotiations and accepts the pattern bargained by others.

Pattern Setter   A union or form that traditionally negotiates the initial or key settlement that becomes the pattern for others. For example, although there are signs that the bargaining structure is changing, the International Typographical Union (ITU) over the years has been the traditional pattern setter in printing and newspaper negotiations.

Patterns of Bargaining   See BARGAINING STRUCTURE.

Pay-for-Knowledge System   A system whereby employees are paid an hourly wage or salary based on their skills, which are not necessarily in the actual job they are performing. When an employee completes a training course for a particular skill or job and the pay-for-knowledge system is applied, the employee's base pay is augmented. If the pay-for-knowledge system is provided for in the labor contract, the pay is a negotiated amount. And when that employee completes a training course that qualifies him/her for still another skill or job, the employee's base hourly wage or salary is further augmented. Proponents of the pay-for-knowledge system contend that (1) it provides employees with an incentive to gain new skills, increase their earnings, and improve their opportunities for upward mobility in the plant and (2) it gives the employer greater flexibility in the use of employees interchangeably throughout the plant. The pay-for-knowledge system was reportedly (1986) used in the GM/UAW Saturn project.

Peaceful Picketing   All lawful picketing must be peaceful—that is, picketers may not forcefully prevent nonstrikers from entering the plant, forcefully prevent deliveries to or from the plant, threaten or exercise violence, and the like.

Permanent Arbitrator   Also referred to as **named arbitrator, contract-named arbitrator, permanent umpire,** or **referee,** the permanent arbitrator, or umpire, or referee is usually designated by the parties at contract negotiations time and is listed in the contract.

Permanent Injunction   See INJUNCTION.

Permanent Umpire   See PERMANENT ARBITRATOR.

Permissive Subjects of Bargaining   Subjects of bargaining that are neither mandatory nor unlawful. Bargaining on permissive subjects may be voluntarily entered into and agreed upon, but it may not be carried to the point of impasse, strike, or lockout by either party. Such subjects as interest arbitration, union representation on a company's board of directors, definition of the bargaining unit as it affects multiplant and multiemployer units, inclusion of foremen and other supervisors in the bargaining unit, presence of a court reporter at negotiations, designation of labor and management representatives at the bargaining table, performance bonds such as requiring a union to post a bond to be forfeited in the event of a strike during the life of the contract or requiring an employer to post a bond to be forfeited in the event of a delinquency in welfare and/or pension payments under the contract, and pensions for retirees are all permissive subjects of bargaining.

Picketing   Posting employees and employee patrols outside an employer's establishment during a labor dispute. The union's use of picketing is multipurposed, to wit: to notify the public that a labor dispute exists; to encourage workers to join in the work stoppage; to discourage patronage of the business establishment; and to dissuade employees and others from entering the premises or making deliveries to or from it.

Piece Rate   A wage paid at a fixed amount per unit produced — for example, $5 per dress, $3 per skirt, $2 per blouse. Often called an **incentive rate** or **incentive wage,** it is traditionally opposed by many unions as conducive to excessive work speeds, grievances, competitiveness among workers, and dissension within the plant, and disruptive of essential union solidarity. Some 20–25% of the work force is estimated to be working in plants where the piece rate system is the predominant method of wage payment. Unions are most likely to accept piece rates when the standard piece rate can be applied uniformly in a large number of competitive shops in an industry nationally or regionally and when changes in the piece rate are made subject to mutual agreement or, in the event of disagreement between the employer and the union, made subject to resolution by a designated impartial chairman or umpire who has become a specialist and is knowledgeable of the industry's needs. Piece rates are prevalent in the men's and ladies' garment industries and in the hosiery, pottery, flint gas, and stove industries.

Piecework   Any work that is assigned which is paid for according to some form of a piece rate system of payment. A large share of the work that is done away from the plant is of this type, and whether paid for by piece or by time rate, it is called **homework.**

Porkchoppers   See LABOR ORGANIZER.

Portable Pension Plan   An arrangement whereby pension rights and benefits under a pension fund or plan are transferable from one employer to another in a given industry. Invariably provided in a multiemployer-bargained pension fund and by some national unions for locally negotiated pension plans. Employers traditionally have been less than partial to portable pension plans. This is understandable since, from an employer's point of view, a distinct advantage of a pension plan is that it serves as an inducement for employees to remain in the company's employ and lessens employee turnover. Notwithstanding traditional employer opposition, the International Typographical Union promoted an industry-wide-portable pension plan in the 1960s and it is now widely provided in newspaper publishing and book and job typographical contracts. The ITU's success here was no doubt partly due to the "printer's ink in one's blood" tradition and the historical acceptance of, and reliance on, the "itinerant printer" by printing and newspaper publishing industry employers. The Employee Retirement Income Security Act (ERISA), with its 10-year vesting of individual employee pension rights, has been a factor in breaking down traditional employer resistance to portable pension plans. Unions, too, have been putting increased pressure on employers to obtain portability in the pension provisions of their contracts. As in the case of cafeteria-style employee benefits, labor's efforts to secure portable pensions have been heightened by the attractiveness of these plans to young employees. The Food and Commercial Workers Union, for example, has been especially alert to the fact that, increasingly, young workers "move about more," and it has been aggressive in getting portability in the pension provisions of its contracts. Also, it has become commonplace for both husband and wife to work, and the two-career interests of many working families have added to the attractiveness of portable pensions.

Portal-to-Portal Pay   Payment that includes travel time from the check-in point at the plant to the actual work area and return. As initially "won" and applied by John L. Lewis in the mines, the shift's pay of a miner included the time spent traveling from the mine's entrance to the place of work, the mine's face or surface, at the start of the shift and back again at the end of the shift. Portal-to-portal payments are currently being provided in several industries in which travel time is a major factor. The Fair Labor Standards Act specifically provides, however, that this is not compensable time in the absence of a union contract.

Posthearing Brief　The brief generally forwarded to the arbitrator by each party within an agreed-upon period following the close of the hearing(s) or the receipt of TRANSCRIPT if taken. Often, the parties arrange for the submission of a **reply brief** after the exchange of post-hearing briefs.

Preactivity　In a sense, preactivity is RETROACTIVITY in reverse since it refers to situations in which the parties reach agreement before the end of the old contract but agree that the settlement terms, usually confined to wage increases, are to be put into effect upon ratification by the union, even though this takes place prior to the date of the old contract's termination and the recorded start of the new contract. Preactivity is not the normal form of early settlement. Generally, when the parties reach agreement on the terms of a new contract early, they do not put them into effect until the old contract expires, this is what is commonly referred to as an **early settlement.**

Preamble Clause　Usually the initial provision in the labor contract identifying the parties involved and often setting forth general objectives, including a statement of intent such as the promotion of harmonious relations.

Preferential Shop　A unionized shop in which there is agreement that the employer will give preference to union members over non-members usually in hiring but sometimes in layoff as well. Now unlawful under the Taft-Hartley Act.

Prehearing Brief　A brief infrequently used in arbitration. When provided, it sets forth the basic issue and position of the parties for the arbitrator's information and review prior to the scheduled hearing date.

Premium Pay　Pay in excess of the regular rate, usually for hazardous, dirty, or unpleasant work; for inconvenience and work on days or at hours employees would normally expect to be off, such as Saturdays, Sundays, sixth and seventh shifts, holidays, night and early morning shifts; for work in excess of normal standards; and the like.

Premium Pay Systems　See BONUS PAY SYSTEMS.

Premium Rates　See OVERTIME RATES; PREMIUM PAY.

Preponderance of Evidence　See QUANTUM OF PROOF.

Prevailing Rate　A regulatory wage rate concept initially adopted in the **Davis-Bacon Act** of 1931 covering federal construction — that is, workers engaged in covered public construction may not be paid less than the rate prevailing in construction in that locality or geographical areas. The prevailing-rate concept has been made applicable to state and local government construction in numerous **Little Davis-Bacon Acts** modeled after the federal law. With some modification, prevailing wages must be paid by employers in manufacturing and service industries performing work for the federal government by contract under the **Walsh-Healy Public Contract Act** of 1936. In recent years, the Davis-Bacon Act has come under especially heavy attack for unduly adding to the already inflated costs of federal construction. The Davis-Bacon Act requires the Secretary of Labor to determine the prevailing wage rates in the area or locality where public works, repair, or alterations are being done. Critics of the Act contend that this results in federal construction's being required to pay the high rates prevailing in Building Trades Union contracts in the area. By contrast, the labor standards established by the Walsh-Healy Public Contracts Act are to be at least the prevailing minimum wage, and this assures consideration of nonunion as well as union rates in the area. In usage other than for established governmental labor standards, the term *prevailing rate* or *prevailing wage* refers to the predominant or composite base wage being paid for particular classifications of work in a given geographical area.

Prevailing Wage   See PREVAILING RATE.

Primary Boycott   See BOYCOTT.

Primary Disputes Arbitration   See INTEREST ARBITRATION.

Primary Labor Organization   See LOCAL UNION.

Production Employee   See PRODUCTION WORKER.

Production Worker   Worker, regardless of his/her skill, in nonsupervisory positions whose job is directly connected with the manufacture of a product or service. Also called **production employee, mechanical worker,** and **mechanical employee,** these workers are distinct from **maintenance workers,** whose basic duties are to maintain and keep in repair the company's plant and equipment. Production and maintenance workers together comprise a company's **blue-collar work force.**

Productivity Bargaining   Bargaining by an employer in which increases in wages and other economic benefits are conditioned on corresponding increases in worker productivity. Usually, in this type of bargaining, wage increases are made the quid pro quo for the union's elimination of work restriction rules and practices.

Profit-Sharing Plans   Wage plans that apportion some amount of a company's net profits to employees. In order to encourage and reward improved productivity and efficiency, the amount to be paid to employees in most profit-sharing plans is stated as a percentage of the profits and is provided as an extra compensation over and above regular salary or base contract hourly earnings. Initially, profit-sharing plans were promoted as a corporate personnel and welfare activity essential to developing a proper "esprit de corps" in the plant and an effective labor force. It is said that profit-sharing plans were first introduced in the United States in 1794 by Albert Gallatin, who served as Secretary of the Treasury under Presidents Jefferson and Madison. Over the years, profit-sharing plans have not been a major factor in American industry for nonexecutive and nonsalaried employees and, with the exception of the 1920s, when many major corporations instituted them along with other welfare plans as an alternative to worker dependency on unions, they have not been widely adopted. From the outset, organized labor has generally taken a dim view toward profit-sharing plans, considering them, along with other unilaterally established welfare programs, as devisive, another device "to get workers to speed up," and generally inimical to trade unionism. There are indications today, however, that a change in attitude toward profit-sharing plans may be taking place. This was evidenced by the adoption of profit-sharing plans in the major automotive contracts negotiated in 1984 and 1985. This has spread to other industries as well. No doubt the adoption of profit-sharing plans in the automotive contracts has been spurred on by Japanese competition and Japan's successes in achieving high levels of worker productivity and efficiency. Much of this has been attributed to the personnel policies of Japanese companies and their heavy reliance on welfare programs of all types. It is still too early to assess whether profit-sharing plans in labor contracts in the United States will outlive the special circumstances and considerations of present-day bargaining or prove as ephemeral as American Motors' Progress Sharing Plan in the late 1950s (Walter Reuther, president of the United Auto Workers at the time, had innovatively proposed the inclusion of profit-sharing plans in automotive contracts). Interestingly, profit-sharing plans like the two-tier wage plans and the lump-sum wage payments negotiated in the 1980s have the distinct advantage of providing increases in workers' earnings without affecting the base contract hourly rate.

Proof Beyond a Reasonable Doubt   See QUANTUM OF PROOF.

Public Employee Relations Laws   Statutes that cover labor-management relations for state and local government employees. The administrative bodies for such laws are usually called **state public employee relations boards** or **commissions**.

Punitive Overtime Rates   See OVERTIME RATES.

Pure Craft Union   See CRAFT UNION.

Pyramiding of Overtime   Payment of more than one overtime or premium rate for the same work. Labor contracts are usually precise in preventing the pyramiding of overtime and premium payments for both daily and weekly overtime or for work on Saturdays, Sundays, holidays, and sixth and seventh days of work.

Quality-of-Work-Life Programs   The quality-of-work-life (QWL) movement, which has flourished in European industry for several decades, has only recently been extended to the United States. Initial impetus to the adoption of QWL programs was provided in 1972 by the report of a task force for the Secretary of Health, Education, and Welfare entitled *Work in America*. The report concluded that serious economic and social problems were resulting from declining productivity and poor job satisfaction and it urged unions and management to address these problems jointly in innovative and experimental shop programs. Encouragement for the adoption of QWL programs was in turn provided by the National Commission of Productivity and its successors, the National Committee on Productivity and Work Quality, and the National Center for Productivity and Work Quality. The efforts to promote QWL programs were only moderately successful, however, and in 1978, following a report by the Government Accounting Office that the National Center for Productivity's accomplishments were limited, the Center was dissolved. Nonetheless, experiments continue to be made with the adoption of this type of joint worker-management shop committee.

Quality-of-work-life programs embrace job enrichment and job enlargement programs as well. In a broad sense, QWL programs extend labor-management cooperation programs, and labor-management relations generally, beyond the traditional union-management concept of wages, hours, and working conditions to such areas as technological change, improving relations between management and workers, improving work habits, participative and team management involving workers and their supervisors, improving the quality of product, productivity, and the like. The essence of the quality of life concept is that worker involvement in decision-making will improve worker satisfaction and that this, in turn, will improve productivity. It is this focus on productivity and concern as to the possible negative impact on jobs that has led organized labor to have mixed reactions to QWL programs. As expressed by Howard D. Samuels, the head of the AFL–CIO's Industrial Union Department, and reported in the *AFL–CIO News*, vol. 29, no. 4 (January 28, 1984), the reasons labor has been more resistant than supportive of QWL programs are that far too frequently the program has been designed primarily to improve productivity and reduce waste and has not been basically concerned with improving the quality of work life in the plant; that the programs have not always provided commensurate benefits to the workers and given them meaningful and lasting participation in decision-making in matters affecting their well-being and that of the plant; and that, in several instances, QWL programs have been utilized to turn workers away from their union or have been put into effect as part of a broad "antiunion" program. On the other hand, albeit an exception to date, unions such as the Auto Workers, Communications Workers, and Steelworkers have been largely pleased with the types of QWL programs they have recently been involved in with several companies in their respective industries.

Whether this interest in QWL programs proves to be short-lived or represents a genuine trend of the future in labor relations in the United States generally, and in labor-management cooperation in particular, remains to be seen. The United States Department of Labor, however, is positive in its assessment. Following a 1983 study of some 200 QWL programs in the private and public sectors, the Labor Department stated that "thousands of companies and unions that have tried these cooperative programs are convinced that there is no other way to operate."

Quantum of Proof   The degree of proof required to justify discharge and less severe disciplinary action. The criminal court's requirement of **proof beyond a reasonable doubt** is the exception rather than the norm in arbitration except in discharge for acts of moral turpitude, criminal intent, and acts of such kind punishable under the law. For the most part, arbitrators use the **clear and convincing proof** standard in assessing whether or not there is just cause for discharge. For suspensions and less severe disciplinary action, arbitrators usually apply the less stringent standard of **preponderance of evidence.**

Quickie Strike   See UNAUTHORIZED STRIKE; WILDCAT STRIKE.

Raiding   A Union's attempt either to organize workers who are within another union's jurisdiction or to enroll the members of another union.

Rank and File   Union members who are not officials or officers of the union. Often called the **grass roots** of the union.

Rat   See RATTING; SCAB.

Rate Cutting   Arbitrarily reducing the established rate on piece work or work incentive standards.

Ratting   A union worker's giving information to an employer which is detrimental to a **brother** or **sister** (another union member) or to the union itself. The informer, in turn, is called a **rat.**

Real Wage   What wages command in goods and services; the purchasing power of the dollar income earned by individuals. Real wages vary in inverse proportion to the cost-of-living Consumer Price Index; when wage rates are unchanged, real wages increase when the Consumer Price Index or prices decline, and vice versa.

Recognition Clause   A contract clause setting forth the union designated as the exclusive representative of, and bargaining agent for, a specified group or groups of employees.

Recognition Picketing   See INFORMATIONAL PICKETING; ORGANIZATIONAL PICKETING.

Recognition Strike   See ORGANIZATIONAL STRIKE.

Red Circle Pay or Rate   Under a special agreement, or a grandfather clause, when a higher rate than the prescribed contractual rate is paid, the higher rate is called a **red circle rate,** and the payment is known as **red circle pay.**

Referee   See PERMANENT ARBITRATOR.

Regional Bargaining   Historically, AREA-WIDE BARGAINING was confined to MULTIEMPLOYER BARGAINING in a city. When it was broadened to include employers of a given industry in a region, as, for example, the paper industry in the Pacific Northwest, it was termed regional bargaining.

Reply Brief   See POSTHEARING BRIEF.

Reporting Pay   Minimum pay to employees who report for work at their regular shift but no work is required and they have not been given prior notice of the unavailability of work. Usually reporting pay is less than a full shift's pay (predominantly 2–4 hours' pay), with the proviso that it is not to be paid if the unavailability of work is due to hurricanes, floods, and other such "Acts of God" beyond the employer's control. Also called **call pay, show-up-time pay,** and **guaranteed minimum shift pay.**

Representation Election   See BARGAINING AGENT; CERTIFICATION.

Res Adjudicata   See RES JUDICATA.

Reserved or Residual Rights Theory of Management's Contractual Rights   A theory which holds that management rights under a contract are all rights that are not expressly denied to the employer; in other words, all rights are reserved for management that are not contractually denied it.

Reserve Fund   See STRIKE FUND.

Reserve Gate   See COMMON SITUS PICKETING.

Res Judicata   A matter that has already been adjudged and ruled upon. In arbitration, as in law, in cases of res judicata the matter is dismissed whatever may be the personal views of the arbitrator as to the merits of the case or the adjudgment in the prior award. This concept is especially important in arbitration since it prevents multiple arbitrations and decisions on the same grievance. Also referred to as **res adjudicata.**

Retroactivity   The effect of reaching agreement subsequent to the end of a contract but making the settlement terms, or stipulated parts of them such as wage increases, effective back to the terminal date of the old contract.

Rights Arbitration   Arbitration dealing with disputes over the rights of the parties under a given contract. Disputes that arise during the life of a contract are essentially of two types: (1) interpretation questions as to the meaning of one or more of the contractual provisions, usually whether in a given instance management's application was in violation of the contract; and (2) discipline questions as to whether management had just cause to render the specific discipline (such as a written warning, suspension, or discharge) that it did. Also referred to as **grievance arbitration, contract interpretation arbitration,** and **minor** or **secondary disputes arbitration.**

Right-to-Work States   See UNION SHOP PROVISO.

Rotating Shifts   In continuous-operation plants with three shifts and in some plants with two shifts, workers are rotated or periodically changed from one shift to another. This rotation is usually set up for periods of one week or longer. Generally, when there is a systematic rotation of shifts, SHIFT DIFFERENTIALS are not paid.

Round-the-Clock Bargaining   A form of CONTINUOUS BARGAINING in which the negotiators, usually at the time settlement appears imminent, negotiate day and night continuously until settlement or impasse is reached.

Rules of Evidence   Rules followed by the courts in evaluating the admissibility of evidence and established largely for the benefit of lay jurors. Arbitrators are not bound by the rules of evidence since the process is quasi-judicial and the arbitrator is presumed to be knowledgeable, capable of sifting out the irrelevant, and evaluating impartially the relative worth of the evidence submitted. For this reason, arbitrators tend to be all-embracing in accepting evidence "for what it is worth" or "subject to connection" and preferring "the sins of commission to those of omission" when ruling on questions as to the admissibility of evidence. Arbitrators need to, and are expected to, know the rules of evidence. While not obligated to apply them, arbitrators nonetheless invariably do so when addressing sensitive areas.

Sabotage   When used in reference to a labor dispute, the deliberate and unlawful destruction or damaging of the property and/or machines and other equipment of an employer or of other employees.

Savings Clause   See LAWS CLAUSE.

Scab   A worker who continues to work in a plant during a strike. Also, frequently called a **rat.** The term *scab,* which is often used interchangeably with STRIKEBREAKER, has also been used in labor circles in referring to workers who have taken a job in a nonunion shop or who work under nonunion conditions at a time when the union is seeking to organize the plant or industry.

Scale   See BASE CONTRACT HOURLY RATE.

Scanlon Plan   See LABOR COST-SAVINGS BONUS PLAN.

Scientific Management   A term popularized in the 1920s by the industrial job evaluation, time and motion, and production studies designed and promoted by such industrial engineers as Frederick

Taylor. Refers broadly to the application of scientific methods and techniques to manufacturing methods and operations in order to increase productivity, decrease cost, reduce spoilage or waste, minimize unproductive time, breakdown or "de-skill" skilled jobs into semiskilled and unskilled components, and the like.

Scope of Arbitration   The range of issues subject to arbitration. In the vast majority of contracts, the scope of arbitration is as broad as the definition of a grievance — that is to say, what is grievable is arbitrable. In some contracts, however, the parties expressly exclude certain issues or provisions from arbitration. For example, a company may be strong enough to exclude from arbitration specific areas of managerial decision-making such as the contracting-out of bargaining unit work while, on the other hand, a strong union may except the jurisdictional provision of the contract from arbitration. This means, in effect, that disputes over contracting-out and/or the union's jurisdiction are not subject to the no strike–no lockout provisions of the contract. If such matters are taken to arbitration and contested by either party, they will be held to be not arbitrable because they are not within the scope of arbitration as provided under the contract, and the arbitrator will not address or adjudge the merits of the dispute. Such disputes, then, because they are outside the scope of arbitration can be resolved only by the parties at the bargaining table or by the pressures of strike or lockout.

Scope of Bargaining   The scope of bargaining encompasses what is being bargained — that is, the subject matter the parties are bargaining over. Within the limits of what is "lawful" under the NLRA and pertinent state and public sector legislation, the scope of bargaining is as broad as "the ingenuity of man" and the willingness of the parties to discuss and negotiate on the subjects raised.

Sea Lawyer   The name colloquially given to a union representative — usually a shop steward or business agent — who is a "stickler" for the contract and who rigidly and uncompromisingly enforces "every letter" and "dot of an *i*" of its provisions in the day-to-day relations with management in the plant.

Secondary Boycott   Boycott pressure exerted against an employer who is not directly involved in a dispute. For example, the concerted decision of workers and a union not directly involved in a labor dispute to refuse to handle, purchase, use, or work with the products of a struck plant or a plant declared to be unfair to labor. Under the Taft-Hartley and Landrum-Griffin acts, certain types of secondary boycotts were made unlawful and restrictions were imposed on other usages.

Secondary Disputes Arbitration   See RIGHTS ARBITRATION.

Secondary Picketing   Picketing directed at an employer who is not directly involved but who does business with the employer with whom the union has a labor dispute. Secondary picketing is unlawful under the Taft-Hartley Act except when it is informational and does not promote a secondary boycott.

Secondary Strike   See SYMPATHY STRIKE.

Second Shift   See SHIFT DIFFERENTIALS.

Selective Strike   A strike in which the union directs the work stoppage at a particular division or plant of a multiplant company operation or at a particular employer or group of employers under a multiemployer contract.

Self-perpetuating Provision   See AUTOMATIC CONTRACT RENEWAL.

Semiskilled Worker   A manual worker who is required to exercise a degree of skill (though not of a high order) which is often limited to a well-defined work routine and does not require the exercise of independent judgment or cause extensive damage to product or equipment if there is a lapse in work performance. Most craft assistants and auxilliary functions are semiskilled—take for example, a proof press operator or a paper handler.

Semistrike   See STATUTORY STRIKE.

Separability Clause   See LAWS CLAUSE.

Sequestering   As practiced in arbitration, the separation of witnesses from the hearing room so that no witness hears another's testimony. When either party requests it, sequestering (sometimes referred to as **invoking the rule**) is generally granted by the arbitrator. Witnesses who leave the hearing room to await their turn to testify are instructed not to discuss the case or their testimony with one another. It is to be noted that the grievant cannot be sequestered. Also, one or the other party frequently requests that the arbitrator exempt a witness from being sequestered; management counsel, for example, may request that the company's director of industrial relations be permitted to remain in the hearing room, or union counsel may request that the union's business manager, agent, or representative remain in the hearing room even though they may ultimately be called to testify. It is wholly within the arbitrator's discretion to grant or deny a party this request, but, if granted, it is generally balanced by the arbitrator's giving the other party the option of also naming a person to be exempt.

Shift Differentials   Premiums for working other than the day shift; usually progressive, as in a 5% shift differential for the **second shift** and a 10% shift differential for the **third shift.** The differential is over the **first shift** rate, and for the workers on the premium shift, it becomes the base rate on which overtime is calculated in that shift. The first shift is uniformly the **day shift** and is generally called that. The second shift invariably starts in the late afternoon and extends into the evening; it is generally called the **night shift** and sometimes the **afternoon shift.** The third shift usually starts at about midnight or just prior to it and is variously called the **midnight shift,** the **morning shift,** the **graveyard shift,** and the **lobster shift.** The term *lobster shift* is not widely used except by printing employees and workers in a few other industries in cities such as New York and Boston which are located near sea waters where commercial lobster fishing is, or was, widely prevalent. The term is an historical carry-over from earlier years when lobster fishing was commonplace and many workers at the completion of their shift at about 6:00 or 7:00 A.M. would tend their lobster pots before going home.

Shop Committee   Some unions handle plant grievances through a shop committee. **Shop committeemen,** like shop stewards, are appointed by union officials or elected by their fellow workers. The **shop committee chairman** is often called the **head steward** or **chief steward** and is frequently a full-time union functionary. Shop committeemen, like stewards, usually handle grievances and represent unit members in the shop on a part-time basis while holding down a regular shop job.

Shop Committee Chairman   See SHOP COMMITTEE.

Shop Committeemen   See SHOP COMMITTEE.

Shop Designation   See UNION SECURITY PROVISIONS.

Shop Steward   Also referred to as the **steward** or **union steward,** the shop steward is the union's representative in the plant. Shop stewards are either appointed by higher officers in the union or elected by higher officers in the union or elected by a group of fellow union members in a department, shop, or area of a shop. There are often several stewards in a large plant, with a designated **head steward** or

chief steward or **chairman,** and frequently with assistants as well. The principal functions of stewards are representing unit members in handling grievances, seeing that the contract's terms are being complied with, collecting union dues, and recruiting new members. **Stewards** usually perform their union duties on a part-time basis while continuing to work at their regular shop jobs. However, in a few contracts, unions have succeeded in obtaining a limited number of **full-time stewards** who are paid by the employer at contract rate.

Short-term Contract   See LONG-TERM CONTRACT.

Show-up-Time Pay   See REPORTING PAY.

Simple Boycott   See BOYCOTT.

Sit-Down Strike   A work stoppage in which the workers refuse to leave the employer's premises. This type of strike was utilized extensively by the auto workers and unions in other mass-production industries in the post–World War II years. Until declared unlawful in the late 1940s, the sit-down strike was held to be labor's most powerful economic weapon, and CIO industrial unions especially viewed it as an effective means of combatting the monopoly power of the "corporate giants" in the mass-production industries.

Skilled Rate, Semiskilled Rate, and Unskilled Rate   Categorization of wage rates by skill.

Skilled Union   See CRAFT UNION.

Special Fund   See STRIKE FUND.

Speed-up   The practice whereby an employer forces workers to increase their production but fails to provide a corresponding increase in wages. Most frequently used in reference to a change and increase in the speed of an assembly or production line, but also used by labor in depicting the general effect of incentive wage plans.

Split Shift   The term has two usages. Primarily, and most frequently, it refers to situations in which the continuity of a shift's working hours is broken and workers are required to take time off without pay during the shift—that is, working from 7:00 A.M. to 11:00 A.M. and then returning at 2:00 P.M. to complete their 8-hour shift. This practice is also referred to as **broken time.** The term *split shift* has also been used by craft unions such as the printing crafts (which insist that a shift be of continuous working hours) to refer to a shift that straddles two normal shifts. For example, a shift that starts at 10:00 A.M. and ends at 6:00 P.M. begins in the normal day shift and ends in the normal night shift. Premium pay is generally required in contracts that permit split shifts of the latter type, and the union usually limits the number of employees allowed to be assigned to it.

Standard Rate   The term given to the BASE CONTRACT HOURLY RATE and popularized in the 1890s and early 1900s by Beatrice and Sidney Webb, the great English scholars and analysts of trade unionism and industrial democracy. In essence, the union's negotiated rate was to become the standard rate throughout the industry, thereby taking wages out of competition over the whole area of competitive production and eliminating the downward pressure on wages exerted by employers in a competitive economy. The term *standard rate* is currently used broadly and often refers to (1) an occupational rate established by regulation, state or federal law, or company rule; (2) a plant or industry rate established by collective bargaining; or (3) a rate upon which incentive pay is computed.

Standard Workday   See BASE CONTRACT HOURS.

State Labor Relations Boards   See STATE LABOR RELATIONS LAWS.

State Labor Relations Laws   Statutes enacted in most states within the framework of the National Labor Relations Act; these laws cover labor-management relations for intrastate industries and are administered by **state labor relations boards.**

State Mediation and/or Conciliation Agencies   Provide mediation services and maintain an arbitration panel for the use of labor and management engaged in intrastate commerce.

State Public Employee Relations Boards or Commissions   See PUBLIC EMPLOYEE RELATIONS LAWS.

Statutory Strike   Also called a **semistrike** or a **nonstoppage strike.** A strike in which there is no work stoppage after impasse is reached, but in which management and labor impose penalties on themselves to pressure an agreement. Usually the penalties take the form of agreed-upon deductions from the workers' pay and matching employer contributions, both of which are put into a special fund. The monies are generally returned if settlement is reached, but are given to charity or used for some other agreed-upon purpose if self-imposed deadlines for settlement are not met. The statutory strike has been suggested by some as a fitting "tool" in an ARSENAL OF WEAPONS available by public statute to deal with emergency strikes. If the statutory strike were to become public policy, the deductions imposed on employees and employer would be forfeited to the U.S. Treasury as a **strike tax.**

Stipulation of Facts   The process by which the parties at the start of the arbitration proceedings agree on certain facts pertinent to the case, as, for example, the grievant's job title and date of hire, the date and time the incident occurred for which the grievant was disciplined, the location of the plant where the incident took place, and the like.

Stool Pigeon   An employee of a detective agency or a company who joins a union in order to spy on it, create dissension, and engage in other activities directed at weakening the union.

Straight   See AGENCY SHOP.

Straight-time Hours   See BASE CONTRACT HOURS.

Straight-time Rate   See BASE CONTRACT HOURLY RATE.

Strategy Strike   A strike by a key or strategic group of employees which affects or ties up the production of a large number of workers in a shop.

Stretch-out   The practice whereby employers require workers to tend more machines, or increase production standards, or take on additional work duties without providing them any increase in their rate of pay.

Strike   A temporary concerted stoppage of work by employees to reinforce a demand for changes in wages, hours, and working conditions or to express a grievance, obtain recognition, or resolve a dispute with management. Also called **economic strike** and **work stoppage.**

Strike Benefits   The monies a union pays its members during a strike. Largely because of the financial cost, but also to put pressure on members to reach a settlement, the union pays strike benefits that rarely approach the level of the worker's base contract wage. There are, of course, exceptions. For example, the pilots union in its strike at Continental Airlines in the early 1980s and the International Typographical Union's "Big Six" in their strike against New York City newspapers in the 1970s provided full-pay strike benefits for their members. More generally, however, strike benefits amount to but a relatively small proportion of the worker's base contract pay, often 50% or less, and are frequently subject as well to periodic reduction as the duration of the strike lengthens. In some instances, unions provide groceries and other essentials to needy striking families. Often this is done in lieu of providing monetary benefits.

Strikebreaker   A person hired to replace a striker. Also called a SCAB.

Strike Deadline   The time and date given by the union for a strike if agreement on a new contract is not reached. Usually announced at "the eleventh hour" prior to a midnight deadline marking the end of an existing collective bargaining agreement and accompanied by the union's traditional warning, "no contract, no work."

Strike Fund   A fund set aside by a union for use during a strike to provide STRIKE BENEFITS and/or assistance to needy striking families, to cover legal fees and the costs of publicity, to promote and "maintain" the strike, and the like. The monies are obtained either from the union's general fund or by a special monthly assessment on all dues-paying members. Sometimes called a **defense fund,** an **emergency fund,** a **special fund,** or a **reserve fund.**

Strike Insurance   Insurance coverage obtained to provide financial aid in the event of a strike. Usually, it is the employer's counterpart to the union's strike fund, although local unions, on occasion, have been known to innovatively subscribe to strike insurance. Strike insurance is widely held by newspaper publishers, and this has given rise to the view among newspaper unions that if a strike is sanctioned, they should be prepared for a long one since insurance coverage is invariably extended over many weeks. Under most strike insurance plans, there is a one-week waiting period before strike benefits are paid.

Strike Notice   Notification that a federal or state law requires a union to file with a designated governmental agency prior to strike. Under the Taft-Hartley Act, notice is to be given to the Federal Mediation and Conciliation Service (FMCS), and the union may not lawfully strike until 30 days after such notice or the termination of the contract, whichever is later.

Striker   An employee who engages in, and is part of, the group of workers on strike. Under the law, workers on an economic strike retain their status as employees but are subject to being replaced and have no legal rights to bump their replacements upon termination of the strike.

Strike Sanction   Union approval of a work stoppage. Local unions often require membership approval in a referendum vote prior to a strike. Some national or international unions require affiliated local unions to obtain the approval of their membership before striking.

Strike Tax   See STATUTORY STRIKE.

Strike Vote   A convening of the union membership to vote on a proposal to "go on strike."

Struck Work   The work performed by or for an employer whose workers are on strike.

Subcontracting   Subletting all or part of the work to be done under a contract to outside contractors. Often called **contracting-out,** this practice is generally resisted by unions, which view the process as a loss or potential loss of jobs, work, and pay for their members.

Subcontracting Clause   See CONTRACTING-OUT CLAUSE.

Submission   Also called the **stipulation,** this is the issue in question before the arbitrator as mutually agreed upon by the parties to a dispute. It is this question, and this question alone, which the arbitrator may legally address in the ARBITRATOR'S AWARD. In fact, if a submission as to discharge is narrowly submitted as to whether there is just cause for the dismissal of the grievant under Article XX of the contract, and the arbitrator states in the opinion that there is question as to whether the grievant failed to conform to the perquisites of Article XX but patently violated the provisions of Article XXI and, hence, was properly discharged for cause, the arbitrator's award is subject to being overturned by the courts as having failed to stay within the arbitral authority provided by the parties.

Subpoena   A writ compelling the appearance of a witness or the submission of certain documents. Often used in arbitration. The arbitrator generally has the legal authority to issue a subpoena when requested to do so by either party. In some instances, the issuance of a subpoena may be on the arbitrator's own authority— that is, the arbitrator subpoenas a witness or documents which neither party intended to present. This is not customary and is questionable as a general practice since arbitration is essentially a proceeding in which the arbitrator, in a sense, is "an instrument of the parties" and his authority stems from the contract. Nonetheless, in a few states the arbitrator has the right to issue subpoenas on his own authority.

Successor Clause   A contractual provision which stipulates that the terms of the COLLECTIVE BARGAINING AGREEMENT shall be binding upon the parties' "successors and assigns." Also called an **assignability clause.** Usually stipulates that in the event of the sale, assignment, or transfer of a business, the employer will incorporate in its contract of sale assignment or transfer a provision requiring the purchaser, assignee, or transferee to assume and be bound by all the terms and conditions of the existing collective bargaining agreement.

Sufficient and Reasonable Cause   See JUST CAUSE.

Sufficient Cause   See JUST CAUSE.

Summation   In the vast majority of arbitration cases, there are no written briefs and each party presents an oral summation of its case at the close of the hearing. This summation is sometimes referred to as a **closing statement.** Unless expedited and specified otherwise, the written OPINION AND AWARD is normally rendered within 30 days (AAA rules) or 60 days (FMCS rules) of the close of the hearing or receipt of briefs as the case may be. As with the OPENING STATEMENT, there is no precise order for the parties in summation. In fact, there is less uniformity here than with the opening statement. However, when the order of summation is not specified by the parties, many arbitrators, unlike the courts, reverse the procedure followed in the opening statement. The view, here, is that in summation what needs be argued first is why the party having the burden of proof in the arbitration has not met that burden.

Sunshine Bargaining   A term that has come into prominence since the advent of collective bargaining in the public sector and the clamor for public (taxpayer) presence or representation at the bargaining table. When the public-at-large is admitted to negotiating sessions, the bargaining is commonly called sunshine bargaining, and in the few states that require it by law, the statutes are known as **sunshine bargaining laws.**

Sunshine Bargaining Laws   See SUNSHINE BARGAINING.

Supplemental Unemployment Benefit Plan   Commonly called **SUB,** this plan contractually provides wage payments to laid-off workers which are made in addition to the unemployment insurance benefits provided by the state. In the mid-1950s, the UAW negotiated a SUB plan when it was unable to secure a guaranteed annual wage.

Swearing-in   The swearing-in of witnesses in arbitration is not required by law. At his/her discretion, however, the arbitrator may require witnesses to testify under oath. The effect of swearing-in witnesses in arbitration is a sobering one, but unlike the courts, the criminal offense of **perjury** has rarely, if ever, been made applicable to false statements by witnesses in an arbitration.

Sweetheart Contract   The "agreement" entered into with an employer by a PAPER LOCAL is known as a *sweetheart contract* since its terms are generally "tailored" to be favorable to the employer as part of the pay-off arrangement made with the officers of the paper local. Frequently, and increasingly so, the term *sweetheart contract* has been loosely used by the rank and file of a legitimate union to describe a contract negotiated with employers whose terms were far less favorable than the membership had expected or included concessions and "give-backs" on labor's part.

Swing Shift   The name given to the **fourth shift** utilized by continuous-operation plants to cover the time-off periods that result from the rotation of the other shifts.

Sympathy Strike   A work stoppage by employees who are not directly involved in the labor dispute. Done to show union solidarity and to put pressure on the employer in support of a strike by another group of employees. Also called a **secondary strike.**

System Boards of Adjustment   See BOARD OF ARBITRATION.

Taft-Hartley Funds   See JOINT WELFARE FUND.

Take-home Pay   The net pay that is actually given an employee or received in the pay check. It includes gross earnings, the regular rate for the period covered plus all overtime and premiums, less deductions such as federal and state income tax, social security tax, pension payments, health insurance premiums, and the like.

Temporary Restraining Order   See INJUNCTION.

10-K Case   See JURISDICTIONAL STRIKE.

Terminal Arbitration   See INTEREST ARBITRATION.

Third Shift   See SHIFT DIFFERENTIALS.

Threshold Issue   See ARBITRABILITY.

Time-and-Motion Study   The study of a job operation to eliminate unessential and wasteful motions and unnecessary time spent in the performance of a given job. Analyzes the motions and measures the time needed by an average worker utilizing specified materials and equipment to complete the job. Often a **time study** or a **motion study** is conducted independently of the other. The term *job study* is sometimes broadly used to refer to all these types of studies.

Timeliness   The critical time frame in which a particular grievance in arbitration is raised or processed. Many contracts provide that a grievance must be raised within a specified period of time—for example, within 30 days of its occurrence. If an employee did not grieve an alleged injustice and violation of the contract until six months after it had taken place, the matter could be contested by management on the grounds of timeliness. If taken to arbitration, absent strong mitigating factors, the arbitrator would more than likely hold the grievance to be untimely, rule the matter not arbitrable, and deny the grievance without addressing the merits of the issue.

Time Rate   Payment of wages at a fixed amount per period of time, as, for example, $5 per hour, $40 per day, and $200 per week.

Time Study   See TIME-AND-MOTION STUDY.

Trade-off   An exchange in which the parties at the bargaining table "trade" concessions to one another. Recently a frequent trade-off has been for the union to gain improvements in job security for unit employees and for the employer to obtain relief from wage increases.

Trade Union   See LABOR ORGANIZATION.

Trampers   See BUSINESS AGENT.

Tramping Committees   See BUSINESS AGENT.

Transcript   The formal record of a hearing made by a court reporter. In arbitration, a transcript is the exception, for generally the arbitrator's notes, exhibits, and briefs when submitted by the parties are deemed to be a sufficient record for study and preparation of an OPINION AND AWARD. When the parties agree to have a transcript, the expense is shared and the arbitrator is provided a copy. When only one party wants a transcript, the arbitrator is provided a copy at that party's expense. Often in such situations, a copy is voluntarily made available to the other party without cost, but if the transcript is to be cited in a posthearing brief, it must be made available.

Tripartite Boards of Arbitration   See BOARD OF ARBITRATION.

Two-Tier Pay Plan   See TWO-TIER WAGE PLANS.

Two-Tier Wage Plans   Wage schedules that specify lower rates for newly hired employees in a given classification. Two-tier wage plans are basically of two types. The first type is often referred to as a "merging" two-tier wage plan since the low-tier rate is like a low hiring-in, probationary, or apprentice rate, which ultimately, in a stated period of time, moves up to the regular classification rate. The stipulated time period for the low-tier rate varies, but generally the "catch up" to the regular rate is over a longer period of time than the typical 30–90-day probationary-rate period; this type of two-tier wage plan is usually measured in years and is frequently tied in to the contract's duration. In the second type of two-tier wage plan, the low-tier rate — usually some 25%–50% below the existing classification rate — is viewed as permanent. In any case, no period is stipulated for this type of low-tier rate to move up to or merge with what hitherto had been considered the regular classification rate. Also, from the worker's standpoint at least, there is no assurance that the low-tier rate will not replace and become, in time, the regular classification rate.

Two-tier wage plans are largely an innovation of collective bargaining in the 1980s, and clearly they prevail where base contract hourly rates have "gotten out of hand" and there is a competitive and economic need for "a more realistic" and lower wage scale. Two-tier wage scales reflect the "swing of the pendulum" toward management in collective bargaining, and they evidence, in the main, employer strength at the negotiating table. But as frequently noted from a union's point of view two-tier wage plans are preferable, in the short run at least, to "taking a wage cut" since the immediate onus is on the new employee. Further, if effective, the two-tier wage plan could result in more jobs over time; in fact, the continuity of a two-tier wage plan may be said to be largely conditioned by its long-term impact. Interestingly, in major contract negotiations during 1985, management carried the two-tier wage concept one step further by proposing a three-tier wage plan. Two-tier plans in the private sector are most prevalent in the airline, automotive, wholesale and retail, transportation, and utility industries. In fact, American Airlines first negotiated a two-tier wage scale with its pilots and machinists in 1983. While considered revolutionary at the time, within two years virtually every major carrier and an increasingly growing number of small carriers as well had obtained some form of two-tier wage system in one or more of its union contracts. It is estimated that in private industry generally, about

10% of the current labor contracts contain provisions for two-tier wage plans of one form or another.

Umpire   See ARBITRATION.

Unauthorized Strike   A strike that is not sanctioned by the union. The term is often used synonymously with **wildcat strike** or **quickie strike,** and because this kind of strike takes place without the union's approval, it is sometimes referred to as an **illegal strike,** an **unlawful strike,** or an **outlaw strike.** Technically, however, from a legal standpoint any work stoppage called for an unlawful purpose, as, for example, to compel a closed shop agreement, is an illegal strike.

Unfair Labor Practice Strike   A lawful strike called to protest an employer's unfair labor practice, or an economic strike prolonged by an unfair labor practice. In contrast to an economic strike, strikers in an unfair labor practice strike cannot be permanently replaced.

Union   See LABOR ORGANIZATION.

Union Administration   See UNION OFFICER.

Union Hierarchy   See UNION OFFICER.

Unionized Shop   A place of work in which the employer recognizes the union as the representative of a majority of its employees and there is a labor contract. Union membership, however, is not a condition of employment; employees are free to join or not join the union and, if members of the union, are free to drop their membership at any time. While the union by law is required to represent all employees in the bargaining unit, only members of the union have the right to attend union meetings or to vote on matters affecting union/management relations such as ratifying a negotiated contract, going out on strike, and the like.

Unionized Worker   See ORGANIZED WORKER.

Union Member   See ORGANIZED WORKER.

Union Officer   A union's officers are generally elected by the membership and include the union's president, vice-president, secretary-treasurer, and recording secretary. The term *union officials* refers to all officers and representatives engaged in conducting the affairs of the union whether selected or elected by the membership, whether part-time or full-time. Full-time union officials are those officers and representatives whose sole responsibilities are the affairs of the union and whose salaries are paid by the union. They are sometimes referred to as the **union administration** and, colloquially, as the **union hierarchy.**

Union Official   See UNION OFFICER.

Union Organizer   See LABOR ORGANIZER.

Union Rights Clause   Unlike management rights, which are largely centered in one clause, union rights are generally set forth in several provisions of the contract. In addition to the implied right to perform the work designated in the RECOGNITION CLAUSE, other provisions include the union's right to in-plant representatives, access to the plant by local union officials and business representatives, bulletin boards, meetings on the plant's premises, and the like.

Union Security Provisions   Union security provisions generally refer to those clauses of a labor contract which protect the union's status under the agreement. These include a UNION SHOP PROVISO, MAINTENANCE-OF-MEMBERSHIP CLAUSE, and the like. Union security provisions are also frequently categorized by shop designation, ranging from the OPEN SHOP, in which there is no union contract, to the AGENCY SHOP, in which union membership is not required but payment of a union representation or service fee is, to the UNION SHOP, which requires union membership in good standing for continued employment.

Union Shop   A unionized shop which requires employees to join the union within a specified period of time and to remain a member "in good standing." Thus, employees need not be a member of the union to be hired, but as a condition of continued employment they must join the union within the designated period—30 days for industry generally, 7 days for construction. Under pertinent NLRB rulings, the requirement to "join a union" and to remain a member "in good standing" under a union shop clause has largely meant that the employee must tender regular dues and initiation fees. An employee who refuses to join the union or to pay dues under a union shop agreement must be discharged when proof is presented and the union requests discharge. However, an employee who has offered to pay dues and appropriate fees and is denied membership by the union has satisfied the prerequisites of the law under a UNION SHOP PROVISO and cannot be discharged because of nonmembership in the union.

Union Shop Proviso   The union shop agreement is an exception to the freedom of an employee under the National Labor Relations Act, Section 8(a), to join or not join a labor organization. As such, the union shop clause is sometimes referred to as the union shop proviso. Further, adoption of the UNION SHOP by the parties to a collective bargaining agreement was made subject to state law under the Taft-Hartley amendments in 1947, Section 14(b). Thus, the union shop—and, indeed, as held by the courts, the AGENCY SHOP and other forms of union security provisions as well—are lawful provided they are not prohibited by state statute. Twenty-one states, mostly in the South, MidWest, and Mountain areas of the United States, have enacted laws prohibiting labor agreements that compel or protect union membership. States with such statutes are commonly referred to as **right-to-work states.** The twenty-one right-to-work states and the year in which each enacted a statute or adopted a constitutional amendment are as follows: Alabama, 1953; Arizona, 1947; Arkansas, 1947; Florida, 1947; Georgia, 1947; Idaho, 1985; Iowa, 1947; Kansas, 1958; Louisiana, 1976; Mississippi, 1954; Nebraska, 1947; Nevada, 1951; North Carolina, 1947; North Dakota, 1947; South Carolina, 1954; South Dakota, 1947; Tennessee, 1947; Texas, 1947; Utah, 1955; Virginia, 1947; and Wyoming, 1963. The states in which right-to-work laws have been defeated and the date(s) of rejection in each are as follows: California, 1944 and 1958; Colorado, 1958; Idaho, 1958; Maine, 1948; Massachusetts, 1948; New Mexico, 1948; Ohio, 1958; Oklahoma, 1964; and Washington, 1956 and 1958.

Union Skate   See ORGANIZED WORKER.

Union Steward   See SHOP STEWARD.

Unlawful Strike   See UNAUTHORIZED STRIKE.

Unlawful Subjects of Bargaining   Subjects of bargaining which by law or the designated administrative agency and the courts may not be bargained. Such subjects may not lawfully be put into a contract and are not enforceable if they are already in the contract. Under the NLRA, the Taft-Hartley amendments, and the Landrum-Griffen Act, unlawful subjects of bargaining include the closed shop, discriminatory or preferential hiring-hall clauses, "featherbedding," secondary boycotts and "hot cargo" clauses. It is unlawful, too, to bargain over provisions that discriminate because of race, creed, origin, national origin, sex, or age. Similarly, the parties may not lawfully bargain provisions in violation of the minimum protection and statutory standards set forth in such pertinent legislation as child-labor laws, minimum wage and maximum-hours laws, and the like; contractual agreements may lawfully improve on these standards, but they may not lawfully provide less.

Unorganized Shop   See OPEN SHOP.

Unskilled Worker   An employee who has no knowledge or experience in a particular craft and is employed on jobs that require no skill, as, for example, janitorial labor, helpers, and sweepers. Also called a **common laborer** or a **nonskilled worker.**

Vertical Job Enlargement   See JOB ENLARGEMENT.

Vertical Parity   See PARITY.

Vertical Unionism   See INDUSTRIAL UNION.

Voir Dire   In arbitration, a process resorted to generally in order to require "the other side" to "speak the truth" or authenticate a matter such as an exhibit that it is submitting in evidence. For example, union counsel requests and obtains the right of voir dire to query the company as to the source of the data it is offering in evidence: Who prepared it? When? For whom was it prepared? and the like.

Voluntary Arbitration   Arbitration that is undertaken by agreement of the parties to a dispute. Thus, all instances of RIGHTS ARBITRATION and INTEREST ARBITRATION which take place under the provisions of a collective bargaining agreement are categorized as voluntary arbitration. The court's rulings as to the enforceability of the contract assures the parties that although arbitration in the contract is voluntarily agreed upon, the parties are legally compelled to comply with it and the ARBITRATOR'S AWARD for the duration of the contract—one year, two years, three years, or longer as the case may be.

Voluntary Checkoff   See CHECKOFF.

Wage Indexing   The term used to refer to any and all measures taken to tie-in an employee's wages to cost-of-living changes. The most commonly accepted procedure for doing this has been through the adoption of cost-of-living clauses in collective bargaining agreements. It has been held by some that the protection of a worker's "real wage" by wage indexing, as with proposals for the indexing of social security benefits and personal income taxes, is a social responsibility. To date, however, there has been no widespread support for the enactment of wage indexing legislation.

Wage-Reopening Clause   Contractual provisions which stipulate that either party, on demand at a specified period, may reopen the contract to negotiate changes in base contract hourly rates. Historically, wage-reopening clauses were agreed to in multiyear contracts and as an alternative to the inclusion of COLA provisions. The reopening period was traditionally limited to the anniversary dates of the contract, and the parties invariably agreed that if their wage differences in reopening were not resolved, the matter would be submitted to arbitration pursuant to the provisions of their grievance procedure. While contract reopenings have become a major subject of interest since their recent use in negotiations in the automot⁻ ⁻ industry, reopening clauses are far from popular today and w' ₋n used are pattern-made to the particular needs of labor and management in a given industry or under an unusual situation: to wit, the wage-hour reopening clause in the last year of the multiyear contract covering New York City hotels; in certain contracts, the wage-reopening clause that becomes applicable when the rise in the cost of living exceeds a specified level; and the wage-reopening clause that would become applicable during federal wage and salary controls if controls were liberalized or eliminated by the government.

Walking Delegate   See BUSINESS AGENT.

Walkout   A term generally used synonymously with *work stoppage* or *strike*. Often applied to a wildcat or quickie strike, which is spontaneous, not planned or authorized.

Wall-to-Wall Unionism   See INDUSTRIAL UNION.

Whipsaw Strike   A union tactic of singling out one employer to strike among the several it is negotiating with simultaneously. Typically, the struck employer is the one believed to be least able to resist the union's demands and to withstand the loss of work to its nonstruck competitors. Once a settlement is reached with the struck employer, the union by whipsaw tactics seeks to make this the pattern of settlement with the other employers one by one.

White-Collar Worker   An employee whose work is nonmanual in nature. This job category includes office, clerical, supervisory, sales, professional, and technical work. As distinct from blue-collar production and maintenance workers, white-collar workers are generally salaried rather than hourly rated employees.

Wildcat Strike   A spontaneous strike usually in violation of the "no strike" provisions of a collective bargaining agreement and unannounced, not planned, and not sanctioned by the union. Most frequently the wildcat strike occurs over some local issue such as health and safety, speed-ups, union rights within the plant, and the like. Also called a **quickie strike.**

Worker Organization   See LABOR ORGANIZATION.

Work-Sharing Provisions   Some contracts make provision for work to be shared in lieu of layoff in reverse order of seniority. Often this is of limited duration, it is applicable only after part-time probationary and other short-time employees have been laid off, and the union must be consulted and be agreeable to its implementation. Work-sharing takes many forms, but the most commonly used provisions divide the day's, week's, or month's work among the work force. Currently, many federal employees who have been retained in the face of budget cuts are being subjected to periodic "payless days" in several governmental agencies as an alternative to being laid off.

Work Stoppage   See STRIKE.

Zipper Clause   A contractual provision which makes it clear that the parties have negotiated on all items pertaining to the contract and that the contract language contains the entire agreement on such matters. Also called a **buttoning-up clause** or **contract finality clause.**

PART II

Compendium of Labor Legislation

Labor Relations Laws:
Union Status, Collective Bargaining,
and Labor Dispute Settlement Legislation
in the Public and Private Sectors

The Conspiracy Doctrine and Its Early Application against
Labor Organizations by the Courts

Philadelphia Cordwainers, 1806

The Conspiracy Doctrine was based on an old English common
law concept: namely, that individuals acting in concert have the
power to injure; that if the objective is unlawful, the combination
to effectuate it is unlawful; and that even if the objective is lawful
for an individual, the combination of individuals to achieve it in
concert is unlawful. American courts for almost fifty years in the
nineteenth-century uniformly accepted the Conspiracy Doctrine in
ruling that labor organizations or any group of workers acting in
concert to increase wages and/or other improvements in working
conditions were an illegal conspiracy against the public. The first
application of the Conspiracy Doctrine against a labor organization in the United States involved Philadelphia cordwainers (journeymen shoemakers) in 1806. The Federal Society of Journeymen
Cordwainers struck when the employers (masters) refused to accept
their demands, and for this the workers were indicted, tried for
criminal conspiracy, found guilty, and fined. In *Commonwealth Pa.
v. Pullis*, 1806, the Pennsylvania Supreme Court applied the English Common law doctrine of criminal conspiracy strictly in holding that "a combination of working men to raise their wages may be
considered in a two-fold point of view: one to benefit themselves .
. . the other . . . to injure those who do not join (the combination) . . . the rule of law condemns both."

Commonwealth v. Hunt, 1842

In *Commonwealth v. Hunt* (45 Mass. (3 Metcalf) 4 (1842)), the Massachusetts Supreme Court dismissed an indictment of conspiracy against a union of cordwainers. The Court rejected the Conspiracy Doctrine as it had previously been applied to labor organizations and held, in brief, that labor combinations were not unlawful in themselves. A conspiracy, as defined by the Court, was "a combination of two or more persons, by some concerted action, to accomplish some criminal or unlawful purpose or to accomplish some purpose not in itself criminal or unlawful, by criminal or unlawful means." The union had struck to obtain a closed shop and was indicted for having "unlawfully, permissively, deceitfully, unjustly and corruptly conspired not to work for any master who employed any workmen not a member of their union." The Court held that the formation of labor organizations for lawful purposes such as to secure wage increases, improvements of working conditions, and, as specifically addressed and ruled upon, to establish a closed shop was legal so long as the means used to obtain the purposes were legal. In effect, the Court modified the English common law Conspiracy Doctrine and substituted the **Doctrine of Legal Ends and Legal Means.** Labor organizations were still subject to indictment, but only if their objectives were illegal or they used unlawful methods in seeking their goals.

Railway Labor Relations Law

The Arbitration Act of 1888

Labor relations in the nation's railways have been the subject of special legislative attention over the years. In fact, the 1888 Act, which was made applicable to railroads, is often cited as the first federal labor relations law. Among other things, as approved by President Cleveland on October 1, 1888, the Act provided for Boards of Investigation appointed by the President to "investigate" labor disputes that threatened to interrupt interstate commerce. In addition to providing for the investigation of railway industrial disputes, it made provision for voluntary arbitration, in which either party, with the concurrence of the other, could submit a dispute to a tripartite board of arbitrators consisting of one arbitrator appointed by each party and a chairman selected by the two. The 1888 Act was largely ignored, however. In the decade of its existence, voluntary arbitration was never entered into by the railway unions and carriers. A Board of Investigation was appointed only once, but even then it was too late for it to be effective; a strike (the Pullman strike of 1894) was already in progress, and the Board's recommendations were ignored.

Erdman Act, 1898

The Erdman Act of 1898 replaced the railway labor relations law of 1888. Unlike its predecessor, the Erdman Act provided specific labor dispute settlement procedures for the railroads in the form of mediation and conciliation as well as voluntary arbitration. And in this regard — namely, the provision of mediation and conciliation services by the government — the Erdman Act was a pioneer. Under the Act, temporary ad hoc boards of mediation and conciliation were established in each railway labor dispute. If a settlement was not reached in mediation, the carrier and union were urged but not compelled by the Act to arbitrate their remaining differences. The avowed purpose of the Erdman Act was to protect interstate commerce through the establishment and maintenance of industrial peace on the railroads. And in addition to providing industrial dispute settlement machinery through mediation and voluntary arbitration, the Act sought to remove some of the major causes of railway strikes. Section 10 of the Act made illegal the "yellow dog" contract, the "blacklisting" of railroad employees, and the discharge of employees for union activities. The Erdman Act was shortly followed by the adoption of labor relations laws in some fifteen states. However, in 1908, the United States Supreme Court in *Adair v. United States* (208 U.S. 191 (1908)) declared Section 10 of the Erdman Act unconstitutional. The Court held that the Act violated the due-process clause of the Fifth Amendment in denying railroads freedom to contract. It declared that the commerce clause did not empower Congress to interfere with the contractual relations of employers and employees. Under Section 10 of the Erdman Act, William Adair of the Louisville and Nashville Railroad had been charged, convicted, and fined for dismissing O. B. Coppage, a fireman, for union membership. Adair appealed, and in specific response to the question of employers' rights, the Court ruled that workers could be discharged for any satisfactory reason, including membership in a labor organization.

The Court's reasoning in *Adair v. United States* was extended to state labor relations laws in 1915. In *Coppage v. Kansas* (236 U.S. 1 (1915)) the United States Supreme Court invalidated a Kansas statute which had made it unlawful for employers to require employees to agree "not to join or become or remain a member of a labor organization" as a condition of employment or remaining in employment. The Court ruled: "Under constitutional freedom of contract, whatever either party has the right to treat as sufficient ground for terminating the employment . . . he has the right to provide against by insisting that a stipulation respecting it shall be a *sine qua non* of the employment or its continuance. . . . [C]onsidering the inherent right of the individual to join the union, he has no inherent right to do this and still remain in the employ of one who is unwilling to employ a union man." This general legal support of the "yellow dog" contract, which began with the Court's invalidation of Section 10 of the Erdman Act, was extended in 1917 to the authorization of injunctions to restrain labor unions from organizing workers in shops with a "yellow dog" contract. *Hitchman Coal Co. v. Mitchell* (245 U.S. 229 (1917)) involved a West Virginia coal company that operated an open shop and required as a condition of employment that employees not be union members and pledge that they would not join a union during their employment. The miners union sought to organize the workers, and the Hitchman Coal Company sought and obtained an injunction restraining the union from continuing its organizing efforts. The United States Supreme Court upheld the Company, ruling that "the employer is as free to make non-membership in a union a condition of employment, as the working man is free to join the union. . . . [T]hat is part of the constitutional rights of personal liberty and private property . . . entitled to be protected." It was not until the Norris-LaGuardia Act of 1932 that the "yellow dog" contract was held to be unenforceable in the courts as it was inimical to public policy, and that the use of labor injunctions was restrained by being made subject to legislative regulation.

Newlands Act, 1913

In 1913, the Newlands Act succeeded the Erdman Act. Like its predecessor, the Newlands Act continued to provide for the mediation and voluntary arbitration of labor disputes in the railroad industry. However, the Newlands Act represented an advance in railway labor dispute settlement procedures. In the first place, the ad hoc or temporary boards of the Erdman Act were replaced by a full-time Board of Mediation and Conciliation. But more importantly, the Board was also given a role in the settlement of disputes that arose during the life of a contract, namely, when requested by either party to render an opinion as to the meaning or application of any disputed provision of the agreement. This was the first recognition and differentiation in railway labor law of disputes arising under a contract, variously referred to as minor, secondary, grievance, interpretation, or rights disputes, and disputes over the terms of a new contract, also referred to as major, primary, terminal, or interest disputes. Prior railway labor legislation dealt with new contract dispute settlement procedures and made no reference to disputes arising over the interpretation of the agreement. This differentiation in the nature of labor disputes is commonplace in labor relations today. Mediation in the classical sense of calling on an outside impartial individual or governmental agency representative to assist the parties through conciliatory efforts in settling their differences is generally not utilized today in the settlement of disputes arising over the interpretation of the provisions of the labor agreement. Instead, the parties provide for a grievance procedure with joint meetings (steps) at progressively higher levels of labor and management in which the parties seek to resolve the dispute themselves. In about 95% of the current labor contracts the final step of the grievance procedure is arbitration. Thus arbitration plays a role in both interpretation disputes and new-contract disputes. Currently, the legal term *rights arbitration* is widely used for the arbitration of contract interpretation grievance disputes and *interest arbitration* is used for the arbitration of new-contract disputes. The Newlands Act was the first labor relations statute to undertake to make this important distinction in the nature of industrial disputes and to establish provisions for the settlement of rights disputes as well as interest disputes.

Transportation Act, 1920

The Transportation Act of 1920 was enacted upon the restoration of the control of the railroads to private management. During World War I, by virtue of a congressional act in August 1916 and a presidential proclamation in December 1917, the federal government took possession and control of the country's railroads. A Director General of Railroads was appointed. In the area of labor relations and employee representation rights, the Director General established the rights of labor to organize without interference by management and gave administrative responsibilities to a tripartite board. For dispute settlement, the Director General established joint, equal-numbered, labor-management Boards of Adjustment and gave them final authority in the resolution of all grievance or rights disputes. The Transportation Act of 1920 incorporated many of these procedures on formal investigation and hearings. The Act established the United States Railroad Labor Board, a tripartite board composed of three representatives each from labor, management, and the public. The dispute settlement authority of the Railroad Labor Board, as specifically set forth in the Act, was "to investigate disputes, publish its findings and interpret existing contracts." In a sense, this was a backward step in the provision of dispute settlement machinery since there was provision for investigation but no provision for the mediation of new contract or interest disputes. Hearings and the investigation of disputes by the Board replaced mediation, with the Board being empowered to embody its recommendations in "decisions," which, it was hoped, would be enforced through the pressure of public opinion. It was expected that the Railway Labor Board would focus primarily on new-contract disputes. For the handling of rights disputes, the Act authorized the establishment of join, equal-numbered, labor-management Boards of Adjustment by mutual consent of the carriers and the railway unions, with such grievance or interpretation disputes going to the tripartite Railway Labor Board for adjudication only if not settled locally. One of the significant reasons for the replacement of the Transportation Act by the Railway Labor Act in 1926 was the ruling of the United States Supreme Court in *Pa. R.R. System and Allied Lines Federation v. Pa. R.R. Co.* (267 U.S. 203 (1925)). Although the Court held, contrary to the decision in the Erdman Act, that the labor sections of the Transportation Act of 1920 were not unconstitutional, it rendered the Act worthless by ruling that no means existed for the enforcement of the decisions and orders of the tripartite Railway Labor Board.

Railway Labor Act of 1926 and Its Amendments

The enactment of the Railway Labor Act was largely the result of labor and management's unhappiness with the Transportation Act of 1920. The provisions of the Act were, in the main, the product of "negotiations" and "compromise" by the railroad employers and unions. The Act was unique in this regard and innovative for its times in protecting the right of employees to unionize and in setting forth enforceable dispute settlement machinery. The Railway Labor Act of 1926 was heralded as a model and pioneering labor relations law. It outlawed the company (company-dominated) union, and its provisions affirming both the right of labor to organize without coercion or interference and the right of employees to bargain collectively through representatives of their own choosing became the basis for the Wagner Act (National Labor Relations Act) for private industry generally in 1935. The constitutionality of the Railway Labor Act was upheld in *Texas and New Orleans R.R. Co. v. Brotherhood of Railway and Steamship Clerks* (281 U.S. 548 (1930)). The Company contended that the Act violated its right under the First and Fifth amendments to decide who to hire and retain in its employ. The United States Supreme Court ruled that the Act "does not interfere with the normal exercise of the right of the carrier to select the employees or discharge them" and that "the statute is not aimed at the right of the employers but at the interference with the right of employees to have representatives of their own choosing." The Court held, importantly, that the enactment of the law was a valid exercise of Congress's legislative authority under the commerce clause of the Constitution. There have been a number of significant court decisions over the years delineating union rights and obligations under the Railway Labor Act. The most significant of these have dealt with the union's duty of fair representation, and the most prominent, although not the first or last Court adjudgment involving railway unions in this regard, was in 1944. In *Steele v. Louisville and Nashville R.R. Co.* (323 U.S. 192 (1944)), and again in the companion case *Tunstall v. Brotherhood of Locomotive Firemen & Enginemen* (323 U.S. 210 (1944)), the United States Supreme Court held that the Railway Labor Act "imposes on the labor organization acting by authority of the statute as the exclusive bargaining representative of a craft or class of railway employees, the duty to represent all the employees in the craft without discrimination because of their race," and that "the courts have jurisdiction to protect the minority of the craft or class from violation of such obligation."

In its dispute settlement procedures, the Railway Labor Act continued the differentiation made in prior railway legislation between new-contract (major) disputes and contract interpretation (minor) disputes. The United States Board of Mediation, which was established in the initial 1926 Act, was replaced by the National Mediation Board in the 1934 amendments. In addition to being given a mediation and dispute settlement role, the NMB was empowered to deal with representation disputes and to certify the designated representative of the employees. In 1936, the Act was amended to extend its coverage to airline carriers and their unions. In 1951, the Act was amended to permit covered unions and carriers to establish union shop agreements and dues checkoff provisions.

For contract interpretation (minor) disputes, the 1934 amendments virtually imposed compulsory arbitration. The regional Boards of Adjustment established in the 1926 Act were replaced by the National Railroad Adjustment Board composed of equal numbers of representatives of the carriers and unions in each of four divisions which, since the amendments in 1970, total 34 members in all. Procedurally, either party by petition may refer a contract interpretation dispute to the appropriate division of the National Railroad Adjustment Board: First Division, 8 members, jurisdiction over train and yard employees, including engineers, foremen, conductors, trainmen, and yard service employees; Second Division, 10 members, jurisdiction over machinists, boiler-makers, blacksmiths, sheet metal workers, electrical workers, car men, coach cleaners, powerhouse workers, and railroad shop laborers; Third Division, 10 members, jurisdiction over station and tower and telegraph employees, train dispatchers, maintenance-of-way men, clerical workers, freight handlers, express and station and store employees, signal men, sleeping car conductors and porters and maids, and dining room employees; Fourth Division, 6 members, jurisdiction over employees of carriers directly or indirectly engaged in transportation of passengers or property by water and all other employees of carriers over which jurisdiction is not given to the other three divisions. The decisions by the National Railroad Adjustment Board in each of its divisions are final and binding. In the event the equal-numbered Board deadlocks, a neutral referee is selected either by the division involved or by the National Mediation Board. The awards of these tripartite boards, like those of a majority in a division of the National Railroad Adjustment Board, are enforceable in the federal courts. The 1936 amendments extending the Railway Labor Act's coverage to airlines specifically excepted the air carriers and unions from the provisions of Section 3, which provide for the National Railroad Adjustment Board. Instead, the air carriers and unions set up their own system boards of adjustment with provision for the selection of neutral referees or impartial chairmen for the adjudication of contract interpretation disputes, including disciplinary grievances. The National Mediation Board is empowered to establish a National Air Transportation Board if needed. Actually, the railroads, too, have been encouraged to set up system boards of adjustment to expedite the adjudication of contract interpretation and disciplinary grievance disputes. In 1966, Section 3 of the Act was amended to provide for the establishment of Special Adjustment Boards upon request of the railroad unions or carriers to resolve disputes otherwise referable to the National Railroad Adjustment Board. The awards of the Special Adjustment Boards, like those of the National Railroad Adjustment Board, are final and binding. Except for the establishment of separate provisions for commuter railroads, there have been no major changes in the law since 1966.

In new-contract (major) disputes, the National Mediation Board, composed of three public members and a professional staff, provides mediation services to carriers and unions during negotiations. There is no statutorily prescribed time limit for mediation, but when an impasse is reached or a strike is threatened, the National Mediation Board proposes voluntary arbitration. If arbitration is refused, the parties are legally free to strike, lock out, or unilaterally change contract terms after 30 days unless the emergency dispute provisions in Section 10 of the Act are invoked. In cases where the National Mediation Board deems that a strike or dispute "threatens substantially to interrupt interstate commerce to a degree such as to deprive any section of the country of essential transportation services," it notifies the President. The President, as empowered by the Act, may in his discretion appoint an emergency board (an ad hoc board of three public members, one of whom is designated chairman by the President). While the emergency board has powers of subpoena and conducts hearings on the issues in dispute, it cannot compel the parties to settle, and it has only investigatory and fact-finding powers. The emergency board is required to render a report to the President within 30 days. The Act does not require that the report contain recommendations, but it does not prohibit them either. From the outset, the President-appointed railway emergency boards have uniformly viewed their function to be fact-finding with recommendation, and their reports to the President have largely focused on recommended settlement terms for new contracts. During the 30-day period in which the emergency board makes its investigation and holds hearings, and for 30 days after it submits its report to the President, the status quo is maintained. Thereafter, the parties are legally free to strike, lock out, or unilaterally change contract terms.

Special action by the President and/or Congress is necessary to prevent or put an end to railway strikes after the 60–90 day cooling-off period. Initially, much faith was placed in the concept of "moral suasion" and the expected impact of "making public" the emergency board's report to the President and the position of the parties if rejected. It was optimistically thought that the ad hoc emergency board would be composed of such prestigious personages — distinguished judges, labor relations experts, prominent arbitrators, and dispute resolution professionals — that the parties would feel obligated to follow the President's report or, with the aid of NMB mediators, use it as the basis for reaching a mutually agreed upon settlement. And for whatever reasons, the "track record" of the impasse provisions of the Railway Labor Act was in the main a successful one for some twenty years. With the advent of World War II, however, and increasingly since then, the failure of the Act's procedures to result in the settlement of emergency disputes has prompted a variety of post-cooling-off actions ranging from government seizure of a struck railroad (while the government operates the railroad, strikes are legally prohibited) to special legislation submitting the dispute to arbitration, enjoining the strike and extending the cooling-off period, imposing the terms recommended to the President by the emergency board, and the like. In recent years this has prompted a myriad of proposed amendments to the Act's impasse procedures, with special emphasis by labor relations and labor law scholars on the need to empower the President to invoke a statutorily prescribed "arsenal of weapons" when the cooling-off period ends without a settlement of the new-contract dispute. To date, however, this and other proposed amendments to the Railway Labor Act have not been supported by the carriers and the railroad unions. Because of the tradition and legislative history of the Act, Congress has been reluctant to enact changes in the law without the mutual approval of railway labor and management.

Antitrust Laws and Unions

Sherman Antitrust Act, 1890

The Sherman Act of 1890 is an antitrust law and not a labor law as such. Its legislative history indicates that its supporters intended that the Act be directed at the growing corporate giants that were dominating American industry and against business practices that restrained trade and interfered with interstate commerce. Nonetheless, while labor unions were not specifically covered in Section 1 of the Sherman Act, they were not specifically excluded either:

Every contract, combination in the form of a trust or otherwise, or conspiracy, in restraint of trade or commerce . . . is hereby declared illegal. Each person who shall make any such contract or engage in any such combination or conspiracy shall be guilty of misdemeanor, and, on conviction thereof shall be punished by fine not exceeding five thousand dollars, or by imprisonment one year or by both punishments in the discretion of the court.

For more than a decade litigation under the Sherman Antitrust Act involved corporations and industry practices only. This was drastically changed when the organizing efforts of the hatters union were resisted by a hat manufacturer in Danbury, Connecticut, who successfully brought litigation against the union under the Act. The hatters union launched an organizing drive in 1897 to enforce the closed shop throughout the industry. D. E. Loewe and Company in Danbury defeated an organizational strike in 1902, and the United

Hatters of Danbury instituted a product (primary) boycott against the Company and put economic pressure (a secondary boycott) on merchants not to use or handle the Company's products. The Company claimed it lost $80,000 and sued the Union for triple damages, charging that the Union's actions were a conspiracy in restraint of trade under the Sherman Act and that its use of the secondary boycott was unlawful. The Court upheld the Company on both counts in *Loewe v. Lawlor* (208 U.S. 274 (1908)), commonly called the *Danbury Hatters* case. In what is still considered to be one of the most important decisions in labor history, the United States Supreme Court stated that the Sherman Act "prohibits any combination whatever to secure action which essentially obstructs the free flow of commerce between states, or restricts, in that regard, liberty of the trader to engage in business," and specifically with respect to the actions of the hatters union, that "the combination charged falls within the class of restraints of trade aimed at compelling third parties and strangers involuntarily not to engage in the course of trade except on conditions that the combination imposes." The secondary boycott was held unlawful under the Sherman Act because it interfered with interstate commerce, and ultimately, in 1915, the United States Supreme Court awarded triple damages, upholding the lower court's decision that the Union's actions were a conspiracy in violation of the Sherman Act. Significant in the assessment of triple damages was the Court's ruling that individual union members were liable to suit—the Company had brought suit against 197 members of the hatters union—and that the employees' personal possessions, including their homes, were subject to seizure for payment of damages. The Company was eventually paid about $250,000 in damages, most of which had been obtained by the AFL in a special Danbury Hatters fund-raising campaign.

Clayton Antitrust Act, 1914

The Clayton Act of 1914 is an antitrust act, but unlike the Sherman Act, it contains provisions that specifically pertain to unions. Both by exempting unions from antitrust legislation and by relieving labor of the indiscriminate use of injunctions, Congress clearly intended that these provisions be favorable to labor. Section 6 of the Act states that "the labor of a human being is not a commodity or article of commerce"; that "nothing contained in the anti-trust laws shall be construed to forbid the existence and operation of labor organizations . . . or to forbid or restrain members of such organizations from lawfully carrying out the legitimate objectives thereof"; and that "neither such organizations, or the members thereof, [shall] be held or construed to be illegal combinations or conspiracies in the restraint of trade under the antitrust laws." Section 20 of the Act forbids the issuance of injunctions in labor disputes "between an employer and employees . . . unless necessary to prevent irreparable injury to property."

The Clayton Act was initially hailed as the "industrial Magna Carta" for the working people. The courts' views differed, however, and labor's expectations were not realized. In 1914, for example, the Coronado Coal Company of Arkansas brought suit against the United Mine Workers Union under the Sherman Act and triple damages, close to $750,000, were sought. The Company had terminated its contract with the Union and was operating as an open shop; the local at one of the mines struck to restore the union shop; there was violence and several lives were lost in battles between the strikers and the mine guards and strikebreakers; the mine was destroyed. The litigation, *Coronado Coal Co. v. the United Mine Workers of America* (259 U.S. 344 (1922) and 268 U.S. 295 (1925)), was lengthy. In 1922, the United States Supreme Court ruled for dismissal under the Sherman Act, claiming there had been no proof of interference with interstate shipments of coal, but later, in 1925, the Court reversed itself upon subsequent testimony that such attempts had been made. The parties settled out of court before the Court's ruling on triple damages.

In *Duplex Printing Press Co. v. Deering* (254 U.S. 443 (1921)), the Court made it clear that despite the enactment of the Clayton Act, unions were not relieved of liability for damages under the antitrust provisions of the Sherman Act. The International Association of Machinists invoked a secondary boycott in support of its organizational strike against the Duplex Printing Company; it was effective in New York City, the Company's major market; the Company obtained an injunction against the secondary boycott; the Machinists contended that the secondary boycott was legal under Section 20 of the Clayton Act and the injunction was vacated; the decision was appealed by the Company. The United States Supreme Court held that the Clayton Act did not wholly exempt labor from antitrust legislation, and using the *Danbury Hatters* case as precedent, it declared the secondary boycott to be in violation of the Sherman Act. In reaching its ruling the Court held that the prohibition against injunctions in labor disputes between "an employer and employees" under Section 20 of the Clayton Act meant "a company and its employees," and inasmuch as other unions honored the Machinists' secondary boycott against the Duplex Printing

Company in New York City, the dispute was enjoinable under the Sherman Act.

In *Bedford Cut Stone Co. v. the Journeymen Stone Cutters' Association* (274 U.S. 37 (1927)), the Company appealed the denial of an injunction against the stone cutters' refusal to handle stone quarried at certain Company sites, and the United States Supreme Court ultimately held that the boycott limited the shipment of stone products in interstate commerce and was "an unreasonable restraint of trade." The *Bedford Cut Stone* case clearly evidenced that the Court's "rule of reason" as to what constitutes a "reasonable" or "unreasonable" restraint of trade under the Sherman Act was applied more stringently to labor than to industry. This apparent "double standard" prompted criticism and was the basis of a strong dissenting opinion by Justice Louis Brandeis.

Labor Relations Law in the Private Sector

Federal Anti-injunction Act (Norris-LaGuardia Act), 1932

The federal Anti-injunction Act, commonly called the Norris-LaGuardia Act, was enacted in 1932 to curb the widespread use of court injunctions and the antitrust provisions of the Sherman Act against labor. The Act's proponents were especially incensed at what they considered to be a distortion of the basic intent of Sections 6 and 20 of the Clayton Act in the Court's decisions in the *Duplex Printing Press, Coronado Coal,* and *Bedford Cut Stone* cases. The Norris-LaGuardia Act declares the "yellow dog" contract unlawful and contrary to public policy. The Act defines a labor dispute broadly so as to negate the narrow interpretation rendered by the courts and to restrict the application of the antitrust provisions of the Sherman Act to labor disputes. The Act regulates the issuance of injunctions by federal courts. It also prohibits the enjoining of certain acts of unions and individuals in a labor dispute; sets conditions that must be met before injunctive relief can be granted, including hearings and testimony in open court, with the union being given the right to testify and cross-examine witnesses; requires the Court to determine that specific unlawful acts had been threatened by the union or will continue and will cause substantial and irreparable damage to company (the complainant's) property; and specifies that the company comply with the law and make every reasonable effort to settle the labor dispute by negotiations and arbitration.

Among the actions of workers and unions which the Act prohibits the federal courts from restraining or enjoining are the following: becoming or remaining a member of a labor union; ceasing
or refusing to perform any work; paying strike or unemployment
benefits; aiding individuals prosecuted for strike activities; publicizing strikes by advertising, speaking, patrolling, or any other nonvi-
olent method; promoting interest in labor disputes through peaceful assembly; indicating intent or agreeing to engage or not to
engage in any of these activities; and advising, urging, or inducing
others to engage in any of these activities.

As is clear from the above, the Norris-LaGuardia Act did not
end the use of federal court injunctions but rather put an end to
their indiscriminate use. The actions of unions and workers can be,
and are, enjoined, under state law when they result in violence,
unlawful acts, and damage to property. According to the provisions
of subsequent legislation, namely, the Labor-Management Relations Act (Taft-Hartley Act) of 1947, court injunctions can be obtained to enjoin strikes for up to 80 days if such strikes are held to
threaten the nation's health and safety, and to enjoin the use of
secondary boycotts, "hot cargo" clauses, and organizational picketing. In two notable decisions, namely, *Allen-Bradley* and *Boys
Markets,* the courts expanded the use of injunctions. As determined in *Allen-Bradley v. Local Union No. 3* (325 U.S. 797 (1945)),
unions and workers can be enjoined under the Sherman and Clayton antitrust laws when their activities are combined with those of
nonlabor groups to restrict interstate commerce; and as provided in
Boys Markets, Inc., v. Retail Clerks (398 U.S. 235 (1970)), strikes in
violation of a contractual "no strike" agreement can be enjoined. In
United States v. Hutcheson (312 U.S. 219 (1941)), the United States
Supreme Court upheld the general purposes of the Norris-
LaGuardia Act by stating that "the underlying aim of the Norris-
LaGuardia Act was to restore the broad purpose which Congress
thought it had formulated in the Clayton Act but which was frus-
trated, so Congress believed, by unduly restrictive judicial construc-
tion." The Court then went on to say that the Norris-LaGuardia
Act expressed disapproval of the *Duplex Printing v. Deering* and
Bedford Stone Co. v. Journeymen Stone Cutters' Association
cases.

Section 7(a) of the National Industrial Recovery Act, 1933

Section 7(a) of the National Industrial Recovery Act was, in
large measure, the precursor of the National Labor Relations Act
(Wagner Act), which was enacted in 1935. Section 7(a) of the NIRA

provided that codes of fair competition should include language providing employees with the right to organize and bargain collectively through representatives of their own choosing. The codes were also to stipulate that employees shall be free from interference, restraint, or coercion by employers in the exercise of these rights. Section 7(a) also required that codes of fair competition provide that employees or persons seeking employment shall not be required either to join a company (company-dominated) union or to refrain from joining, organizing, or assisting a labor organization of their own choosing. A National Labor Board with an equal number of employer and union representatives was established by executive order by President Franklin Roosevelt to implement the provisions of Section 7(a) and to settle disputes under it. This was replaced by a National Labor Relations Board composed of three impartial members. The latter, however, lacked statutory authority, was challenged by industry, and its effectiveness was minimal. Although the National Industrial Recovery Act was short-lived and the provisions of Section 7(a) were weakened by the lack of statutory enforcement procedures, congressional efforts to enact legislation extending the labor relations objectives of Section 7(a) to all industries were under way before the Act's invalidation in the *Schecter* decision of 1935.

National Labor Relations Act (Wagner Act), 1935

The National Labor Relations Act, commonly called the Wagner Act, was enacted in July 1935. As set forth in Section 1, the Wagner Act incorporated the objectives of Section 7(a) of the National Industrial Recovery Act, and avoiding the frustrating experience of the two labor relations boards that had been established to implement the provisions of Section 7(a), founded the National Labor Relations Board, giving it the power to administer and enforce the Act. The declared purpose of the Wagner Act was to promote industrial peace by encouraging collective bargaining and to establish equality of bargaining power between employees and employers. The Act states that "the inequality of bargaining power" between workers, who are not free to form associations, and employers "tends to aggravate recurrent business depressions by depressing wage rates and the purchasing power of wage-earners in industry and by preventing the stabilization of competitive wage rates and working conditions." Thus, it gives employees the right to organize, and obliges employers to bargain with their chosen representatives. The rights of workers, specified in Section 7, include "the right to self organize, to form, join or assist labor organizations, to bargain collectively through representatives of their own choosing, and to engage in other concerted activities for the purpose of collective bargaining or other mutual aid or protection." And in order to protect the rights of workers, the Act sets forth in Section 8 a list of unfair labor practices by employers.

The Wagner Act, with its intent to correct inequality at the bargaining table by giving workers rights and strengthening labor's position, made no provision for unfair labor practices by unions. Thus, the closed shop was attainable by unions, and no limitations were imposed on labor's use of the boycott. The NLRB is empowered to rule on charges of unfair labor practices by employers. Also, Section 9 of the Act authorizes the NLRB to determine the chosen representative of the workers in a bargaining unit, and to conduct elections to this end if necessary. In 1937, the Wagner Act was held to be constitutional in *NLRB v. Jones and Loughlin Steel Co.* (301 U.S. 1 (1937)). In a far-reaching decision by a narrow, 5 to 4 margin, the United States Supreme Court affirmed the broad concept of the commerce clause that "although activities may be intrastate in character when separately considered, if they have such a close and substantial relation to interstate commerce that their control is essential or appropriate to protect that commerce from burdens and obstructions, Congress cannot be denied the power to exercise that control." The National Labor Relations Act, as amended, has continued to date, and it applies to all establishments in the private sector whose activities affect interstate commerce except the railroads and airlines, which are covered by the Railway Labor Act. As will be noted, however, certain of the objectives and labor-favoring provisions of the Wagner Act were modified and prohibited by the amendments set forth in the Labor-Management Relations Act (Taft-Hartley Act, 1947) and in the Labor-Management Reporting and Disclosure Act (Landrum-Griffin Act, 1959).

Labor-Management Relations Act (Taft-Hartley Act), 1947

The Labor-Management Relations Act, commonly called the Taft-Hartley Act, was enacted in June 1947. Its amendments to the National Labor Relations Act (Wagner Act) are contained in Title I of the Act and reflect, in major part, the reaction to the stormy labor relations and rash of strikes of the postwar years following the lifting of wartime controls. More basically, however, the Taft-Hartley Act represents a shift in public policy toward labor relations and collective bargaining which has continued to date. Unlike the Wagner Act, the Taft-Hartley Act curbs labor's "excesses" as well as management's, and protects the rights of employees to refrain from joining a union. In a sense, the "rules of the game" of collective bargaining are set by the National Labor Relations Act. The proponents of the Taft-Hartley amendments viewed, and continue to view, its provisions restoring some of management's pre-Wagner Act bargaining strength as essential to a balanced labor relations policy. The Taft-Hartley Act was enacted over President Truman's veto and the opposition of organized labor, which denounced the Act as a "Slave Labor Act."

The Taft-Hartley amendments prohibit the closed shop, secondary boycotts, jurisdictional and sympathy strikes, and strikes by employees of the federal government. The Act permits the union shop, but limitedly, as Section 14(b) in effect subjects its usage to the proviso "unless prohibited by State law." To date, 21 states have enacted prohibitions against the union shop along with other union security provisions in legislation commonly called right-to-work laws. The basic rights of employees to organize and to engage in collective bargaining and lawful strikes, picketing, and other concerted action are continued in Section 7, but the Taft-Hartley amendments add the right of employees "to refrain from any or all such activities except to the extent that such right may be affected by an agreement requiring membership in a labor organization as a condition of employment."

The five categories of unfair employer labor practices initially set forth in Section 8 of the Wagner Act are continued in Section 8(a) as follows: it is an unfair labor practice for an employer "to interfere with, restrain or coerce employees in the exercise of their rights guaranteed by Section 7" (Section 8(a)(1)); "to dominate or interfere with the formation and administration of any labor organization or contribute financial or other support to it" (Section 8(a)(2)); "to discriminate in regard to hire or tenure of employment or any term or condition of employment to encourage or discourage union membership" (Section 8(a)(3)); "to discharge or otherwise discriminate against an employee because he has filed charges or given testimony under the Act" (Section 8(a)(4)); and "to refuse to bargain collectively with the representatives of the employees" (Section 8(a)(5)).

In keeping with its objective, the Taft-Hartley Act has added a list of unfair union labor practices in Section 8(b). Initially there were six, the seventh being added subsequently by the Landrum-Griffin Act in 1959. It is an unfair labor practice for a labor organization "to restrain or coerce (A) employees in the exercise of the rights guaranteed in Section 7 or (B) an employer in the selection of his representatives for the purpose of collective bargaining or the adjustment of grievances" (Section 8(b)(1)); "to cause an employer to discriminate against an employee" (Section 8(b)(2)); "to refuse to bargain with an employer" (Section 8(b)(3)); to engage in activities with the illegal objective of requiring a self-employed person to join a union, or requiring a person to stop using, selling, or handling the products of, or otherwise dealing with, a primary employer (secondary boycott), or requiring an employer to recognize or bargain with a particular labor organization when another union has already been certified as the employees' bargaining representative, or requiring an employer to assign work to members of a particular labor organization rather than to some other labor organization (jurisdictional dispute) or to engage in or encourage employees of a secondary employer to strike or refuse to handle or use the products of a primary employer (Section 8(b)(4)); to charge excessive or discriminatory initiation fees or dues (Section 8(b)(5)); "to cause or attempt to cause an employer to pay . . . for services which are not performed or not to be performed [featherbedding]" (Section 8(b)(6)); and to engage in picketing or to threaten to picket an employer unless certified as the employee's bargaining representative (Section 8(b)(7)).

Other significant provisions of the Taft-Hartley amendments include: permitting employers to make precertification election statements to employees, providing they do not contain "threats of reprisal or force or promise of benefit" (Section 8(c)); requiring the parties to bargain in good faith and to meet and confer at reasonable times and reduce their agreements to writing (Section 8(d)); prohibiting "hot cargo" agreements by making it unlawful for a union and an employer to make an agreement that the employer "ceases or refrains from handling, using, selling, transporting or otherwise dealing in the products of any other employer" (Section 8(e)); setting procedures for employees in a bargaining unit to decertify their union representative, increasing the size of the National Labor Relations Board from three to five members, and establishing an independent office of General Counsel; establishing a Federal Mediation and Conciliation Service (FMCS); and setting procedures for dealing with labor disputes that "imperil national health and safety." Strikes by federal employees are prohibited. The FMCS was established under Section 203 of the Labor-Management Relations Act to "profer its [mediative] services in any labor dispute in any industry affecting commerce, either upon its own motion or upon the request of one or more of the parties to the dispute, whenever in its judgment such dispute threatens to cause a substantial interruption in commerce." As a condition of bargaining in good faith under the provisions of Section 8(d) of the Act, a party is obligated to notify the FMCS that a dispute exists within 30 days of notifying the other party that it proposes to terminate or modify the contract, and for 60 days after such notice to keep the existing contract in full force without strike or lockout. When mediation fails to resolve the labor dispute, the parties are urged to submit the unresolved issues to arbitration, but the FMCS is not empowered to compel the parties to do so.

When labor disputes affect an entire industry or substantial part thereof, Section 206 of the Taft-Hartley Act empowers the President to intervene if the nation's health and safety are imperiled. To cite the statute,

Whenever, in the opinion of the President of the United States, a threatened or actual strike or lockout affecting an entire industry or a substantial part thereof engaged in trade, commerce, transportation, transmission or communication among the several states or with foreign nations, or engaged in the production of goods for commerce will, if permitted to occur or continue, imperil national health and safety . . .

The Act provides for an 80-day "cooling off" period as described in the following procedures. The President appoints an ad hoc Board of Inquiry if he believes a threatened or actual strike or lockout imperils the nation's health and safety. The Act does not permit the Board of Inquiry to make recommendations, but the Board makes a written report to the President on the issues in dispute and a statement from the parties as to their respective positions. No time frame is specified for this, but the report to the President is rendered promptly, usually within a matter of days. The President may then direct the Attorney General to petition for an enjoinment of the actual or threatened strike or lockout. The federal district court will issue the injunction upon a showing that an entire industry or substantial part thereof is affected and that a strike imperils the nation's health and safety. Upon issuance of an 80 day injunction, the Board of Inquiry is reconvened and the parties are obliged to make every effort to settle their differences with the assistance of the FMCS. After 60 days, the Board of Inquiry reports to the President on the parties' current positions, the efforts made to settle the dispute, and the employer's last offer of settlement. The President makes the report available to the public, and the NLRB conducts a secret ballot within 15 days on whether the employees accept the employer's last offer. Within 5 days thereafter, the NLRB certifies the result of the vote. If the employer's last offer is rejected, the Attorney General is required to request the court to vacate the injunction; the court is required to discharge the injunction; and the parties are legally free to resume, or go forward with, their strike or lockout unless Congress takes special action. The President is required by the Act to report to Congress the findings of the Board of Inquiry and the NLRB's certified results of the vote on the employer's last offer with such recommendations as he may care to make. Organized labor has strongly criticized the government's use of the injunction in these procedures, but with the notable exception of the defiance of the coal miners in the early years of the Act resulting in heavy fines being imposed on John L. Lewis and the United Mine Workers, labor has largely complied with the injunctions that have been issued.

The emergency strike procedures, however, can hardly be held to be successful. They have been invoked infrequently over the years and with mixed results. In the 31 instances in which the emergency strike procedures have been invoked since the Act's passage in 1947, 4 were settled prior to the issuance of an injunction, 15 were settled during the 80-day cooling-off period, 6 were settled thereafter without strike, and in 6 the strike was resumed. Particular criticism has been leveled against the procedures required during the last 20 days of the injunction for a secret vote among unit employees on the employer's final offer. This procedure has been viewed not only as a waste of time, since invariably the vote has resulted in an affirmation of the union leadership, but also as a deterrent to effective mediation efforts and what should be "last ditch, eleventh-hour" negotiations to settle differences. The Board of Inquiry has been criticized since, unlike the presidential emergency board under the Railway Labor Act, it is professionally limited by the statutory prohibition against its making recommendations. As in the case of the emergency strike provisions of the Railway Labor Act, many have urged amendment of the Taft-Hartley Act to provide the President with the power to invoke an "arsenal of weapons" following the cooling-off period. It has been suggested, too, that railway employees also be subjected to these amended emergency strike provisions. To date, however, little interest has been shown in these and other proposed changes in impasse procedures except, perhaps, among scholars and professionals in labor dispute resolution.

Labor-Management Reporting and Disclosure Act (Landrum-Griffin Act), 1959

The Labor-Management Reporting and Disclosure Act, commonly known as the Landrum-Griffin Act, was enacted in 1959. It is not a labor relations law as such since its primary focus is on the regulation of unions, their officers, and their internal operations. Among the Act's miscellaneous provisions in Title VI, there are amendments to the Taft-Hartley Act. Section 8(b)(7), which prohibits organizational picketing by noncertified unions, was added to the list of unfair union labor practices. As stated by proponents of the Landrum-Griffin Act, "loopholes" in Section 8(b)(4) of the Taft-Hartley Act were closed by outlawing the "hot cargo" clauses in labor contracts (except limitedly in the construction and garment industries), which permitted employees to refuse to handle goods shipped from a struck plant or to perform services benefiting an "unfair employer," and by tightening the restrictions on the use of the secondary boycott. In the main, however, the Landrum-Griffin Act represents a new direction of the public regulation of labor in (1) its protection of the individual union member from improper practices on the part of union officers and the labor organization; (2) its requirement that unions follow democratic procedures in their internal operations; and (3) its provision for public reporting and disclosure on the part of unions and officers.

The Landrum-Griffin Act was prompted by the findings of the United States Senate Committee on Improper Activities in the Labor or Management Field (McClellan Committee). Although the McClellan Committee concluded that the vast majority of unions were honest, democratic organizations and that most employer-employee relations were conducted with integrity, it did uncover malpractices within several large international unions and among certain union officers. "Paper locals," "sweetheart contracts," and misuse of union funds were especially condemned, and the Landrum-Griffin Act was passed to give the federal government vast regulatory authority over the internal affairs of unions in order to prevent and make unlawful such abuses. Specifically, Title I of the Act sets forth a "Bill of Rights for Members of Labor Organizations." Among its provisions is the right of union members to nominate candidates; vote in elections; attend, participate, and speak freely at union meetings subject to reasonable rules and regulations; meet freely and assemble; sue the union or its officers; participate in union decisions on dues, initiation fees, and assessments; and be extended due process in disciplinary matters — members cannot be fined, suspended, expelled, or disciplined except for nonpayment of dues without the charges being put in writing, a reasonable amount of time being allowed for the preparation of a defense, and a full and fair hearing being granted. Title IV deals with union elections and similarly sets forth standards to assure union democracy in the administration of its internal affairs. Officers of unions are required to be elected by secret ballot not less than once every three years for local union officers and not less than once every five years for national or international union officers. All members who have fulfilled the requirements for union membership shall be provided the right to vote in the election of union officers.

Title II sets forth the requirements for reporting by "Labor Organizations, Officers and Employees of Labor Organizations, and Employers." Unions are required to provide to the United States Department of Labor copies of their constitution and bylaws; the names of officers, a tally of initiation fees and dues, and a list of membership requirements; the procedures for levying assessments, auditing financial transactions, disciplining officers, and ratifying contracts; financial reports of assets and liabilities, the salaries and allowances of union officers and employees, and receipts and their source; and an accounting of loans made to union officers and employees and to employers and business establishments. Union officers and employees are required to report any financial arrangement, including ownership of stock or securities, they or their family have involving firms at which the union is, or is seeking to be, the bargaining agent. Employers are required to report loans made to union officers, employees, or business establishments; payments to employees to persuade other employees to exercise or not exercise their rights to organize and bargain collectively; and payments for the purpose of interfering with, restraining, or coercing employees in the exercise of the right to organize and bargain collectively. Violators of the provisions of Title II are subject to fines of up to $10,000 and imprisonment for up to one year.

Title III, "Trusteeships," requires national unions to report the establishment of a trusteeship to the United States Department of Labor within 30 days, and to provide semiannual reports thereafter indicating the reasons for establishing or continuing the trusteeship; and to file a full and complete report of the local union's financial condition. During the trusteeship, the transfer of funds from the local union to the national union is prohibited, and delegates from the local union in trusteeship are prohibited from voting at conventions or for national officers unless they had previously been chosen by the vote of the local union membership in a secret ballot.

Title V is entitled "Safeguards for Labor Organizations." It imposes fiduciary responsibility on the union officers; permits members to sue to recover damages or secure a financial accounting; requires union officers and employees to be bonded; limits the indebtedness of union officers and employees to the union to $2,000; provides a fine of up to $10,000 and imprisonment for up to five years for embezzling or stealing union funds; and prohibits the holding of union office by persons who have been convicted of a variety of crimes such as robbery, bribery, extortion or embezzlement, violation of narcotics law, arson, rape, murder, and assault with intent to kill. Initially, communists were also barred from holding union office, but this provision of the Landrum-Griffin Act was declared unconstitutional by the United States Supreme Court in 1965 in *United States v. Brown* (380 U.S. 278 (1965)).

Postal Reorganization Act, 1970

The Postal Reorganization Act of 1970 made the postal service an independent agency and, in matters of labor relations, removed postal unions from the limitations of Executive Orders 10988 (1962) and 11491 (1969), which regulated federal employees and their rights to organize and bargain collectively at the time. In large measure, the Act was the result of labor unrest in the postal service and the pressure for greater bargaining rights. Under the Postal Reorganization Act, the scope of bargainable issues was broadened to include wages, hours, and other economic conditions as in the private sector, but the right to strike was not extended to postal employees. Many of the provisions of the Labor-Management Relations Act were incorporated in the Postal Reorganization Act, with the NLRB's being given jurisdiction over questions of union representation and alleged unfair labor practices by the unions and management. Unlike the Labor-Management Relations Act, however, the Postal Reorganization Act bans all forms of union security provisions except the voluntary checkoff of union dues. Because strikes are prohibited, the impasse provisions of the Act differ from those in the Labor-Management Relations Act by providing for mediation, fact-finding, and arbitration of new-contract disputes if necessary. There has been some resistance by the postal unions to the compulsory arbitration provisions of the Act, and there have been some unlawful strikes. Nonetheless, by and large, the Postal Reorganization Act has been well received and has given impetus to other federal employees to seek similar legislation to expand their union rights and to broaden the scope of bargaining. To date, however, federal employee unions have had little success in promoting such legislative changes, and there appears little likelihood that the Reagan administration or Congress will support such changes in the present law.

Labor-Management Relations Act as Amended, 1974:
The Health Care Industry under the NLRA

In July 1974 Congress enacted Public Law 93-360 amending the Labor-Management Relations Act, effective August 25, 1974, to cover all private health care institutions whether or not they are operated for profit. The exclusion of "any corporation or association operating a hospital, if no part of the net earnings inures to the benefit of any private shareholders or individual" was deleted from Section 2(2) and a new subsection, (14), was added to Section 2 which defines covered health care institutions as follows:

The term "health care institutions" shall include any hospital, convalescent hospital, health maintenance organization, health clinic, nursing home, extended care family, or other institution devoted to the care of sick, infirm, or aged persons.

Federal, state, county, city, and other government-operated health facilities are not covered under the Act. In its administration of the Act, the National Labor Relations Board applies the same representation election procedures to covered health care facilities as are provided for other establishments. Similarly, the same statutory provisions that relate to unfair labor practices for employers and unions generally are applicable in the health care industry. However, a new unfair labor practice was added in 1974 — Section 8(b)(g) — requiring unions in health care institutions to give at least 10 days notice prior to any strike or picketing in order that the FMCS might extend its services in warding off work stoppages and assuring continuity of patient care. Section 8(b)(g) reads as follows:

A labor organization before engaging in any strike, picketing, or other concerted refusal to work at any health care institution shall, not less than ten days prior to such action, notify the institution in writing and the Federal Mediation and Conciliation Service of that intention. . . . The notice shall state the date and time that such action will commence. The notice, once given, may be extended by the written agreement of both parties.

An exception was provided in the above notice requirement of Section 8(b)(g): "[I]n the case of bargaining for an initial agreement following certification or recognition," the 10-day notification required in Section 8(b)(g) "shall not be given until the expiration" of the 30-day dispute-notice period stipulated in Section 8(d)B. Thus, in negotiating an initial contract in health care institutions, a union is required to give the FMCS at least 30 days written notice of the existence of a dispute prior to giving the employer and the FMCS the required 10 days notice of its intention to engage in any strike, picketing, or other concerted refusal to work at the institution.

When a contract renewal or reopener is negotiated, the party seeking to terminate or modify the existing contract must notify the other party at least 90 days prior to the contract's expiration date and notify the FMCS in writing at least 60 days prior to the expiration date.

A new provision, Section 19, "Individuals with Religious Convictions," was added to the Act in the 1974 amendment. It provides that "any employee of a health care institution who is a member of and adheres to established and traditional tenets or teachings of a bona fide religion, body or sect which has historically held conscientious objections to joining or financially supporting labor organizations shall not be required to join or financially support any labor organization as a condition of employment." Section 19 further provides that "such employee may be required, in lieu of periodic dues and initiation fees, to pay sums equal to such dues and initiation fees to a nonreligious charitable fund exempt from taxation . . . chosen by such employee from a list of at least three such funds, designated in a contract between such institution and a labor organization, or if the contract fails to designate such funds, then to any such fund chosen by the employee."

Finally, the Act was amended to provide for the "Conciliation of Labor Disputes in the Health Care Industry." These new dispute-settling procedures, as set forth in Section 213, may be invoked "if, in the opinion of the Director of the Federal Mediation and Conciliation Service a threatened or actual strike or lockout affecting a health care institution will, if permitted to occur or to continue, substantially interrupt the delivery of health care in the locality concerned. The FMCS director, in his/her discretion, is empowered "to assist in the resolution of the impasse by establishing . . . an impartial Board of Inquiry to investigate the issues involved in the dispute and to make a written report thereon to the parties within fifteen (15) days after the establishment of such a Board." The individuals and number of members of the Board are determined by the director as he/she "may deem desirable." Unlike the report of the Board of Inquiry in national emergency disputes generally, the written report of the Board of Inquiry selected for a health care industry dispute "shall contain the findings of fact together with the Board's recommendations for settling the dispute, with the objective of achieving a prompt, peaceful and just settlement of the dispute." Under Section 213, the Board of Inquiry has broad powers; it is authorized to investigate, mediate, find fact, and make recommendations. While the FMCS can, and does, urge voluntary arbitration for the settlement of unresolved items, the parties are not obligated to accept the Board of Inquiry's recommendations, may reject them wholly or in part, and are free to strike or lock out thereafter. The Board of Inquiry is appointed for a statutory limit of 15 calendar days from date of written notice of appointment. If a Board of Inquiry is to be appointed in a contract renewal or reopener impasse, the director of the FMCS must do this no later than 30 days prior to the expiration date of the contract or within 30 days of receipt of the 60 days notice to the FMCS, whichever date is later. If the impasse is reached in the negotiating of an initial contract, the Board of Inquiry must be appointed within 10 days of receipt of the 30 days notice to the FMCS that a dispute exists.

The fact-finding recommendation responsibility and authority of the Board of Inquiry in the health care industry has, in the view of most professionals, been a marked improvement over the impasse procedures under the Labor-Management Relations Act for national emergency disputes generally. There is some criticism that the 15-day limit for the Board's written report and recommendations is too short, but by and large there appears to be no major drive for changes in the impasse procedure at this date. Initially, and to some extent it has continued in certain quarters, there was concern that putting the health care industry under the National Labor Relations Act and negating state compulsory arbitration laws for hospitals and health care institutions such as had been provided in New York State would result in a rash of strikes and a continuing disruption of essential patient care. However, neither the employers nor the unions in the health care industry wanted compulsory arbitration. And to date, at least, the public well-being and the medical needy in the main do not appear to have been unduly affected by the reliance on mediation, fact-finding, and voluntary arbitration in the impasse procedures for the settling of labor disputes in the health care industry.

Bankruptcy Law and the Labor Contract

In recent years, differences over the impact of bankruptcy proceedings — specifically, Chapter 11 reorganization proceedings — on collective bargaining agreements have been the subject of heated and often bitter and acrimonious legal contention. Section 365 of the bankruptcy code states that trustees may assume or reject executory contracts. Initially, it was assumed that Section 365 applied to commercial contracts, the contention being that because the National Labor Relations Act both promoted and protected collective bargaining, the labor contract had a preeminent status and, in any event, was different from an executor contract. This assumption was challenged, and well before the *Bildisco* decision of the United States Supreme Court in 1984 (*NLRB v. Bildisco & Bildisco*, 465 U.S. 513, 104 S. Ct. 1188 (1984)), the courts uniformly held that labor contracts are executory contracts; that the legislative history did not reveal any intent to exclude the labor contract from Section 365 coverage; and that collective bargaining agreements, like other executory contracts, could be rejected in bankruptcy proceedings. Extended litigation then ensued over what test should be applied in the rejection of a collective bargaining agreement in a bankruptcy proceeding. The commonly used test in bankruptcy proceedings is "the business judgment test," in which the sole burden on a debtor is to show that the rejection of the agreement will benefit the estate. The courts rejected "the business judgment test" as inappropriate to labor contracts and sought other tests. The United States Court of Appeals, Second Circuit, enunciated a "thorough scrutiny and balancing of the equities test" in *Kevin Steel (Shopmen's Local Union No. 455, etc., v. Kevin Steel Products, Inc.,* 465 U.S. 513 (1975), 104 S. Ct. 1188, 519 F.2d 698 (CA 2 1975)). However, in *REA Express (Brotherhood of Railway Clerks, etc., v. REA Express, Inc.*, 523 F.2d 164 (2d Cir. 1975), cert. denied, 423 U.S. 1017 (1975), cert. denied; and *International Association of Machinists and Aerospace Workers v. REA Express, Inc.*, 423 U.S. 1073 (1976)), the Second Circuit used a "threat of imminent collapse test." Here the Court ruled that a labor contract could be rejected only if it was determined that the contract was burdensome and threatened the debtor with collapse. Clearly these tests were at variance. The "thorough scrutiny and balancing of the equities test," because of its ambiguities, eased the task of obtaining rejection of collective bargaining agreements in bankruptcy proceedings, while the "threat of imminent collapse test," because of its stringency and the ease of showing that the contract's labor costs could be met if a business was reorganized and run efficiently, made it very difficult to establish a convincing basis for the rejection of the collective bargaining agreement. The Second Circuit did not follow the "threat of imminent collapse test" in its decisions subsequent to *REA Express*; it, along with the courts of appeal in the other circuits, applied the *Kevin Steel* test of "thorough scrutiny and balancing of the equities." Litigation over the status of the labor contract in bankruptcy reached the United States Supreme Court in *Bildisco* after a ruling of the National Labor Relations Board that was largely favorable to labor in protecting the sanctity of the collective bargaining agreement in bankruptcy proceedings. In its ruling, the Supreme Court embraced the "thorough scrutiny and balancing of the equities test" in rejecting collective bargaining agreements in bankruptcy proceedings. Given the test's acceptance and widespread application by the courts of appeal, this ruling was not unexpected, even by the most ardent proponents of the "threat of imminent collapse test."

But a second question was at issue before the Court in *Bildisco*—namely, whether a debtor (employer) petitioning for bankruptcy under Chapter 11 could reject a labor contract and unilaterally impose his/her own terms prior to the approval of rejection by the bankruptcy court. Hitherto, it had been widely thought that a bankruptcy proceeding did not alter an employer's obligation under the National Labor Relations Act to bargain in good faith and that it was an unfair labor practice for the employer to unilaterally impose terms and conditions of employment. This viewpoint, however, was challenged by management in several quarters and received national prominence when Continental Airlines and Wilson Foods unilaterally imposed new terms and conditions upon the unions with which they had collective bargaining agreements the day after they filed a Chapter 11 petition. The Supreme Court sided with management, holding that the National Labor Relations Act did not take precedence over the bankruptcy code and that the National Labor Relations Board lacked the jurisdiction to rule that an employer (debtor in possession) acted illegally in unilaterally rejecting the labor contract and imposing its own terms and conditions of employment.

Labor reacted strongly to the *Bildisco* decision, contending, among other things, that it gave employers in bankruptcy proceedings unconscionable freedom to reject collective bargaining agreements and to impose whatever terms and conditions of employment they chose and predicting that it would bring a rash of bankruptcy petitions by employers intent on undermining the labor contract and "getting rid of the union." The unions put pressure on Congress "to remedy" *Bildisco*, and to this end Congress enacted the Bankruptcy Amendments and Federal Judgeship Act of 1984 (P.L. 98-353, 98 Stat. 33 (July 10, 1984)). The Act establishes the steps that must be followed before a debtor may reject a collective bargaining agreement. And in this regard the Act partially supersedes *Bildisco*, since it stipulates that there can be no automatic rejection of a labor contract or the imposition of unilateral terms and conditions of employment by an employer upon the filing of a bankruptcy petition. Further, the Act provides that the employer/debtor must make a proposal to modify the collective bargaining agreement when he/she files a petition to reject it and that the proposed modifications must be "necessary to permit the reorganization of the debtor." The expectation here, at least on the part of unions, is that the "necessity" standard will deter employers from seeking to reject a labor contract and that it will stimulate collective bargaining—albeit quite different from labor negotiations in a period of economic normalcy—during bankruptcy proceedings in preference to the procedure of seeking a court order rejecting the agreement.

Duffy v. Wheeling-Pittsburgh Steel Corp. (738 F.2d 1393 (Ct. App. Pa. 3d), *cert. denied,* 469 U.S. 1087 (1984)) was the initial test following the 1984 enactment of the Bankruptcy Amendments Act. The Wheeling-Pittsburgh Steel Corporation filed for bankruptcy under Chapter 11 and began its reorganization effort in April 1985. The Corporation contended that it needed to lower the base contract hourly rate in the steelworkers contract from $21.40 to $15.20 and that even though there were 13 months remaining in the duration of the contract, this decrease, along with a five-year wage freeze and certain other benefit reductions, was necessary for reorganization. The Union argued that the cut in compensation and the wage freeze were not necessary for the Corporation's survival as the payment of the contract hourly rate of $21.40 until the contract's end would not deplete the Corporation of cash on hand to meet current operating expenses. The bankruptcy judge approved the Corporation's reorganization plan, denying the Union's contention by ruling that the Corporation "may emerge with enough cash on hand to meet its current operating expenses, but if a successful reorganization necessitates more cash than that the proposed modification is necessary for reorganization." The Steelworkers Union resisted the imposition of these terms, and after a strike of 98 days involving 9 steel plants in West Virginia, Pennsylvania, and Ohio, a new contract was negotiated which included, among other things, the USWA's gaining two seats on the Corporation's Board of Directors and being given "a voice in management" along with a bonus plan linked to future increases in steel prices and profits. The USWA's appeal of the decision of the bankruptcy court (*supra*) resulted in the United States District Court's affirming and the United States Court of Appeal's reversing the bankruptcy court. The Court of Appeals held that the Wheeling-Pittsburgh Steel Corporation had failed to follow the 1984 Bankruptcy Amendments Act, which requires that an employer make a proposal to the union, bargain in good faith, and try to reach an agreement before repudiating the union contract; that the Corporation never showed that the reorganization plan was necessary for its financial survival or that its plan was "fair and equitable" to all parties; that the workers were "being asked to take a five-year agreement under a worst-case scenario without any possibility for restoration or share in the event of a better-than-anticipated recovery"; that the bankruptcy judge "failed to give any persuasive rationale for the disproportionate treatment of the employees"; and that a bankruptcy court could not "authorize rejection of a labor contract" for the convenience of management and creditors. (See also *Wheeling-Pittsburgh Steel Corp. v. United Steelworkers of America*, Ct. App. Pa. 3d, 791 F.2d 1074 (1986).)

The courts will undoubtedly address these issues further in subsequent litigation over the status of the labor contract in bankruptcy proceedings. Clearly, clarification is needed as to the meaning and application of the "necessity test" in Section 1113 of the 1984 Bankruptcy Amendments Act. Also needed is greater preciseness in defining the procedures and steps a debtor and a union must follow when the debtor petitions for the rejection of the labor contract. A final point that remains unsettled is the status of public sector collective bargaining agreements in bankruptcy proceedings. Chapter 11 covers establishments in the private sector. Bankruptcy proceedings for a public institution are covered by Chapter 9. On its face, Section 1113 of the Bankruptcy Act is not applicable to public sector bankruptcy proceedings. To date, there has been no ruling to the contrary, and it would appear that it remains for Congress to address the question of whether public policy would be best served if the provisions of Section 1113 of the 1984 Bankruptcy Act were extended to public institutions.

Federal Employee Labor Relations Law

Executive Orders 10988 and 10987, 1962

On January 17, 1962, President John Kennedy issued Executive Order 10988 giving federal employees the protected right to join or refrain from joining an employee organization. The limitation on the right to organize was the proviso that the labor organization (1) not assert the right to strike against the United States government; (2) not advocate the overthrow of the constitutional form of government in the United States; and (3) not discriminate with regard to membership on the basis of race, color, creed, or national origin. On the same day, President Kennedy issued Executive Order 10987, which required federal agencies to develop a procedure for the appeal of administrative decisions adversely affecting their employees.

Executive Order 10988 was initially hailed as the Magna Carta of public sector unionism. While this proved to be an overly optimistic view, Executive Order 10988 was a pioneering effort that encouraged public sector unionization and bargaining at state and local government levels as well as among federal agencies. Federal employee collective action and unionization dates back to the mid-1800s, but it was not until Executive Order 10988 that the Postal Service and federal agencies generally were required to bargain with the labor organizations representing their employees.

The scope of bargaining permitted federal employees under Executive Order 10988, and under its successor, Executive Order 11491, and the Civil Service Reform Act, does not include working conditions determined by law. These are essentially the same primary economic issues that are bargained in the private sector — namely, salaries, pensions, health and welfare insurances, and other key fringe benefits provided to all federal government employees by congressional action. Bargaining on other important working conditions such as hours of work and paid holidays is largely limited to issues of scheduling since federal employees are prohibited from bargaining on shorter hours or increasing the number of holidays and the pay for working on a holiday. A major limitation of Executive Order 10988 to federal employee unions was that it provided for three forms of union recognition. In addition to **exclusive recognition**, which could be attained by a majority vote of the unit employees in a secret ballot representation election, **formal recognition** was provided to a union if it got the support of less than 50% but more than 10% of the unit employees, and **informal recognition** was provided to unions that demonstrated that they represented some of the unit employees. While only the union with exclusive recognition was empowered to bargain with the federal agency, the unions with formal and informal recognition could be consulted and share their views with the agencies. This multiplicity of employee representation in a given federal agency was viewed as favorable to management and divisive of that union solidarity which is so essential for effective employee representation.

Executive Order 11491, 1969

President Richard Nixon responded to the above criticisms by issuing Executive Order 11491 in October 1969. The changes promulgated by this order brought labor relations law for federal employees closer to that for workers in the private sector. Multiplicity of union representation for a unit of employees in a federal agency was eliminated. However, when a union failed to get exclusive recognition through a majority vote of unit employees, it could attain **national consultative rights** if the union got more than 10% of the vote. Under Executive Order 11491, federal agencies were required to bargain with unions that had the exclusive recognition of their employees but were not obligated to do so if the union had attained only national consultative rights. For implementation purposes, Executive Order 11491 established three administrative units with functions modeled along the lines of private sector law: the Federal Labor Relations Council (FLRC) was given general administrative responsibilities similar to those of the NLRB; the Federal Service Impasses Panel (FSIP) was to assist the parties in the resolution of interest disputes with fact-finding and arbitration if necessary; and the office of the Assistant Secretary of Labor for Labor-Management Relations was granted powers analagous to those of the NLRA's General Counsel.

Civil Service Reform Act, 1978:
Title VII, Federal Service Labor-Management Relations

Title VII of the Civil Service Reform Act of 1978 replaced Executive Order 11491 and its predecessors, Executive Orders 10988 and 10987. Title VII codified and impoved regulations governing federal employee labor relations. It specifically declared labor organizations and collective bargaining in the civil service to be "in the public interest." The opening section of Title VII of the Act, "Findings and Purpose," reads as follows:

(a) The Congress finds that—
(1) experience in both private and public employment indicates that the statutory protection of the right of employees to organize, bargain collectively, and participate through labor organizations of their own choosing in decisions which affect them—
(A) safeguards the public interest
(B) contributes to the effective conduct of public business, and
(C) facilitates and encourages the amicable settlement of disputes between employees and their employers involving conditions of employment; and
(2) the public interest demands the highest standards of employee performance and the continued development and implementation of modern and progressive work practices to facilitate and improve employee performance and the efficient accomplishment of the operations of the Government.
Therefore, labor organizations and collective bargaining in the Civil service are in the public interest.

Title VII of the Civil Service Reform Act specifically provides the federal employee with "the right to form, join, or assist any labor organization, or to refrain from any such activity, freely and without fear of penalty or reprisal, and each employee shall be protected in the exercise of such right." This includes the employee's right "to act for a labor organization in the capacity of a representative and the right, in that capacity, to present the views of the labor organization to heads of agencies and other officials of the executive branch of the Government, the Congress, or other appropriate authorities" and the right "to engage in collective bargaining with respect to conditions of employment through representatives chosen by employees."

The federal agencies covered by Title VII of the Reform Act are largely those previously governed by Executive Orders 10988 and 11491—namely, the executive branch agencies and the Veterans' Administration, the Library of Congress, and the Government Printing Office. The federal agencies specifically excluded from coverage by Title VII are the General Accounting Office, the Federal Bureau of Investigation, the Central Intelligence Agency, the National Security Agency, the Tennessee Valley Authority, the Federal Labor Relations Authority, and the Federal Service Impasses Panel. Close to three million federal employees in all are in agencies covered by Title VII.

The new law makes no major change in the definition of "conditions of employment" for bargaining purposes, and the scope of federal employee bargaining largely remains as it was under the above-mentioned executive orders. "Conditions of Employment" in Title VII of the Reform Act are stated to mean "personnel policies, practices, and matters, whether established by rule, regulation, or otherwise, affecting working condition." Specifically excluded from the scope of federal employee bargaining are "policies, practices, and matters" relating to prohibited political activities, the classification of any position, and "matters . . . specifically provided for by Federal statute." Thus, as with the prior executive orders, federal employees are precluded from bargaining their wages, basic hours of work, and employee benefits, as these are all determined by congressional enactment.

Under Title VII, Congress formed the Federal Labor Relations Authority to "establish policies and guidance" and generally to administer the labor-management relations provisions of the Act. The Authority replaces the Federal Labor Relations Council, which had virtually the same basic responsibility under the executive orders. The Authority is "composed of three members, not more than two of whom may be adherents of the same political party." The members serve terms of five years, and one is appointed to serve as chairman. The members, and the General Council as well, are appointed by the President with the advice and consent of the Senate.

The executive director and the directors of regional offices are appointed by the Authority.

The duties of the Authority include the following: determine the appropriate bargaining unit; supervise or conduct representation elections; resolve issues relative to a labor organization's eligibility for, and continuance of, national consultation rights, and conduct hearings to resolve complaints of unfair labor practices; resolve issues relating to the duty to bargain in good faith; and resolve exceptions to arbitrators' awards.

The provisions of Title VII of the Civil Service Reform Act specifically provide that it is an unfair labor practice for a federal agency to interfere with, restrain, or coerce any employee in the exercise of his/her provided rights; to encourage or discourage membership in any labor organization by discrimination in connection with hiring, tenure, promotion, or other conditions of employment; to sponsor, control, or otherwise assist any labor organization; to discipline or otherwise discriminate against an employee for filing a complaint, affidavit, or petition, or for giving information or testimony under employee rights as provided; to refuse to consult or negotiate in good faith with labor organizations as required; to fail or refuse to cooperate in impasse procedures and decisions; and to enforce any rule or regulation conflicting with provided employee rights.

Unfair labor practices for a labor organization as set forth in Title VII of the Reform Act are as follows: to interfere with, restrain, or coerce any employee in the exercise of his/her provided rights; to cause or attempt to cause an agency to discriminate against an employee for exercising such rights; to coerce, discipline, fine, or attempt to coerce a member of the labor organization as punishment, reprisal, or for the purpose of hindering or impeding the member's work performance or productivity; to discriminate against an employee with regard to the terms or conditions of membership in the labor organization on the basis of race, color, creed, national origin, sex, age, preferential or nonpreferential civil service status, political affiliation, marital status, or handicapping condition; to refuse to consult or negotiate in good faith with an agency as required; to fail or refuse to cooperate in impasse procedures and decisions; and to call, or participate in, a strike, work stoppage, or slowdown, or in the picketing of an agency in a labor-management dispute if such picketing interferes with an agency's operations, or to condone any such activity by failing to take action to prevent or stop it. Under the "Standards of Conduct" provisions for labor organizations, it is specified that "an Agency shall only accord recognition to a labor organization that is free from corrupt influences and influences opposed to basic democratic principles." To this end, labor organizations are required to maintain democratic procedures and practices and to provide for periodic elections; to exclude from organization office persons affiliated with communist or other totalitarian movements and persons identified with corrupt influences; to prohibit organization officers from having financial interests or engaging in business in conflict with their duty to the organization and its members; and to maintain fiscal integrity through accounting and financial controls and regular financial reports or summaries made available to members.

Title VII of the Reform Act makes specific provisions for dealing with negotiation impasses. The Federal Mediation and Conciliation Service is designated to provide services and assistance to federal agencies and exclusive representatives in the resolution of such bargaining impasses. The Service is authorized to determine under what circumstances and in what manner it will provide such assistance. In the event the services of the FMCS or any other third-party mediation fails to resolve a negotiation impasse, either party may request the Federal Service Impasses Panel to consider the matter or the parties may jointly refer the matter to binding arbitration providing the procedure is approved by the Federal Service Impasses Panel.

The Federal Service Impasses Panel is an entity within the Federal Labor Relations Authority with the express function, under Title VII of the Reform Act, "to provide assistance in resolving negotiation impasses between agencies and exclusive representatives." The Panel is composed of a chairman "and at least six other members, who shall be appointed by the President solely on the basis of fitness to perform the duties and functions involved from among individuals who are familiar with Government operations and knowledgeable in labor-management relations." The powers of the Panel are broad—namely, to "promptly investigate any impasse presented to it"; to "recommend to the parties procedures for the resolution of the impasse or assist the parties in resolving the impasse through whatever methods and procedures, including fact-finding and recommendations, it may consider appropriate"; and if the parties do not arrive at a settlement after assistance by the Panel, to hold hearings, administer oaths, take testimony or deposition or any person under oath, issue subpoenas, "and take whatever action is necessary and not inconsistent" with the responsibility to resolve the impasse. The parties are to be notified promptly of any final action of the Panel, "and the action shall be binding on such parties during the term of the agreement unless the parties agree otherwise." ·

Clearly, the power given to the Panel in dealing with federal negotiation impasses is broad and virtually unlimited. From the outset, the Panel has exercised this authority commendably with an innovative blend of flexibility and restraint. In developing its implementing rules and regulations, the Panel has drawn on its extensive experience under the prior executive orders. The Panel has endeavored to promote self-help and problem-solving by the parties themselves and to discourage dependence upon, and use of, a "third party outsider."

Finally, it needs to be reiterated that there are four major differences between "labor relations law" set forth for employees in the private sector under the National Labor Relations Act, as amended, and for employees in the federal sector under Title VII of the Civil Service Reform Act of 1978. These differences are:

(1) Federal employees are denied by statute the right to strike.

(2) The right of federal employees to picket is limited to informational picketing since it is an unfair labor practice for an organization to picket an agency in a labor-management dispute if such picketing interferes with an agency's operations.

(3) The scope of collective bargaining for federal employees is limited to personnel employment practices; basic working conditions such as wages, basic hours of work, and employee benefits are still subject to statutory provisions.

(4) Union and agency provisions as well as other forms of union security, with the exception of the checkoff, are prohibited in the federal civil service.

Federal labor-management relations under Title VII of the Civil Service Reform Act of 1978 differ from those under the prior executive order in the following important ways:

(1) The 3-member Federal Labor Relations Authority, which is responsible under Title VII of the Reform Act for determining the appropriate bargaining unit, conducting representation elections, and adjudicating unfair labor practice complaints, is an independent authority whose members are appointed by the President with the advice and consent of the Senate. Its predecessor under the prior executive orders, the Federal Labor Relations Council, was composed of three members, all heads of executive branch agencies, and was often criticized as being promanagement.

(2) Under Title VII of the Reform Act, the General Council of the Federal Labor Relations Authority investigates and prosecutes unfair labor practices. Back pay, reasonable attorney's fees, and resto-

ration of annual leave are remedies to which employees are entitled if found to have suffered from unfair personnel actions.

(3) Under Title VII of the Reform Act, the checkoff is permitted and dues will be automatically withheld from a federal employee's paycheck at his/her request.

(4) Under Title VII of the Reform Act, a federal agency must prove that a compelling need exists for a particular rule or regulation in order to prohibit negotiations on it; government-wide regulations, however, are still nonnegotiable.

(5) Under Title VII of the Reform Act, official time is to be granted to organization representatives for contract negotiations, grievance handling, and the resolution of negotiation impases.

(6) Under Title VII of the Reform Act, grievances are handled, at the employee's option, under either a negotiated grievance procedure or a statutory procedure, but not both. When discrimination is alleged or questions of constitutionality are involved, final decisions on a grievance, including arbitration awards, are subject to judicial review.

Protective Labor Legislation:
Maximum Hours, Minimum Wages, Child and Women's Labor, Workers' Compensation, and Social Insurance

The 1836 Reorganization Act:
"Shop Hours" for Federal Employees

The 1836 law reorganizing the General Land Office had the effect, among others, of regulating the hours of work of federal government employees. As such, it predates President Martin Van Buren's Executive Order of 1840, which is commonly held to be the first public regulation of hours of labor. The Reorganization Act required government offices to be open at least 8 hours a day in the winter months (October 1–April 1) and 10 hours a day in the summer months (April 1–October 1). These mandated "shop hours" tended to become the regular working hours, which meant that federal employees enjoyed a basically shorter workday than employees in private industry, who generally worked 10–12 hours a day at the time. It is interesting to note that the 1836 Act was never officially superseded by another; was incorporated into the revised statute of 1874; and was not repealed as obsolete until December 1930.

President Van Buren's Executive Order of 1840:
10-Hour Day for Federal Employees, Laborers, and Mechanics

On March 31, 1840, President Martin Van Buren issued an executive order directing the observance of "the 10-hour system" for laborers and mechanics employed on government public works. The term *public works* was used in its broadest sense and included employment in federal navy yards as well as on roads, bridges, buildings, and government construction of all sorts; it did not apply to clerical, administrative, and fiscal employees. President Van Buren's action was prompted by "the 10-hour movement," which had been initiated by, and met with some success in, private industry in the mid-to-late 1830s. The limiting of hours of work to the number prescribed by "the 10-hour system" was not the introduction of a 10-hour workday as we would currently define it. At that time, working hours referred to total hours of presence rather than to actual hours worked, and included meal times along with other authorized nonwork periods that were the custom of the day under "the 10-hour system." President Van Buren's executive order did not mention hourly rates of pay, but it was not his intention that compliance with "the 10-hour system" would occasion a reduction in daily wages. The President made this clear at a meeting with a group of citizens in Philadelphia in September 1840. In response to a query as to whether he favored "reducing the standard of wages," President Van Buren responded "no" and stated that "the 10-hour system had been uniformly carried out at all the public establishments, and this mitigation of labor had been accompanied by no corresponding reduction of wages." Key among the economic consequences of reductions in hours of work is whether hourly wage rates or the base pay for the workday or workweek are maintained. When base hourly rates are unchanged as the workday or workweek is shortened, additional leisure time is attained by the worker, but at the expense of a reduction in base pay from that received under the former (longer) workday or workweek. Prior to the successes of the 10-hour movement in the 1830s, reductions in hours of work were generally of this type. President Van Buren's Executive Order of 1840 and its implementation established as government policy that when the length of the basic workday was reduced, hourly rates of pay would be increased proportionately in order to maintain the base wage paid for the former (longer) workday. This policy on the maintenance of daily wages as hours decreased was not automatic, and because it did not bind future administrations, proved to be short-lived. In fact, wages were not initially maintained as hours of work for public employees were successively reduced to 8 per day.

New Hampshire 10-Hour Law, 1847

In 1847, New Hampshire enacted the first state 10-hour law. Ten hours was promulgated as the legal workday in the state. The New Hampshire law covered all employment and prompted efforts at shortening working hours, establishing minimum wages, setting working standards for child and women's labor, and promulgating other forms of protective labor legislation at the state and local government levels. It was generally considered unconstitutional, at the time, for the federal government to enact maximum-hours and minimum-wage laws for private employment.

Pennsylvania Child Labor Law, 1848

In 1848, Pennsylvania enacted the first state child labor law by establishing a minimum age for workers in commercial operations. The minimum age was set at 12 years, and in 1849 it was raised to 13 years.

Ohio 10-Hour Law for Women, 1852

In 1852, Ohio enacted the first state women's labor law. The Ohio law limited the working hours of women to 10 a day.

Federal Wage-Hour Law for Navy Shipyards, 1861

By 1861, advances in state protective labor legislation and in private industry generally were such that hours of labor and wages were, for the most part, less favorable in public employment than in the private sector. For some two decades, Congress and suceeding presidents evidenced no interest in emulating President Van Buren's "model" hours regulation of 1840. President Lincoln, however, urged remedial action. Congressmen who were considering legislation to promote the efficiency of the navy supported him, contending that an improvement in working conditions for public employees would contribute to the national defense. The 1861 law required that working hours, and within limits wages, of employees in government navy ship-yards conform to those of the nearest private shipyard. The commandant in each government yard was empowered to make the wage-hour determination. In 1862, the law was amended to ease the task of making wage-hour determinations comparable to those in private establishments.

8-Hour Day for Federal Employees, 1868

The first 8-hour law was enacted by the federal government in 1868. The Act covered "all laborers, workmen, and mechanics . . . employed by or on behalf of the government of the United States." The inclusion of workers "employed by or on behalf of" the government was an innovation in federal labor legislation. Proponents of the Act intended for it to cover the employees of government contractors as well as government agencies and hoped that it would encourage a general acceptance of the 8-hour day in both the public and the private sector. The Attorney General and the courts, however, did not share this view. In 1869, the Secretary of the Treasury refused to enforce the Act against a government contractor who was working his laborers 10 hours a day on the construction of a post office. The matter was referred to the Attorney General, who in a decision some three years later upheld the Secretary of Labor and ruled that the Act, as a general principle, covered only the immediate employees of the government (14 Op. Att'y Gen. 37 (1872)). In 1876, the United States Supreme Court virtually emasculated the 8-Hour Law of 1868 when it ruled (*United States v. Martin*, 94 U.S. 400 (1876) that the law was not a contract between the government and its laborers; that it was a "direction" and therefore was intended as a "guide"; and that its 8-hour provision was not mandatory. Congress, which consolidated several 8-hour bills into the 1868 law, clearly intended that daily wages would be protected. However, this was not specifically provided for in the Act, and government agencies uniformly reduced the daily earnings of their employees proportionally as they reduced working hours to 8 per day. Again the matter was referred to the Attorney General's Office and the ruling was unfavorable to labor, to wit, "the law did not require Federal agencies to pay employees as high wages for an eight-hour day as private industry paid employees doing similar work for ten or even twelve hours a day" (12 Op. Att'y Gen. 530 (November 25, 1868)). In May 1869, at the urging of organized labor, President Ulysses Grant issued a proclamation requesting compliance with the 8-hour provisions of the 1868 law without reduction in daily wages because of reduction in working hours (Proclamation No. 3, 16 Stat. L. 1127 (May 19, 1869)). President Grant's proclamation was largely ignored, however, and he issued another in May 1872 calling attention to the 8-Hour Law of 1868 and his prior proclamation and directing all appropriate officers of the executive branch of the government to comply with their provisions (Proclamation No. 10, 117 Stat. L. 955 (May 11, 1872)). The possibility of a further ignoring of President Grant's proclamation was avoided by the appropriation of funds in 1872 for the use of government agencies to compensate employees for wage decreases resulting from the introduction of the 8-hour day. Similar appropriations were made intermittently until the law was replaced in 1892. Although the 8-Hour Law of 1868 never proved to be the "model" its proponents had intended it to be, and its provisions had been virtually nullified by the Martin decision, it was nonetheless a major advance in protective labor legislation. The leader of the Knights of Labor, Terence V. Powderly, summed it up this way: "[T]he principle had been recognized by the Government that eight hours were sufficient for men to toil."

8-Hour Law for Laborers and Mechanics on Public Works, 1892, and 8-Hour Law for Federal Contractors, 1912

Enactment of the 8-Hour Law of 1892 followed a congressional inquiry into the effectiveness of the 1868 law. Except for legislation extending the 8-hour provision to employees of the Printing Office (March 30, 1888) and to letter carriers (May 24, 1888), the 1868 law by the end of the 1880s was either ignored or only partially complied with. The 1892 law was intended to remedy this by (1) making it unlawful for any officer of the government to require or to employ covered employees in excess of 8 hours per day except in emergencies and (2) providing that intentional violations be deemed misdemeaners subject to a fine of $1,000 or 6 months imprisonment, or both. The Act covered all laborers and mechanics employed by the government of the United States or the District of Columbia, or by any contractors or subcontractors upon any of the public works of the United States or the District of Columbia. At the time, the 1892 law, like its predecessor, was a "model" law since the 8-hour day in private industry was by no means prevalent even in construction. Further, it was recognized that 8 hours, unlike 10 hours, from a practical as well as a protective consideration could not be an absoltue, and provision was made in the 1892 law for overtime work beyond 8 hours in emergencies.

The 8-Hour Law for Federal Contractors, enacted in 1912, supplemented the 1892 law. It was intended to extend the 8-hour principle to all work done for the government of the United States. It remedied a defect of the 1892 law by clearly indicating the enforcement obligations of the contracting or procurement agencies of the government.

State 8-Hour Law for Hazardous Industries, Utah, 1898

Shorter-hours laws for private industry were enacted in the 1800s by several states. For the most part, however, they were "guides" and were not considered enforceable. This was partially reversed in 1898 when the United States Supreme Court in *Holden v. Hardy* (169 U.S. 336 (1898)) upheld a Utah statute that limited the workday to 8 hours per day in the mining and smelting industries. The Court held that protection of the health of workers was a proper exercise of police power by the state.

8-Hour Day and 48-Hour Week for Letter Carriers: The 1900 Law and Subsequent Maximum-Hours Legislation for Postal Workers

In 1900, the 8-Hour Law of 1884 for letter carriers was replaced by legislation that provided both weekly and daily hours protection. In addition to an 8-hour day, hours were "not to exceed forty-eight hours during the six working days each week and such number of hours on Sunday, not exceeding eight, as may be required by the needs of the service." In 1911, the law was amended to authorize the Postmaster General to allow compensatory time off during the regular workweek for hours worked on Sundays.

The Reilly 8-in-10 Act for Postal Service Employees was enacted in 1912. The law covered clerks in first- and second-class post offices and letter carriers in the city delivery service and provided for "eight hours of service per day provided it does not extend over a longer period than ten consecutive hours." This became the basic maximum-hours law for postal employees. It has been supplemented over the years to broaden its coverage to virtually all postal employees; to provide for the working of overtime and compensation for such work; and to extend its maximum-hours protection to weekly hours. Key among these supplemental provisions was the amendment to permit overtime in emergencies, "provided it was not practicable to employ substitutes," and compensatory time or pay for such overtime work (1925); provision of the basic 44-hour week with Saturday a half-holiday (1931); establishment of the basic 40-hour week with Saturday a holiday (1935); and provision that the 40-hour week for postal employees was to be "introduced without reductions in weekly earnings" so that in reducing the basic workweek from 44 hours to 40 hours "remuneration was to equal that paid for the 44-hour week" (1936).

Workmen's Compensation Law, Maryland, 1902, and Other Early Workers' Compensation Legislation

Although workers' compensation laws had been enacted in Germany in 1884 and in England in 1897, it was not until Maryland's 1902 law that legislative steps were taken in this direction in the United States. The Maryland law covered employees in mines, quarries, public utilities, and municipal contract work. The 1902 law was short-lived, however, as it was held to be unconstitutional two years later even though under its provisions participation by employers was voluntary. The same fate befell a 1908 Montana workmen's compensation law for miners. New York State enacted a workers' compensation law that was voluntary for manufacturing but compulsory for hazardous industries. The law became the subject of intense litigation that ultimately resulted in workmen's compensation legislation being held constitutional under federal law. The law was initially held to be unconstitutional by the New York Court of Appeals, and New York State amended its constitution to meet the state court's objection. Largely encouraged by President Theodore Roosevelt's messages urging industrial accident compensation laws, 30 states enacted workmen's compensation laws from 1910 to 1915. A number of these states followed New York State's action and amended their constitutions. The question still remained, however, whether compulsory workers' compensation laws violated the due-process clause of the federal constitution. In 1917, the United States Supreme Court ruled that the Fourteenth Amendment does not prevent states from enacting such protective legislation and in three major test cases it upheld the New York State Workers' Compensation Law (*New York Central R.R. Co. v. White*, 243 U.S. 188), an Iowa law (*Hawkins v. Bleakley*, 243 U.S. 212), and a Washington law (*Mountain Timber v. Washington*, 243 U.S. 238).

State Maximum-Hours Laws for Nonhazardous Industries: New York State Bakery Workers, 1905, and Oregon Manufacturing Employees, 1916

Although maximum-hours laws for hazardous industries were declared constitutional in 1898, state hours legislation for employees were generally held to be unconstitutional until 1916. The early ruling differentiating nonhazardous industries was rendered by the United States Supreme Court in *Lochner v. New York* (198 U.S. 45 (1905)). Following a report of the state's Commissioner of Health that the excessively long hours of bakery workers made them susceptible to tuberculosis, New York enacted a law prohibiting work in excess of 10 hours per day or 60 hours per week for bakery workers. In declaring the law unconstitutional and in violation of the right of freedom of contract under the Fourteenth Amendment, the Court held that "there can be no fair doubt that the trade of a baker, in and of itself, is not an unhealthy one to that degree which would authorize the Legislature to interfere with the right of labor and with the right of free contract on the part of the individual either as employer or employee."

In 1916, the United State Supreme Court reversed itself when it upheld an Oregon 10-hour law. The law covered employees in "mill, factory, or manufacturing establishments" and permitted up to three hours a day of overtime provided penalty rates of time and one-half were paid for such overtime work. In declaring the law constitutional, the Court held in *Bunting v. Oregon* (243 U.S. 426 (1916)) that the penalty overtime rate of time and one-half deterred employers from working employees excessive hours and that inasmuch as 10 hours was generally observed as the normal workday, the law could not be held to be unreasonable or arbitrary.

Hours of Service Law for Railroad Employees, 1907, and the Adamson 8-Hour Act, 1916

In 1907, Congress enacted the first maximum-hours law for railroad employees engaged in interstate commerce. The Hours of Service law prohibited trainmen from being on duty longer than 16 consecutive hours or from going on duty before having had 10 hours rest. The legislation and the right "to enact laws for the safeguarding of the persons and property . . . transported . . . and of those who are employed in transporting them" was upheld under the power to regulate interstate commerce in *Baltimore & Ohio R.R. Co. v. Interstate Commerce Commission* (221 U.S. 612 (1911)).

Railroad workers pressed for the 8-hour day, and following a threatened national strike by the railway brotherhoods, the Adamson Act was enacted in 1916. The Act established a basic 8-hour day for interstate train service employees and was held to be constitutional by the United States Supreme Court in *Wilson v. New* (243 U.S. 323 (1917)).

State Minimum-Wage Laws for Women and Minors: Massachusetts Law of 1912 and Subsequent Legislation

Massachusetts enacted the first state minimum-wage law in 1912. It covered women and minors, and its provisions were nonmandatory. No penalties were provided in the statute, but the names of violators were to be publicized, and public disapproval was expected to bring about compliance. The National Consumers' League at the time spearheaded the legislative campaign for minimum-wage protection for minors and women.

Following the Massachusetts legislation, several states and the District of Columbia enacted mandatory minimum-wage laws with penalty provisions for violators. In *Stettler v. O'Hara* (243 U.S. 629 (1917)), the United States Supreme Court was divided in a test case on the Oregon law, but in *Adkins v. Children's Hospital* (226 U.S. 525 (1923)), it held the District of Columbia's minimum-wage law to be unconstitutional. The Court's reasoning in the *Adkins* case was largely followed in subsequent decisions invalidating minimum-wage laws for women and minors in Arizona, Arkansas, and New York. Finally, in 1937, the United States Supreme Court reversed the *Adkins* Case in upholding a 1913 minimum-wage law for women in the state of Washington. In its majority decision in *West Coast Hotel Co. v. Parrish* (300 U.S. 379 (1937)), the Court held that the exploitation of women is injurious to their health and imposes a burden upon the community and that reasonable regulations adopted in the interests of the community do not violate the restraints of due process under the Constitution. This line of reasoning of the United States Supreme Court persisted and served as a basis for the Court to hold as constitutional state minimum-wage and maximum-hours laws for workers generally so long as the coverage was limited to establishments engaged in intrastate commerce. As with federal hours legislation, the "maximum hours" nomenclature was a misnomer for laws establishing hours of 8 per workday and/or 40 per workweek since work beyond those basic hours "was largely unrestricted" so long as time and one-half was paid for all such hours of overtime.

Davis-Bacon Act, 1931

The Davis-Bacon Act covers federal construction contracts and requires that workers employed in the construction of public works or buildings for the federal government or the District of Columbia may not be paid less than the wage rate prevailing in construction in that area or geographical locality. A number of state and local governments have enacted similar prevailing-wage laws for workers engaged in the construction of public works and government buildings. These laws have also been referred to as **"Little Davis-Bacon Acts."** In recent years, but especially with the advent of large non-union construction contractors and companies, the Davis-Bacon Act has come under heavy attack for unduly adding to the already inflated costs of federal construction. The Act requires the Secretary of Labor to determine the prevailing wage rates in the area or locality where the public works or federal building construction, repair, or alterations are being done. Critics of the Act contend that this has resulted in the federal government's being required to pay the high wage rates prevailing in the Building Trades Union contracts in the area.

Efforts to repeal the Davis-Bacon Act have persisted over the years but they have been met with strong resistance by organized labor and to date have not been successful. Early in 1983, the Secretary of Labor modified and relaxed the regulations for determining prevailing wage rates. The use and calculation of rates for semiskilled helpers vis-à-vis journeymen and apprentices was expanded and the requirement that federal construction contractors submit payroll data to the Labor Department for verification of their conformity to the prevailing-wage requirement was eliminated. Organized labor, namely, the Building and Construction Trades Department and the AFL–CIO got a court injunction prohibiting the new regulations from being put into effect by the Labor Department. As stated in the *AFL–CIO News* (Vol. 28, No. 27

(July 9, 1983)), it is labor's view that "the Reagan Administration is trying to undercut prevailing wage protection by changing the rules even though Congress has not changed the law." The United States District Court largely upheld labor's position. The United States Court of Appeals, however, held that the Act gives the Secretary of Labor the authority to determine prevailing wages "in the broadest terms imaginable," and the Supreme Court refused to review the lower court's decision. Organized labor maintains that this is a "radical" change in the prevailing-rate concept. It contends that under the pretext of "cost-effectiveness" and essential budget saving, the Reagan administration and the Department of Labor have departed from the basic protective objective of the Act, which, as expressed in the *AFL–CIO News* (Vol. 29, No. 3 (January 21, 1984)), is "to prevent cutthroat competition based on wages among contractors and to protect reputable, established area contractors from unfair competition from fly-by-night, out-of-state operations who snared government contracts by low-balling wage costs in bids." In its decision, however, the Court of Appeals restricted the use of semiskilled helpers as partial replacement for journeymen and apprentices to localities where this was the prevailing practice. Also, the United States Court of Appeals rejected as unsatisfactory the modified regulation that would have reduced employer (contractor) reports on conformity to the mere submission of weekly statements of compliance. Further, the appellate court held that the required wage information submitted did not have to be in the form of actual payroll records.

National Industrial Recovery Act, 1933: Maximum Hours, Minimum Wages, and Codes of Fair Competition

Under the National Industrial Recovery Act enacted in June 1933, maximum hours and minimum wages were established by industry to "put a floor on wages and a ceiling on hours"; to "end cut-throat competition"; to "increase purchasing power" and "spread work"; to "combat depression"; and to "induce recovery." The hours and wages standards were developed individually industry by industry and were then embodied in **codes of fair competition,** which numbered 557 codes and 201 supplementary codes in all by the time the Act was declared unconstitutional in May 1935. The minimum wages in the codes varied by industry and by geographic area, population, and sex. The objective was to provide a "living wage" and to increase the purchasing power "of the lowest paid classes." The industry differences in minimum wages established in the codes was wide-ranging, from a low of 12½¢ per hour for Puerto Rican needle workers to a high of 70¢ per hour for workers in the wrecking and salvaging industry in New York City. Maximum-hours provisions in the codes of fair competition also varied, but a little over half of the industry codes provided for a 40-hour workweek, and about a third of the codes stipulated a maximum of 48 hours. It is significant to note with respect to the development of the public regulation of hours of work and wages that the commerce clause was the basis for the United States Supreme Court's decision that the National Industrial Recovery Act was unconstitutional. The Court did not hold or even infer that the regulation of wages and hours by the federal government was unlawful. The crux of the Court's ruling in *Schecter Poultry Corp. v. United States* (295 U.S. 495 (1935)) was that the codes of fair competition had been extended to poultry firms that were engaged in intrastate business only, and that this exceeded the interstate commerce powers of the federal government.

State Unemployment Insurance Act, Wisconsin, 1932

In 1932, Wisconsin enacted the first state unemployment insurance law. The Wisconsin Unemployment Reserve Act was passed in the spring of 1932 but did not become compulsory until July 1, 1934. Although over the years the Wisconsin legislature has been liberal in outlook and socially minded, its pioneering effort in unemployment insurance conservatively followed the pattern of existing workers' compensation acts in requiring that contributions be made by employers only and be based on the employers' experience rating. This was contrary to the unemployment insurance experience of Great Britain and other European countries. Critics have contended that this practice falsely assumes that employers are as much to blame for unemployment as they are for industrial accidents. Great Britain, in 1911, was the first country to enact a compulsory unemployment insurance law. While our states have followed the Wisconsin pattern, other countries have generally modeled their unemployment insurance laws after that of Great Britain, which does not rely on experience rating; which generally divides the cost among the employers, employees, and the state; and which varies the amount of weekly unemployment benefit with the size of the employee's family.

Federal Social Security Act, 1935

Essentially a social insurance law, the Federal Social Security Act was passed in August 1935 at the urging of President Franklin

Roosevelt. As initially enacted, the Act set up a national old-age insurance system; provided for federal grants-in-aid to approved state plans for old-age relief, care of dependent and crippled children, assistance to the blind, maternal and child health, and public health services; and encouraged state unemployment insurance laws by leveling a uniform federal payroll tax on employers and allowing a credit of up to 90 percent for payroll taxes into an approved state unemployment compensation fund. The Social Security Act has been amended several times over the years, and until recently, this was done largely to improve benefits and coverage. The Act was amended, for example, in 1956 to improve disability benefits, among others; in 1965, to adopt the medicare plan providing partial coverage for hospitalization, nursing home care, home nursing, and diagnostic expenses for employees over 65 years of age; and, in 1974, to provide automatic cost-of-living adjustments in social security payments and raise the tax base. There has been periodic concern over the years for the fiscal soundness of the Act. This reached its zenith early in the eighties, and the Reagan administration has promoted major steps to improve the Act's financial position with some resultant modification in benefits.

Walsh-Healy Public Contracts Act, 1936: Maximum Hours, Minimum Wages, and Labor Standards for Employees Working on Federal Contracts

The Walsh-Healy Public Contracts Act as enacted in June 1936, effective September 1936, covers employees working under federal contracts exceeding $10,000. The Act regulates both hours of work and minimum wages and establishes certain other labor standards as well, including provisions governing the employment of child and convict labor. The hours provision sets up a basic 8-hour day and 40-hour workweek for employees on federal contracts and requires that overtime rates be paid for all hours worked in excess of 8 hours per day or 40 hours per week, whichever is greater. The Act did not establish the rate of pay for overtime, but the overtime rate of time and one-half was stipulated by the Secretary of Labor. The Act superseded the 1912 8-Hour Law for all federal contracts jointly covered. The wage provisions of the Act require that federal contractors pay covered employees at least the amount determined by the Secretary of Labor to be the prevailing minimum wage in the industry or branch of the industry. Although there have been complaints about the length of time taken in making wage determinations and about their "out-of-dateness," the standard of the Walsh-Healy Public Contracts Act has not drawn the heated criticism that has been levied against the Davis-Bacon Act. This is largely because the wage standard of the Walsh-Healy Public Contracts Act is a "prevailing minimum wage" standard rather than a "prevailing wage" standard. The penalties under the Walsh-Healy Public Contracts Act for noncomplying federal contractors include cancellation of contract, denial of the right to bid on federal contracts for three years, and liability to liquid damages for underpayments to employees and for additional charges incurred by the Federal contracting agency because of the cancellation of the original contract. Historically, the Walsh-Healy Public Contracts Act represents one of several laws that President Franklin Roosevelt and supporters of the "New Deal" sponsored and designed with the intent of restoring government controls over terms of employment, especialy maximum hours and minimum wages, which had been lost through the invalidation of the codes of fair competition of the National Industrial Recovery Act.

Bituminous Coal Conservation Act (Guffey Act), 1935

The Bituminous Coal Conservation Act (Guffey Act) of 1935 established wages, hours, and labor standards as provided in collective bargaining agreements "to stabilize the coal industry," but was held unconstitutional by the United States Supreme Court in *Carter v Carter Coal Co. et al.* (298 U.S. 238 (1936)). The Guffey Act and the Fair Labor Standards Act of 1938 had been sponsored by the Roosevelt administration with the broad objective of restoring government controls over terms of employments.

Fair Labor Standards Act (Federal Wage-Hour Law), 1938

The Fair labor Standards Act of 1938 is also known as the Federal Wage-Hour Law since it established maximum-hours and minimum-wage standards for most employees in establishments engaged in interstate commerce. The provision on hours established a basic 40-hour workweek with time and one-half for overtime. Unlike the Walsh-Healy Public Contracts Act, the Fair Labor Standards Act did not regulate hours for the workday. As initially enacted in 1938, the basic 40-hour workweek was to be reached gradually: for the first year, 1938–1939, the basic workweek was 44 hours; for the second year, 1939–1940, the basic workweek was 42 hours; and thereafter it was 40 hours. The Fair Labor Standards Act was promoted in the Depression with the same objective for its hours standards as had been stated for the hours provisions of the codes of fair competition of the National Industrial Recovery Act and those of the Walsh-Healy Public Contracts Act, namely, to "spread the work." However, with the advent of emergency defense production in 1940 and World War II following the attack on Pearl Harbor on December 7, 1941, the basic 40-hour workweek standard with its provision for time and one-half for overtime soon became a source of increased earnings rather than a means of spreading the work. As with the Walsh-Healy Public Contracts Act, the hours provision of the Fair Labor Standards Act has remained at 40 hours per week despite periodic efforts to reduce it.

The minimum-wage provisions of the Fair Labor Standards Act also were put into effect gradually. As enacted in June 1938, the Act established an absolute minimum wage of 25¢ per hour for the first year and 30¢ per hour thereafter. However, the statute also stipulated that the minimum wage was to be raised to 40¢ per hour "as rapidly as is economically feasible without substantially curtailing employment." And to this end, temporary industry committees composed of representatives of the public and of the employers and workers were set up in industries to determine when it would be "feasible" to raise the minimum wage above 30¢ an hour but not to exceed 40¢ an hour. The minimum wage was an "absolute" with no differentials for sex or regions as such. The statute further provided that "the universal minimum wage of 40¢ an hour" would automatically go into effect seven years after the effective date of the Act, namely in 1945, except for any industry in which it had been found that the 40¢ per hour minimum was not economically feasible. The concerns over the impact of the minimum wage on employment were based on the "Depression economics" that prevailed at the time Congress was considering the several House and Senate bills for a federal wage-hour law. As with the gradualness of reaching the 40-hour workweek standard, the advent of defense and war production increased employment by leaps and bounds, and minimum wages in industry rose rapidly to the point that the 40¢ per hour standard was largely obsolete long before the Act's target date of 1945. Unlike the 40-hour basic workweek standard, the minimum-wage standard of the Act has been raised often by amendment over the years. Currently, the minimum wage of the Fair Labor Standards Act is $3.35 per hour. The persistence of a high rate of unemployment in the early 1980s has given rise to periodic efforts to amend the Fair Labor Standards Act to provide a lower minimum-wage standard for younger workers and student employees. The Reagan administration has for the most part favored these efforts, but to date, the proposal has not met with general support, and the Act has not been amended to provide such an exception in its minimum-wage standard.

Although there were several legal challenges to the law, the constitutionality of the Fair Labor Standards Act was settled early. In *United States v. Darby Lumber Co.* (312 U.S. 451 (1941)), the United States Supreme Court upheld the general power of Congress to regulate the hours of work and wages of employees in establishments producing goods for interstate commerce and to prohibit the shipment of goods in interstate commerce which had been produced in violation of the law. In its ruling on the constitutionality of the Act, the Court specifically upheld the power to set child labor standards and overruled the prior ruling in *Hammer v. Dagenhart* (247 U.S. 251 (1918)), which had invalidated the first child labor law. The delegation of authority to the Wage and Hour Administration and the procedures for setting minimum wages without differentials by region or sex were affirmatively ruled on by the United States Supreme Court in *Opp Cotton Mills, Inc., v. Administrator of the Wage and Hour Division* (312 U.S. 524 (1941)). The prohibition of "homework" by child labor under the Fair Labor Standards Act was upheld by the United States Supreme Court in *Gemsco et al. v. Walling* (324 U.S. 244 (1946)), and in 1949 the Act was amended to prohibit child labor altogether.

Over the years the coverage of the Fair Labor Standards Act has been broadened. In 1961, the Act was amended to extend coverage to more than 3.5 million workers, mostly in the retail trade and construction industries; in 1966 the Act was amended to extend coverage to about 10 million more workers who had previously been excluded; and in 1968 the United States Supreme Court held in *Maryland v. Wirtz* (392 U.S. 183) that it was a lawful exercise of the commerce clause of the Constitution to cover employees of state and local government hospitals. The *Maryland v. Wirtz* precedent and later amendments that added some 3.5 million public workers to the coverage of the Fair Labor Standards Act were overturned by the United States Supreme Court in 1976 in *National League of Cities v. Usery* (426 U.S. 833). In the *National League of Cities* case the Supreme Court held that because of the primacy of states' rights, Congress lacked the authority to set minimum wages, maximum hours, and overtime standards for public sector workers who were employed in "traditional government functions." After this decision, the San Antonio Metropolitan Transit Authority stopped complying with the wage, hour, and overtime provisions of the Fair Labor Standards Act. The Transit Authority challenged a ruling of the U.S. Labor Department which held that the Authority was still covered by the Fair Labor Standards Act because the operation of a bus system is not a "traditional function of government."

Joe G. Garcia was one of several affected employees, and because he was the first named, the case reached the Supreme Court as *Garcia v. San Antonio Metropolitan Transit Authority* (469 U.S. 528 (1985), *reh. denied, Donovan v. San Antonio Metropolitan Transit Authority*, 471 U.S. 1049 (1985)). The Supreme Court, in a 5 to 4 decision, overturned its 1976 ruling in the *National League of Cities* case. The Court majority in 1985 rejected the states' rights doctrine it had previously relied upon. It held that there is no reason for state governments to be immunized from the constitutional authority of Congress to regulate commerce. The majority stated, further, that federalism is built into the constitutional frame-work of government through such provisions as equal representation of states in the Senate and the electoral vote system of choosing the President. The minority of the Court stoutly maintained that the majority were in error and that the states' rights doctrine would, in time, once again prevail. Meanwhile, pursuant to the Court's decision, efforts were made to apply the provisions of the Fair Labor Standards Act to public employees. State and local governments resisted, contending that the increases in overtime costs would be especially burdensome, and sought congressional relief in the form of legislation removing public sector workers from the overtime pay requirements of the Fair Labor Standards Act. In the fall of 1985, a compromise was effected allowing state and local governments to make overtime payments in compensatory time off at the same time and one-half rate as cash payments for work beyond 40 hours a week. Public sector unions hailed the legislation providing "comp time" at the time and one-half rate as "a major break through" for state and local government employees. The legislation, which was made enforceable as of April 1986, sets limits on the amount of compensatory time that can be paid to a public worker—480 hours for public safety and emergency workers and 240 hours for workers generally, after which hours of overtime worked are to be paid for in cash.

Welfare and Pension Disclosure Act, 1958

The Welfare and Pension Disclosure Act of 1958 requires administrators of health and welfare insurance, pension, and supplementary unemployment compensation plans to file descriptions of the plan and annual financial reports with the Secretary of Labor. The reports are to be available for public inspection and are also to be made available to plan participants. As amended in 1962, the plans that are subject to the Act are those which cover more than 25 workers.

Equal Pay Act, 1963

The Equal Pay Act of 1963 prohibits wage differentials based on sex. The Act covers all workers who are subject to the provisions of the Fair Labor Standards Act.

Civil Rights Act, 1964: Title VII,
Equal Employment Opportunity (EEO)

Title VII of the Civil Rights Act of 1964 prohibits discrimination on the basis of race, color, religion, sex, or national origin in hiring, apprenticeship, compensation and the terms, conditions, or privileges of employment, and union membership. The **Equal Employment Opportunity Commission** was established to investigate and adjudicate discrimination complaints.

Occupational Safety and Health Act (OSHA), 1970

The Occupational Safety and Health Act was signed by President Richard Nixon on Decmeber 29, 1970, and became effective on April 18, 1971. The Act empowers the Secretary of Labor to establish occupational safety and health standards in the nation's workplaces. The Act promotes the establishment and enforcement of state occupational safety and health standards with the approval of the Secretary of Labor. The Secretary of Labor and an independent review commission appointed by the President are authorized to impose civil penalties and fines, and criminal action is authorized in cases of willful violations resulting in death.

Employee Retirement Income Security Act (ERISA), 1974

The Employment Retirement Income Security Act subjects private pension plans to rigid public regulation. The Act also covers private welfare plans but less extensively. Among other things, pension plans are required to comply with certain funding standards to assure the adequacy of contributions and the attainment of vesting by an employee after 10 years of coverage under the plan. The purchase of termination insurance also is required. To this end, a **Pension Benefit Guaranty Corporation** has been established. The PBGC is headed by the Secretary of Labor and in the event a plan is terminated with insufficient funds to pay all of its nonforfeitable benefits, the insurance provided by the Pension Benefit Guaranty Corporation is to pay pension benefits up to a specified individual amount initially set at $750 a month.

PART III

Arbitration:
Major Court Decisions
and Arbitration Standards

The Labor-Management Relations Act and Arbitration: Sections 201(b), 203(d), and 301

The Labor-Management Relations Act of 1947 makes it clear that voluntary arbitration is the preferred method of settling labor-management impasses both as the final step of the grievance procedure in rights disputes and after mediation has failed to bring about an agreement on new-contract terms in interest disputes. The role of voluntary arbitration is evidenced in Sections 201(b), 203(d), and 301 of the Act. Section 201(b) refers to the settlement of new-contract disputes as follows:

The settlement of issues between employers and employees through collective bargaining may be advanced by making available full and adequate governmental facilities for conciliation, mediation, and voluntary arbitration to aid and encourage employers and the representatives of their employees to reach and maintain agreements concerning rates of pay, hours, and working conditions, and to make all reasonable efforts to settle their differences by mutual agreement reached through conferences and collective bargaining or by such methods as may be provided for in any applicable agreement for the settlement of disputes.

Section 203(d) refers to the settlement of grievance disputes as follows:

Final adjustment by a method agreed upon by the parties is hereby declared to be the desirable method for settlement of grievance disputes arising over the application or interpretation of an existing collective bargaining agreement. The Service [Federal Mediation and Conciliation Service] is directed to make its conciliation and mediation services available in the settlement of such grievance disputes only as a last resort and in exceptional cases.

151

Section 301, which the United States Supreme Court has held permits suits to be brought in any federal district court to enforce the provisions of the collective bargaining agreement, including the arbitration provisions, reads as follows:

(a) Suits for violation of contracts between an employer and a labor organization representing employees in an industry affecting commerce as defined in this chapter, or between any such labor organizations, may be brought in any district court of the United States having jurisdiction of the parties, without respect to the amounts in the controversy or without regard to the citizenship of the parties.

(b) Any labor organization which represents employees in an industry affecting commerce as defined in this chapter and any employer whose activities affect commerce as defined in this chapter shall be bound by the acts of its agents. Any such labor organization may sue or be sued as an entity and in behalf of the employees whom it represents in the courts of the United States. Any money judgment against a labor organization in a district court of the United States shall be enforceable only against the organization as an entity and against its assets, and shall not be enforceable against any individual member or his assets.

Section 301 brought uniformity in the enforcement of arbitration provisions. Prior to 1947 and the Taft-Hartley amendments, the parties were forced to rely on the state courts, and the application of common law to arbitration varied widely among the states. In many states, the contractual provision to arbitrate was not enforceable in the courts, and the parties were free "to renege" on the arbitration agreement in their labor contract and to take their dispute directly to the courts. The United States Supreme Court in what have often been called the landmark court decisions in arbitration—namely, the *Lincoln Mills* case in 1957 and three cases involving the United Steelworkers of America, referred to as the *Steelworkers Trilogy*, in 1960—established that grievance (rights) arbitration is enforceable in the federal district courts and ruled on several questions involving arbitrability, the enforceability of the arbitrator's award, and the role of arbitrators vis-à-vis that of the courts. Summaries of these and other key Court decisions dealing with the role of arbitration in industrial disputes follows.

Landmark Court Decisions

Textile Workers Union v. Lincoln Mills, 1957

The basic issue to be decided in the *Lincoln Mills* case (353 U.S. 448, 40 L.R.R.M. 2113 (1957)) was whether the Court could compel a company to arbitrate a dispute under a union contract. The essential background facts are as follows:

(1) The existing contract between the Textile Workers Union and the Lincoln Mills Company had an arbitration clause and a no-strike clause.

(2) The grievance arose over the Company's reassignment of work loads.

(3) The dispute was duly processed through the grievance steps, not settled, and the Union sought arbirtration.

(4) The Company refused to arbitrate, contending that the assignment of work was management's prerogative, and it used the management rights clause in the contract to support its position.

(5) The Union sued in the federal district court under Section 301 of the Labor-Management Relations Act to enforce the arbitration provision.

(6) The District Court sustained the Union, but the Court of Appeals reversed, holding that while Section 301 gave the federal courts jurisdiction, it did not authorize the courts to grant a remedy.

(7) The Supreme Court granted a writ of certiorari.

The Supreme Court held in brief as follows:

(1) that arbitration is the quid pro quo for the no-strike provision in a collective bargaining agreement;

(2) that the arbitration provision is enforceable in the federal court under Section 301 of the Labor-Management Relations Act, and that Section 301 gave the court the authority to grant a remedy;

(3) that it is the federal court and not the state courts which has the basic jurisdiction over these questions so long as the parties to the collective bargaining agreement are covered by the Labor-Management Relations Act; and

(4) that the provisions of the Norris-LaGuardia Act prohibiting the use of labor injunctions do not apply in matters pertaining to the enforceability of the provisions of a collective bargaining agreement.

In reaching its decision, the Court drew on the provisions of the Labor-Management Relations Act, namely, the law's preference for the peaceful settlement of labor disputes by voluntary arbitration as expressed in Sections 201(b) and 203(d) and the obligation of the courts under Section 301 to enforce the arbitration provisions of a collective bargaining agreement. With respect to the anti-injunction provisions of the Norris-LaGuardia Act, it is of interest to note that in spite of the Court's holding in the *Lincoln-Mills* case, it was not until *Boys Markets, Inc., v. Retail Clerks* (74 L.R.R.M. 2257 (1970)) that the Court made it clear that the Norris-LaGuardia Act does not bar the granting of injunctive relief to an employer against a strike by a union in breach of the arbitration and no-strike provisions of the collective bargaining agreement. In reaching this conclusion, the Supreme Court overruled its decision in *Sinclair Refining Co. v. Atkinson* (370 U.S. 195, 50 L.R.R.M. 2420 (1962)) and stated as follows:

> The Sinclair decision . . . seriously undermined the effectiveness of the arbitration technique as a method peacefully to resolve industrial disputes without resort to strikes, lockouts, and similar devices. Clearly employers will be wary of assuming obligations to arbitrate, specifically enforceable against them, when no similarly efficacious remedy is available to enforce the concomitant undertaking of the union to refrain from striking. On the other hand, the central purpose of the Norris-LaGuardia Act to foster the growth and viability of labor organizations is hardly retarded—if anything, this goal is advanced—by a remedial device which merely enforces the obligation that the union freely undertook under a specifically enforceable agreement to submit disputes to arbitration.

The Steelworkers Trilogy

United Steelworkers v. Warrior & Gulf Navigation Co., 1960

The *Warrior & Gulf Navigation* case, (363 U.S. 574, 46 L.R.R.M. 2404 (1960)) was the first of the *Steelworkers Trilogy* cases. Basically, the question before the Court was what is the Court's role when there is doubt that the dispute between the parties is covered under the arbitration clause. The Warrior & Gulf Navigation Company had contracted-out work and laid off 20 maintenance employees. The contract was silent on subcontracting but contained a clause which stated that matters which are strictly a function of management are not subject to arbitration. The employees grieved the contracting-out of work; the matter was not settled in the grievance procedure; the Union invoked arbitration and the Company refused, citing the provision that the contracting-out of work was a function of management and contending that therefore the dispute was not arbitrable. The Union brought suit. The District Court granted the Company's motion to dismiss after reviewing the merits of the grievance and ruled that the aribtrator is not empowered to review the Company's business judgment in contracting-out work. The Court of Appeals affirmed.

The United States Supreme Court reversed the lower courts, however, holding that the dispute over contracting-out should be arbitrated. The arbitration clause in the collective bargaining agreement was broad, applicable to any difference between the parties, and the Court held that the contracting-out dispute was just such a difference. The Court held that the lower courts had erred in getting into the merits of the dispute, making the decision that contracting-out was a function of management, and ruling that it was therefore excluded from arbitration. Such determinations, the United States Supreme Court reasoned, are the function of the arbitrator; the Court should not inquire into the merits of a dispute or seek to interpret the arbitration provision. The rights of a party to arbitrate a dispute under the arbitration provision of the collective bargaining agreement "should not be denied," stated the Court, "unless it may be said with positive assurance that the arbitration clause is not susceptible of an interpretation that covers the asserted dispute. Doubts should be resolved in favor of coverage." In commenting on the qualifications of the arbitrator vis-à-vis the courts in the adjudication of the merits of a labor dispute, the Court stated:

The labor arbitrator performs functions which are not normal to the courts. . . . The labor arbitrator's source of law is not confined to the express provisions of the contract, as the industrial common law—the practices of the industry and the shop—is equally a part of the collective bargaining agreement although not expressed in it. The labor arbitrator is usually chosen because of the parties' confidence in his knowledge of the common law of the shop and their trust in his personal judgment to bring to bear considerations which are not expressed in the contract as criteria for judgment. . . . The ablest judge cannot be expected to bring the same experience and competence to bear upon the determination of a grievance, because he cannot be similarly informed.

United Steelworkers v. American Manufacturing Co., 1960

The basic question in the *American Manufacturing Company* case (363 U.S. 564, 46 L.R.R.M. 2414 (1960)) as in *Warrior & Gulf Navigation*, involved the Court's role when asked to enforce the arbitration provision of a collective bargaining agreement. Here, however, the doubt was not whether the dispute was covered by the arbitration provision but, rather, whether it had merit. The contract provided for the arbitration of any unsettled dispute "as to the meaning, interpretation and application of the provisions" of the agreement and provided job seniority rights to the employees. The grievant, Sparks, had been out on disability due to a plant accident; settled a workmen's compensation claim against the Company for a 25% permanent partial disability benefit; and sought to return to work on the basis of the seniority provisions of the contract. The Company refused to arbitrate, on the ground that Sparks's grievance was without merit and patently frivolous since he had settled his claim on the basis of being disabled. The Union brought suit under Section 301 of the LMRA to compel arbitration; the federal district court upheld the Company on the basis that the permanent partial disability settlement estopped the claim of seniority and employment rights; and the Court of Appeals affirmed, holding that the grievance was "a frivolous, patently baseless one, not subject to arbitration under the collective bargaining agreement."

As in the *Warrior & Gulf Navigation* case, the Supreme Court reversed the lower courts, holding that the courts had no business weighing the merits of the grievance since their sole function in determining whether to order arbitration was to ascertain whether the parties had agreed to arbitrate such disputes; and that even though the grievance was without merit and frivolous, it had to be arbitrated since the parties had agreed to arbitrate any dispute over the provisions of the contract. The Court stated as follows:

> The function of the court is very limited when the parties have agreed to submit all questions of contract interpretation to the arbitrator. It is confined to ascertaining whether the party seeking arbitration is making a claim which on its face is governed by the contract. Whether the moving party is right or wrong is a question of contract interpretation for the arbitrator. . . .
>
> The courts, therefore, have no business weighing the merits of the grievance, considering whether there is equity in a particular claim, or determining whether there is particular language in the written instrument which will support the claim. The agreement is to submit all grievances to arbitration, not merely those which the court will deem meritorious. The processing of even frivolous claims may have therapeutic values of which those who are not a part of the plant environment may be quite unaware.

United Steelworkers v. Enterprise Wheel & Car Corp., 1960

Enterprise Wheel & Car (363 U.S. 593, 46 L.R.R.M. 2423 (1960)) the last case of the *Steelworkers Trilogy*, concerned the Court's role in questions pertaining to the enforcement of an arbitration award. In brief, the facts of the case are as follows:

(1) An employee was discharged and a group of employees went out on a wildcat strike in protest.

(2) The Union ordered the employees to return to work, but when they did the Company refused to take them back.

(3) The Union grieved, the matter was not settled in the grievance steps, and the Union invoked arbitration.

(4) The Company refused to arbitrate, even though the contract clause provided for it as the final settlement of any dispute over the meaning and application of the provisions of the contract.

(5) The Union sued under Section 301 of the LMRA to compel the Company to arbitrate and the arbitration was held.

(6) The arbitrator ruled that the expiration of the contract had not barred reinstatement; that while the employees had acted improperly, discharge was too severe a penalty; that the appropriate pen-

alty was a 10-day suspension; and that the employees were to be reinstated with back pay less pay for the suspension period and monies earned elsewhere if any.

(7) The Company refused to comply with the arbitrator's award and the Union brought suit to enforce compliance.

(8) The District Court ordered compliance, but the Court of Appeals reversed on the ground the employees had no right to reinstatement or back pay subsequent to the contract's expiration.

The Supreme Court reversed the Court of Appeals, holding that so long as the arbitrator's decision "draws its essence" from the contract, the Court should enforce it, even though the arbitrator's decision may be ambiguous and the Court may disagree with it. The Supreme Court stated:

As we . . . emphasized, the question of interpretation of the collective bargaining is a question for the arbitrator . . . and so far as the arbitrator's decision concerns construction of the contract, the courts have no business overruling him because their interpretation of the contract is different from his.

With respect to the arbitrator's responsibility in interpreting the contract, the Court held:

Nevertheless, an arbitrator is confined to interpretation and application of the collective bargaining agreement; he does not sit to dispense his own brand of industrial justice. He may of course look for guidance from many sources, yet his award is legitimate only so long as it draws its essence from the collective bargaining agreement. When the arbitrator's words mainfest an infidelity to this obligation, courts have no choice but to refuse enforcement of the award.

In a recent case, *AT&T Technologies, Inc., v. Communications Workers of America* (— U.S. —, 106 S. Ct. 1415, 89 L. Ed. 2d 648 (1986)), the Supreme Court in a unanimous decision cited the *Steelworkers Trilogy* in holding that questions of arbitrability are for the Court and not the arbitrator to decide. The matter was triggered by a 1981 layoff of 79 telephone installers in Chicago by Western Electric (later renamed AT&T Technologies). The Company replaced the laid-off employees with installers transferred from Wisconsin and Indiana. The CWA protested that the labor contract had been violated since the layoffs had not been for lack of work as required under Article 20. The dispute was not settled and the Union sought arbitration pursuant to the grievance and arbitration provisions of the contract. The Company refused to arbitrate the dispute, citing Article 9, the management rights provision of the contract, and contending that Article 20 dealt only with the order of layoff. The Union sought to compel the Company to arbitrate and sued in federal court under Section 301 of the Taft-Hartley Act, contending that the dispute over the layoffs was an arbitrable issue under its contract with the Company.

The United States District Court for Northern Illinois ruled that "it was for the arbitrator, not the Court, to decide whether the Union's interpretation has merit" and directed the Company to submit the threshold issue to an arbitrator. The Company appealed and the Seventh Circuit affirmed, holding that an arbitrator and not the Court should decide threshold issues of arbitrability because "deciding the issue would entangle the Court in interpretation of substantive provisions of the collective bargaining agreement and thereby involve consideration of the merits of the dispute." The Company's petition for review of the decision was granted by the Supreme Court, and oral argument was held on January 22, 1986.

The Supreme Court reversed the Seventh Circuit, holding, in brief, that the lower court's interpretation of the "precepts" set forth in the *Steelworkers Trilogy* was in error and that "these precepts have served the industrial community well, and have led to continued reliance on arbitration, rather than strikes or lockouts, as the preferred method of resolving disputes arising during the term of a collective bargaining agreement. ". . . [W]e see no reason either to question their continued validity, or to eviscerate their meaning by creating an exception to their general applicability." Among the "precepts" that were referenced by the Supreme Court as having been established in the *Steelworkers Trilogy* are (1) that parties cannot be compelled to arbitrate issues they have not agreed to submit to arbitration in their contract and (2) that where there are disputes as to whether an issue is arbitrable, the Court should decide in the first instance whether that issue should be submitted to arbitration.

Speaking for the Court, Justice White stated that "the question of arbitrability—whether a collective bargaining agreement creates a duty for the parties to arbitrate the particular grievance—is undeniably an issue for judicial determination. . . . [U]nless the parties clearly and unmistakably provide otherwise, the question of whether the parties agreed to arbitrate is to be decided by the court, not the arbitrator." Justice White went on to add that if an arbitrator is permitted to rule on arbitrability, he/she may seek "to impose obligations outside the contract limited only by [his/her] understanding and conscience." The Supreme Court remanded the case for the Seventh Circuit or the District Court to decide "whether, because of express exclusion or other forceful evidence, the dispute over the interpretation of Article 20 of the contract, the layoff provision, is not subject to the arbitration clause."

Justice Brennan, in a concurring opinion joined by Chief Justice Burger and Justice Marshall, stated that the Seventh Circuit

was mistaken insofar as it thought that determining arbitrability required resolution of the parties' dispute with respect to the meaning of Article 9 and 20 of the collective bargaining agreement. . . . [T]he judicial inquiry required to determine arbitrability is much simpler. . . . [T]he question for the court is "strictly confined" to whether the parties agreed to submit disputes over the meaning of Article 20 to arbitration. . . . [B]ecause the collective bargaining agreement contains a standard arbitration clause, the answer must be affirmative unless the contract contains explicit language stating that disputes respecting Article 20 are not subject to arbitration, or unless the party opposing arbitration—here AT&T—address "the most forceful evidence" to this effect from the bargaining history. . . . [U]nder [*Steelworkers v.*] *Warrior & Gulf Navigation Company*, determining arbitrability does not require the Court even to consider which party is correct with respect to the meaning of Article 20.

In referencing the *Warrior & Gulf Navigation* case, the Court cited the holding that "an order to arbitrate the particular grievance should not be denied unless it may be said with positive assurance that the arbitration clause is not susceptible of an interpretation that covers the asserted dispute. Doubts should be resolved in favor of coverage." By and large, since the enunciation of these views by the Supreme Court in 1960, arbitrators have considered them to be precepts they are obligated to follow in addressing questions of arbitrability that are submitted to them. And judging by the large number of arbitrability issues arbitrators have been required to adjudge, the parties also seemingly felt that the arbitral process was as capable of dealing with the threshold issue as of addressing the merits of a dispute. There is of course the possibility, as Justice White stated, for an arbitrator "to impose obligations outside the contract limited only by [his/her] understanding and conscience." But that is the nature of the arbitrator's profession, and the curb, in any event, is judicial review. It would appear that the Supreme Court in 1960 had this in mind when it stated in *Enterprise Wheel & Car* the following: "Nevertheless, an arbitrator is confined to interpretation and application of the collective bargaining agreement; he does not sit to dispense his own brand of industrial justice."

On its face, the Supreme Court ruling in the *AT&T Technologies* case does not preclude arbitrators from ruling on threshold issues of arbitrability. It is hoped that in the interest of minimizing delays in the arbitral resolution of industrial disputes the parties will, in the main, continue to take questions of arbitrability to the chosen arbitrator. However, given the Supreme Court's explicit enunciation in *AT&T Technologies* that questions of arbitrability are for the Court and not for the arbitrator to decide, there is a grave danger that this may well prove to be little more than a pious hope. Certainly, if one or the other party to a labor contract is intent for one reason or another on delaying an adjudgment of the merits of a dispute and there is some basis on which to raise the threshold question of arbitrability, the courts will be used. As a minimum timewise, with the use of the courts there is an imposed bifurcation of the hearing of the threshold issue from the hearing of argument on the merits which the parties may waive, and most often have done so, when placing the matter before an arbitrator.

The National Labor Relations Board and Arbitration: Deferral Policy

It is inevitable that certain types of contract violations will also be unfair labor practices in contravention of the Labor-Management Relations Act. Hence, the decisions of an arbitrator in an arbitration proceeding and those of the National Labor Relations Board in an unfair labor practices proceeding can overlap. The vast majority of contract violations are not unfair labor practices, and here there is no conflict, for the law is clear. As stated in Section 10(a) of the LMRA, the NLRB is given the power to prevent unfair labor practices, and the Board's authority cannot be modified or negated by the provisions of a collective bargaining agreement or an arbitrator's role in a contract interpretation dispute. According to Section 301 of the LMRA, the arbitrator is given the authority to rule on contract interpretation decisions, and the NLRB has no jurisdiction over such disputes unless there is a question as to whether an unfair labor practice has been committed. The Board has ruled that it is a violation of the duty to bargain in good faith and, hence, an unfair labor practice if a union or a management abrogates or totally repudiates the collective bargaining agreement. In order to minimize conflict with contract arbitral procedures, the NLRB has established a policy of deferral to arbitration which was initially embodied in two doctrines, namely, the Spielberg Doctrine of 1955 and the Collyer Doctrine of 1971. It is to be noted that the Board has subsequently modified and limited its deferral policy, especially in cases involving discipline for union activity and other disputes in which there is an alleged interference with an employee's Section 7 rights under the Act. On several occasions, some members of the Board have strongly urged that the deferral policy be rescinded altogether. This notion persists. To date, however, except for prohibiting deferral in certain types of cases, the policy enunciated in the Spielberg and Collyer doctrines continues as the basic deferral policy of the Board in its relationship to the arbitral process.

The Spielberg Doctrine, 1955

The Spielberg Doctrine is applied in cases in which there has been a prior arbitration decision on a contract dispute and one or the other party to the contract or the grievant brings the mattter before the NLRB on the charge that there has been an unfair labor practice. Briefly, the facts of the case, *Spielberg Manufacturing Co.* (112 N.L.R.B. 1080 (1955)), were that after an economic strike the Company discharged four employees for misconduct; the matter was grieved, taken to arbitration, and the arbitrator sustained the discharge; the Union filed an unfair labor practice charge with the NLRB. The Board refused to hear the case, ruling that it would defer to an arbitrator's decision without rehearing the matter if the following conditions were met: (1) the arbitration proceedings were fair and regular, providing the employee a fair hearing as would be the case if the matter were tried before the Board; (2) the arbitration was mandatory under the contract and binding on the parties; (3) the arbitrator's decision was not repugnant to the Act, which thus assured employees that rights guaranteed by the LMRA would not be denied by an arbitrator's decision that is inconsistent with the policies and principles of the Board; and (4) the arbitrator has considered and expressly addressed the unfair labor practice issue in reaching the decision rendered.

The principle of deferral to arbitration awards rendered in the *Spielberg* case was extended to pending arbitration proceedings in *Dubo Manufacturing Corp.* (142 N.L.R.B. 431 (1963)).

The Collyer Doctrine, 1971

The Collyer Doctrine, rendered some sixteen years after the Spielberg Doctrine, extends the NLRB's deferral policy to cases in which a party to a collective bargaining agreement goes directly to the Board to seek redress for an alleged unfair labor practice which is also a contract violation matter subject to final and binding arbitration. Under the Collyer Doctrine, when an issue is brought to the Board which is susceptible to being resolved in arbitration under a collective bargaining agreement, the Board will not hear the case and will defer the matter to arbitration under the contract. However, the Board will retain its jurisdiction over the case and apply the Spielberg criteria in evaluating the arbitrator's decision. If any one of the four requirements of the Spielberg Doctrine is not met, the case will then be heard, ruled upon by the Board, and the

Board's decision will prevail over the arbitrator's. The facts in *Collyer Insulated Wire* (192 N.L.R.B. 150 (1971)) were that the collective bargaining agreement between the parties provided that management could make individual wage changes to correct inequities; that pursuant to this provision management gave a general wage increase to all maintenance workers to bring them closer to the wage level of production workers; that the Union protested, since in contract negotiations it had opposed raising the wages of maintenance workers to the level of production workers; and that instead of taking the matter to arbitration, the Union had filed unfair labor practice charges with the Board against management for refusal to bargain.

The Duty of Fair Representation Doctrine and Arbitration

One of the more significant of judicial and legislative trends in recent decades has been the protection of individual employee rights. This has led to the United States Supreme Court's intervention in internal union affairs and union-management relations under the collective bargaining agreement. Specifically, with respect to contract dispute resolution machinery, the courts have ruled on the rights of individual employees in grievance and arbitration proceedings. In adjudging whether or not a union had represented unit employees fairly in processing their greivances or had afforded them due process in arbitration, the Supreme Court has developed criteria commonly referred to as the Doctrine of the Duty of Fair Representation. The early development and application of the doctrine came in a series of cases affecting railroad workers and unions (see the reference to the Court's 1944 decision in *Steele v. Louisville & Nashville R.R. Co.* in the earlier discussion of railway labor relations legislation). The landmark court decision on the duty of Fair Representation Doctrine, however, is *Vaca v. Sipes* (386 U.S. 171, 64 L.R.R.M. 2369 (1967)), and it and two important subsequent court decisions, *Hines v. Anchor Motor Freight, Inc.* (424 U.S. 554, 91 L.R.R.M. 2481 (1976)) and *Bowen v. United States Postal Service* (81 S. Ct. 525, 112 L.R.R.M. 2281 (1983)), will be summarized below.

Vaca v. Sipes, 1967

In *Vaca v. Sipes,* Benjamin Owens brought a class action suit on February 13, 1962, against the officers and representatives of his union, the National Brotherhood of Packinghouse Workers (later known as the National Brotherhood of Packing House and Dairy Workers), Local 12. Owens alleged that he had been discharged by Swift & Company's Kansas City Meat Packing Plant in violation of the collective bargaining agreement and that the union had "arbitrarily, capriciously and without just or reasonable reason or cause" refused to take his grievance to arbitration. Briefly, the background facts are as follows:

(1) Owens, a long-time high blood pressure patient, became ill in mid-1959, entered the hospital on sick leave, and after a long rest, during which Owens's weight and blood pressure were reduced, he was certified by his own physician as fit to resume his heavy work in the packing plant.

(2) Swift's doctor examined Owens and concluded that his blood pressure was still too high to permit reinstatement.

(3) Owens secured a second favorable authorization from an outside doctor and was permitted to work by a Company nurse on January 6, 1960.

(4) Following the Company doctor's discovery that Owens was working, Owens was permanently discharged on January 8, 1960, on the ground of poor health.

(5) Owens appealed to his Union and a grievance was filed in his behalf.

(6) The third-step grievance meeting was held in November 1960, and when the Company reiterated that Owens's poor health justified the discharge, the Union on February 6, 1961, sent Owens to a new doctor at the Union's expense "to see if we could get some better medical evidence so that we could go to arbitration with his case."

(7) The examination did not support Owens's contention, and when the Union's executive board received the medical report it voted not to take the grievance to arbitration.

(8) At the fourth grievance step — the fifth and final step was arbitration — the Company offered to refer Owens to a rehabilitation center, but Owens refused and demanded that the Union take the grievance to arbitration.

(9) The Union refused and the grievance was stalled at the fourth step.

(10) Owens took action in the courts and ultimately the matter reached the United States Supreme Court.

The Supreme Court ruled in favor of the Union, but in so doing it set forth basic considerations in assessing a union's duty of fair representation. The Court held that "a breach of the statutory duty of fair representation occurs only when a union's conduct toward a member of the collective bargaining unit is arbitrary, discriminatory, or in bad faith." The Court also held that a union need not take all matters to grievance, and that employees do not have an absolute right to have their greivances taken to arbitration, to wit:

Though we accept the proposition that a union may not arbitrarily ignore a meritorious grievance or proceed in a perfunctory fashion, we do not agree that the individual employee has an abolute right to have his grievance taken to arbitration regardless of the provisions of the applicable collective bargaining agreement. . . .

If the individual employee could compel arbitration of his grievance regardless of its merit, the settlement machinery provided by the contract would be substantially undermined, thus destroying the employer's confidence in the union's authority and returning the individual grievant to the vagaries of independent and unsystematic negotiation.

Hines v. Anchor Motor Freight, Inc., 1976

In *Hines v. Anchor Motor Freight, Inc.,* the employees (Hines et al.) were discharged for alleged dishonesty. The discharge was upheld in arbitration before a joint labor-management arbitration committee. The employees, who were truck drivers in the employ of Anchor Motor Freight, Inc., brought action against the Employer under Section 301 of the LMRA for being improperly dismissed and against Local 377 of the International Brotherhood of Teamsters, Chauffeurs, Warehousemen, and Helpers of America for breach of the duty of fair representation. In the discharge of June 6, 1967, the employees were charged with having sought reimbursement for motel expenses in excess of the actual charges sustained by them while on the road overnight. The employer presented motel receipts that were in excess of the charges shown on the motel's registration cards along with the motel clerk's notarized statement as to the accuracy of the registration cards and the motel owner's affidavit that the registration cards were accurate. Although the Union supported the employees in their plea of innocence, it did not investigate the motel and it told the employees they need not hire their own attorney as "there was nothing to worry about." Following their discharge, the employees retained an attorney and subsequently it was discovered that the motel clerk had falsified the records and pocketed the difference between the sums shown on the receipts and the registration cards. The District Court held that the decision of the arbitration committee was final and binding on the employees and that although the acts of the Union "may not meet professional standards of competency, and while it might have been advisable for the Union to further investigate the charges," the facts demonstrated at most bad judgment on the Union's part and this was insufficient to prove a breach of the duty of fair representation. The Court of Appeals affirmed the judgment in favor of Anchor Motor Freight and the International Union, but held that there were sufficient facts to infer bad faith or arbitrary conduct on the part of the Local Union.

The Supreme Court reversed the District Court's dismissal of the employees' action against Anchor Motor Freight and held that if the employees "prove an erroneous discharge and the Union's breach of duty tainting the decision of the joint committee, [they] are entitled to an appropriate remedy against the Employer as well as the Union." In commenting on the employer's liability for the reinstatement of the employees with back pay, the Supreme Court stated:

Anchor would have it that petitioners are foreclosed from judicial relief unless some blameworthy conduct on its part disentitles it to rely on the finality rule. But it was Anchor that originated the discharges for dishonesty. If these charges were in error, Anchor has surely played its part in precipitating this dispute. Of course, both courts below held there were no facts suggesting that Anchor either knowingly or negligently relied on false evidence. As far as the record reveals it also prevailed before the joint committee after presenting its case in accordance with what were ostensibly wholly fair procedures. Nevertheless there remains the question of whether the contractual protection against relitigating an arbitral decision binds employees who assert that the proceess has fundamentally malfunctioned by reason of the bad-faith performance of the union, their statutorily imposed collective bargining agent.

In holding Anchor liable, the Supreme Court then went on to state:

[W]e cannot believe that Congress intended to foreclose the employee from his Section 301 remedy otherwise available against the employer if the contractual processes have been seriously flawed by the union's breach of its duty to represent employees honestly and in good faith and without invidious discrimination or arbitrary conduct.

Bowen v. United States Postal Service, 1983

In *Bowen v. United States Postal Service,* Charles V. Bowen, a member of the American Postal Workers Union, was suspended without pay by the United States Postal Service following an altercation with another employee on February 21, 1976. On March 30, 1976, Bowen was discharged by the Service and he filed a grievance. The Union refused to carry his grievance forward to arbitration and Bowen brought suit in the United States District Court charging the Union with having breached its duty of fair representation and the Service with having discharged him without just cause. The evidence at the trial showed that the Local Union officers at each step of the grievance had recommended pursuing Bowen's grievance but that the National Union had refused to take the matter to arbitration.

The jury found in favor of Bowen, and the District Court held that the Service had discharged Bowen without just cause; that the

Union had handled Bowen's "apparently meritorious grievance
. . . in an arbitrary and perfunctory manner"; that both the Service
and the Union had acted "in reckless and callous disregard of [Bo-
wen's] rights"; that Bowen could not have proceeded independently
of the Union; and that if the Union had arbitrated Bowen's grievance, he would have been reinstated. The Court ordered that Bowen be reimbursed for lost benefits and wages. In assessing the
Union as well as the Service, the Court stated: "Although there is
authority suggesting that only the employer is liable for damages in
the form of back pay . . . this is a case in which both defendants,
by their illegal acts, are liable." The District Court found as fact
that if Bowen's grievance had been arbitrated, he would have been
reinstated by August 1977, and it therefore ruled that Bowen's loss
of wages after that date was the fault of the Union:

While the [Service] set this case in motion with its discharge, the [Union's]
acts, upon which [Bowen] reasonably relied, delayed the reinstatement
. . . and it is a proper apportionment to assign fault to the [Union] for
approximately two-thirds of the period [Bowen] was employed up to the
time of trial.

The Service and the Union appealed. The United States Court of
Appeals affirmed the District Court's findings of fact and apportionment of fault. However, it held that as a matter of law Bowen's
compensation was at all times payable by the Service and that reimbursement of his lost earnings continued to be the obligation of the
Service.

The United States Supreme Court reversed the Court of Appeals. It held that inasmuch as the findings of fact were that damages had been caused initially by the Service's unlawful discharge
and increased by the union's breach of its duty of fair representation, apportionment of the damages was required. The Court rejected the Union's argument that the governing principle of the
Vaca case required that the employer be solely liable for the damages from a wrongful discharge and that the Union could be liable
only for an employee's litigation expenses resulting from the Union's breach of its duty of fair representation. The United States
Supreme Court stated that "[a] Collective Bargaining Agreement is
much more than traditional common law employment terminable
at will. Rather, it is an agreement creating relationships and interests under the federal common law of labor policy"; and that, as
noted in the *Vaca* decision, "[d]amages attributable solely to the
employer's breach of conduct should not be charged to the union,
but increases if any in those damages caused by the union's refusal
to process the grievance should not be charged to the employer."

The Supreme Court's decision in *Bowen v. United States Postal Service* has occasioned grave concern on the part of both practitioners and professionals in industrial dispute resolution. The Duty of Fair Representation Doctrine has been largely accepted as essential to the protection of individual employee rights even though it has the disturbing consequences of negating the desired finality of arbitration. But the *Bowen* decision has been especially disturbing and has given rise to questions as to the Court's role, first, in its hypothetical assumption of an award if an arbitration had been held, and, second, in its holding unions liable for a grievant's losses incurred subsequent to an arbitrator's hypothetically assumed award. In fashioning remedy, an arbitrator has broad powers, and in an altercation such as Bowen was involved in it cannot be assumed with any degree of certainty that the arbitrator would have reinstated Bowen and "made him whole." Indeed, even without finding just cause for Bowen's dismissal, an arbitrator might, alternatively, have reinstated him without back pay since he was guilty of having been involved in an altercation, or commuted his discharge to a suspension of some specified period of days or weeks, or even reduced the penalty to a disciplinary warning. In addition to the concern over the Court's conjectural determination of an arbitrator's award, unions are deeply concerned over the Court's imposition of liability. Union proponents maintain that the result of the Court's ruling that both employer and union share liability when ultimately just cause is not shown and the union is adjudged to have breached its duty of fair representation is a disproportionate burden on the union. As the Court defined liability in the *Bowen* case, the employer is liable for the loss of a grievant's wages and benefits from the date of discharge up to the date of the actual or projected arbitration hearing. The losses, thereafter, as ruled by the Court in *Bowen,* are accountable to the union. And, as is argued on behalf of unions, this cost is more than likely the major part of a grievant's loss of wages and benefits because of the delay in the processing of court cases involving appeals through to the United States Supreme Court.

Title VII of the Civil Rights Act of 1964 (Equal Employment Opportunity Law) and Arbitration

Alexander v. Gardner-Denver Co., 1974

In *Alexander v. Gardner-Denver Co.* (415 U.S. 36, 7 F.E.P. 81 (1974)) the finality of arbitration was set aside by the United States

Supreme Court for employment discrimination cases. From a practical standpoint, however, this was partially a rejection of the arbitrator's finality. The Court held that a prior submission of an employment discrimination dispute with a company to arbitration did not foreclose the employee's right of access to federal court under the provisions of Title VII of the Civil Rights Act of 1964. And clearly the times an employee would exercise this right of access to the courts are those when the arbitrator rules against the employee and holds that there was no employment discrimination. In commenting on the role of arbitration in discrimination cases, the United States Supreme Court stated that "arbitral procedures, while well suited to the resolution of contractual disputes, make arbitration a comparatively inappropriate forum for the final resolution of rights created by Title VII."

In reversing the judgment of the Court of Appeals, the United States Supreme Court concluded as follows:

We think, therefore, that the federal policy favoring arbitration of labor disputes and the federal policy against discriminatory employment practices can best be accommodated by permitting an employee to pursue fully both his remedy under the grievance-bargaining agreement and his cause of action under Title VII. The federal court should consider the employee's claim *de novo*. The arbitral decision may be admitted as evidence and accorded such weight as the court deems appropriate.

And in the now-well-known and frequently cited footnote 21 of the *Gardner-Denver* decision, the Court elaborated as follows on the varying degrees of weight that would be accorded the arbitrator's decision on employment discrimination:

We adopt no standards as to the weight to be accorded an arbitration decision, since this must be determined in the court's discretion with regard to the facts and circumstances of each case. Relevant factors include the existence of provisions in the collective bargaining agreement that conform substantially with Title VII, the degree of procedural fairness in the arbitral forum, adequacy of the record with respect to the issue of discrimination, and the special competence of particular arbitrators. Where an arbitral determination gives full consideration to an employee's Title VII rights, a court may properly accord it great weight. This is especially true where the issue is solely one of fact, specifically addressed by the parties and decided by the arbitrator on the basis of an adequate record. But courts should ever be mindful that Congress, in enacting Title VII, thought it necessary to provide a judicial forum for the ultimate resolution of discriminatory employment claims. It is the duty of courts to assure the full availability of this forum.

The background facts of the *Gardner-Denver* case are as follows:

(1) Harrell Alexander, Sr., a black, was hired by Gardner-Denver Company in May 1966.

(2) In June 1968, Alexander was awarded a trainee position as a drill operator and remained at that job until discharged by the company on September 29, 1969, for too much spoilage and excessive scrap.

(3) Alexander filed a grievance on October 1, 1969, pursuant to the provisions of the collective bargaining agreement between Local 3029 of the United Steelworkers of America and Gardner-Denver Company.

(4) Alexander's initial grievance did not explicitly claim racial discrimination but stated: "I feel I have been unjustly discharged and ask that I be reinstated with full seniority and pay." In the final step of the grievance procedure prior to arbitration, however, Alexander claimed the discharge resulted from racial discrimination.

(5) At the arbitration hearing on November 20, 1969, Alexander testified that his discharge was the result of racial discrimination and that he had filed a charge with the Colorado Equal Employment Opportunity Commission. The Union placed into evidence a letter in which Alexander claimed that "in the same plant others have scrapped an equal amount and sometimes in excess, but . . . I . . . have been the target of preferential discriminatory treatment."

(6) The arbitrator's award on December 30, 1969, ruled that Alexander had been discharged for just cause. The arbitrator did not address Alexander's claim of racial discrimination. The arbitrator stated that the Union had failed to produce evidence of a practice of transferring rather than discharging trainee drill operators who accumulated excessive scrap, but sugggested that the Union and the Company consider whether transfer was feasible.

(7) The Equal Employment Opportunity Commission on July 25, 1970, determined that there was not reasonable cause to believe that there had been a violation of Title VII of the Civil Rights Act of 1964.

(8) Alexander was subsequently notified of his right to institute a civil action in a federal court within 30 days and he did so.

(9) The lower courts held that since Alexander had voluntarily elected to pursue his grievance to final arbitration under the discrimination clause of the collective bargaining agreement, he was bound by the arbitral decision and thereby precluded from suing the Company under Title VII.

(10) The Court of Appeals affirmed the District Court in its finding that it could not "accept a philosophy which gives the employee two strings to his bow when the employer has only one."

(11) The United States Supreme Court reversed, as noted, by holding in effect that an individual's civil rights under Title VII are controlling and cannot be preempted. The Court also specifically rejected the proposal that the federal courts should defer to arbitral decisions on discrimination claims when (1) the claim is before the arbitrator; (2) the collective bargaining agreement prohibits the form of discrimination charged in the suit under Title VII; and (3)

the arbitrator has authority to rule on the claimant to fashion a remedy.

The Supreme Court's test for determining the weight to be accorded arbitral decisions in Title VII claims which are also contractual issues is often referred to as the *Gardner-Denver* balancing test. The Supreme Court has subsequently applied the test in its decisions affecting other federal employment statutes such as the Fair Labor Standards Act (Federal Wage-Hour Law) and the Occupational Safety and Health Act (OSHA). In *Barrentine v. Arkansas-Best Freight System, Inc.* (101 S. Ct. 1437 (1981)) the Court held that wage claims under the Fair Labor Standards Act were not barred by the fact that they had been contractually grieved to arbitration. As in *Gardner-Denver,* the Court held that there should be deferral to arbitral decisions when the employee's claim is based on rights arising out of the collective bargaining agreement. However, the Court also determined that different considerations apply when the employee's wage claim is based on rights arising out of the protective provisions of the Federal Wage-Hour Law; that an arbitrator effectuates the intent of the parties rather than the intent of the statute; and that the range of relief available under the statute is broader than that which an arbitrator may award under the collective bargaining agreement.

In *Marshall v. N. L. Industries, Inc.* (618 F.2d 1220 (7th Cir. 1980)) the Seventh Circuit applied the *Gardner-Denver* test to an arbitration involving considerations under the Occupational Safety and Health Act. An employee had been terminated for refusing to comply with a work order. The Secretary of Labor charged the Company with having violated the provisions of the Occupational Safety and Health Act by discharging an employee for refusing to work under unsafe conditions. The arbitrator's award had reinstated the employee with seniority but without back pay. The Court rejected the finality of the arbitration and held that the arbitration did not bar the Secretary of Labor from the judicial relief sought by the Secretary of Labor under the provisions of the statute. As stated by the Court, "OSHA legislation was intended to create a separate and general right of broad social importance existing beyond the parameters of an individual labor agreement and susceptible of full vindication only in a judicial forum."

The Bases for Vacating Arbitration Awards

In the main, the courts have deferred to arbitration awards and have not substituted their adjudgments for those of the arbitrator in matters involving disputes under a collective bargaining agreement. Nonetheless, the awards of arbitrators may be vacated. The primary bases for vacating an arbitrator's award are found in the Federal Arbitration Act and in the view of the United States Supreme Court expressed in the *Steelworkers Trilogy* cases, especially in *Enterprise Wheel & Car Corp.*

As set forth in the Federal Arbitration Act (United States Arbitration Act of July 30, 1947, P. L. 80-282, 61 Stat. 669 as amended, § 10), an arbitrator's award may be vacated under the following circumstances:

(a) when the award was procured by corruption, fraud, or undue means;

(b) when there was evident partiality or corruption in the arbitrators, or in either of them;

(c) when the arbitrators were guilty of misconduct in refusing to postpone the hearing, upon sufficient causes shown, or in refusing to hear evidence pertinent and material to the controversy; or of any other misbehavior by which the rights of any party have been prejudiced; and

(d) when the arbitrators exceeded their powers, or so imperfectly executed them that a mutual, final, and definite award upon the subject matter submitted was not made.

Section 10 (e) provides that "where an award is vacated and the time within which the agreement required the award to be made has not expired the court may, in its discretion, direct a rehearing by the arbitrators." It is important to note that in the recent ruling of the United States Supreme Court in *Southland Corp. v. Keating* (U.S. 104 S. Ct. 852 (1984)), the United States Arbitration Act was held to be applicable to both federal and state courts and to supersede conflicting state law. While the case arose not under a labor contract but in a suit alleging, among other things, breach of contract and violations of the disclosure requirements of California's Franchise Investment Act, the Court's decision is applicable to all forms of arbitration. As stated by Chief Justice Warren E. Burger, "In enacting Section 2 of the federal Act, Congress declared a national policy favoring arbitration."

To these acts of misconduct and procedural unfairness set forth in the United States Arbitration Act, the United States Supreme Court has added the prequisite that the labor arbitrator be confined to the interpretation and application of the collective bargaining agreement and that his/her award "draw its essence" from that agreement. As stated by the Court in *United Steelworkers v. Enterprise Wheel & Car Corp.* (363 U.S. 593, 46 L.R.R.M. 2423 (1960)), "[A]n arbitrator . . . may of course look for guidance from many sources, yet his award is legitimate only so long as it draws its essence from the collective bargaining agreement."

Standards (Tenents) of Arbitration

There are no set "rules" that arbitrators apply in evaluating issues in dispute and fashioning an award. Nonetheless, over the years arbitrators have developed standards in addressing certain contract interpretation and disciplinary issues which have come to serve as guidelines. These are sometimes referred to as "tenents of arbitration" since they are more generally followed than not.

Tenets in Contract Interpretation Disputes

Among the tenets of arbitration which frequently serve as guidelines or standards for arbitrators in addressing contract interpretation questions are the following:

(1) When the contract language is clear and unambiguous, it prevails over past practice.

This is the "basic past practice rule." Even if a practice has been followed for many years, arbitrators will generally set it aside when challenged in the face of the clear and unambiguous contract language that is contradictory to the practice. For example, eligibility-for-holiday-pay provisions in collective bargaining agreements often stipulate that a doctor's certificate or some other appropriate proof of illness is required for payment of holiday pay in the event of illness. Even though management may have been lax over the years in requiring proof of illness, it will more than likely be upheld if there is challenge to its having taken "corrective measures" and uniformly applied the contract's proof of illness requirement. The arbitrator might well modify the application of this basic past practice standard, if not negate it, however, if the contract contains a past practice or maintenance of standards clause requiring the continuance of practices favorable to employees for the duration of the agreement.

(2) When a given managerial action conforms to clear and unambiguous contract language but is contrary to past practice, the former prevails except that arbitrators in the interest of equity often permit the instant application of past practice to prevail as "a pass through" on the ground that there has been no forewarning or timely notice of discontinuance of the past practice.

This is a fairly common exception to the basic past practice rule. While by no means universally invoked, arbitrators often apply the exception if management has failed to provide forewarning of its discontinuance of a past practice of long standing. The reasoning here is that management must apply a contract right equitably, and this would not be the case if a past practice that employees had come to rely upon was discontinued without timely notice. This exception might be invoked by an arbitrator, for instance, if in the above-cited example employees were not told beforehand that management would no longer provide holiday pay to employees who had been out ill unless they provided a doctor's certificate or some other proof of illness. Such a ruling by an arbitrator is called a "pass through"since it is "one time" in nature and will not be exercised in continuing applications of the contract provisions by management.

(3) Past practice, to be controlling, must be long-established, well-known to both parties, and accepted.

When contract language is ambiguous, arbitrators frequently look to the past practice of the parties for guidance as to meaning and intent. Hence, it is frequently said with respect to the interpretation of ambiguous contractual provisions that "what the parties do under a collective agreement might be even more important than what they say in it." But in order for past practice to be controlling in an arbitrator's determination, it must be shown that it is a practice of sufficient generality and duration to imply acceptance as to meaning and intent by the parties. The continued application of a past practice or the failure to object to its application is often regarded by arbitrators as evidence of its having been mutually accepted. However, if it can be shown that the failure to object to a practice was due to an unawareness of the practice or of contractual rights, arbitrators may be persuaded that the failure to object to the practice under such circumstances did not constitute acceptance.

(4) Even though the contract is silent and contains no "past practices" clause, past practice in the provisions of an employee benefit may require its continuance unless timely notice has been given.

Past practice plays a role in arbitral decisions involving disputes over management's discontinuance of a noncontractual benefit. For example, management may have given employees two hours off with pay to allow them to vote or one-half hour off with pay so that they can cash checks on pay day, even though there is no provision in the contract which requires the employer to do so. Arbitrators' awards reveal that it cannot be assumed that the controlling stand-

ard here is that if an employer voluntarily provides a noncontractual employee benefit, he is free to discontinue it at any time. Many
rulings qualify management's freedom to discontinue the past practice of providing a noncontractual employee benefit by requiring
that timely notice of the discontinuance be provided. Frequently,
too, timely notice for the discontinuance of the past-practice
benefit is held to be at a time the union can do something about it,
namely, at contract negotiations time. Generally, for the discontinuance of the past practice of providing such noncontractual
benefits as a Thanksgiving turkey or a Christmas bonus, "timely
notice" has not been so stringently applied. but in any event, the
employer's notice must be clear, unequivocable, and made available
to all employees and the union well in advance of the discontinuance of the benefit if it is to fully satisfy past-practice and timely
notice standards in arbitration.

(5) When the contract is silent on contracting-out, and a dispute arises
over its use by management, the arbitrator is often governed by considerations of reasonableness and the consequences of the subcontracting of the
work.

If a contract contains a provision on subcontracting, the arbitrator must rely on it and base his award on its meaning. Most contracts, however, do not contain a contracting-out provision, and the
arbitrator must rely on other standards in addressing disputes over
the employer's recourse to subcontracting. In addressing subcontracting disputes, some arbitrators have rigidly applied the reserved
(residual) rights theory of management when the contract is silent
on the subject of contracting-out. In brief, it is held that all rights
not expressly prohibited by the contract are reserved for management; hence, in the absence of a provision prohibiting or limiting
subcontracting, management is free to contract-out work. A countervailing theory is that management's recognition of the union has
given the union the implied right of performing the designated
work; thus, subcontracting is impliedly prohibited if it is for work
covered in the recognition clause of the contract. Most arbitrators
balance the theories and hold that contracting-out may be properly
entered into by an employer provided that there is economic justification for its doing so, that it is entered into in good faith, and
that the subcontracting would not undermine the union or erode
the contract. Among the factors considered in such determinations
are whether the subcontracting is temporary or permanent; whether
it is emergency or regular work; whether it is work that unit em-

ployees are capable of performing; whether it is work frequently performed or marginal and incidental to unit work; whether the equipment and facilities necessary to perform the work are available or can be obtained readily and economically; whether the work has been subcontracted in the past without objection; whether the union is being discriminated against; whether the status and integrity of the bargaining unit is impaired; and whether unit employees are discriminated against, displaced, laid off, or deprived of jobs and/or overtime earnings regularly available to them prior to the subcontracting.

(6) When there is no management rights clause or the contract is silent as to a specific managerial action affecting covered employees at the workplace, arbitrators often consider and endeavor to balance the reserved (residual) rights theory of management rights and the countervailing theory of the implied (recognition) rights of the union.

The prior discussion of standards applied in contracting-out disputes in which the contract is silent on subcontracting touches on this point.

(7) In a dispute over a contract interpretation, when there is a choice as to the applicability of either the general or the specific in contract language, the specific prevails. Conversely, a general provision prevails in the absence of specific language.

Contracts frequently contain a broad provision of intent which states, among other things, that "no covered employee" will be denied the benefits and "all employees" will be extended the privileges of the contract. Arbitrators, however, by way of an application of the "specific over the general" standard would not hold that this broad language supersedes an express provision limiting such contract benefits as holiday pay, jury duty, and paid sick leave to "regular, full-time employees." Under the "specific over the general" standard, arbitrators would hold that management did not violate the contract in denying holiday pay, jury duty, and paid sick leave to temporary, part-time, and probationary employees. By the same token, arbitrators would not sustain management when it similarly limited the payment of bereavement leave if that contractual provision read: "Employees are entitled to 3 days leave with pay upon the death of . . ."

(8) In contract interpretation questions, arbitrators often find that not only what is "in a given contract," but what is excluded and prevails in related contracts, is controlling.

There are many situations in which an arbitrator looks to other contracts for clarity in interpreting a provision in dispute. Again, a case in point is the contract that is silent on the requirement of proof of illness for eligibility for holiday pay. Management's contention that this right is covered broadly by the contract's management rights clause will lose some of its persuasiveness if it is shown that employers in competitive shops with the same union have specific proof-of-illness requirements in their holiday pay provisions. The union is doubly persuasive here if it shows, additionally, that the industry practice of requiring proof of illness was not initiated until after employers had "won" the inclusion of the specific contractual requirement clause at the bargaining table.

(9) In the interpretation of a given provision of a contract, arbitrators generally do not allow parties "to get in arbitration" what was expressly denied them at the bargaining table.

If a party unsuccessfully tries during contract negotiations to include a specific clause or a specific interpretation of a clause in the agreement, the arbitrator is likely to be hesitant to accept the contention that such a clause or interpretation can be read into the existing language of the contract. For this reason, records of negotiations and bargaining "proposals" or "demands" can be, and often are, most important in the evolution of contract interpretation standards. Again, to cite the contract that is silent on requiring proof of illness, if the employer had sought but failed at the bargaining table to secure the insertion of that eligibility qualification in the holiday pay provision, the arbitrator would more than likely be dissuaded from reading it into the broad rights given the employer in the management rights clause of the contract.

(10) When the meaning of a word or clause used in a contract is not clear, arbitrators tend to assume, if there is no conflicting evidence, that the parties intended the word or clause to have the same meaning as that given it during the negotiations leading up to the agreement.

This is, in large measure, a variation of the standard discussed above. It is also another example of the importance of records and notes relative to oral testimony in arbitration as to the "intent" of the negotiators with respect to a disputed provision of a contract. When the testimony or notes relative to contract negotiations are not definitive, "meaning" can be, and often is, imputed to the contract language in dispute from industry usage, custom, and practice.

(11) In threshold questions of arbitrability, arbitrators frequently hold grievances that are untimely "on the face" as arbitrable because the parties have been lax and have not strictly applied the time limits in the past.

In large measure, this standard is a past-practice modification of clear and unambiguous contract language. Contracts often require that a grievance be filed within a specified period of time, as, for example, within 10 days of when the grievance occurred or, in the case of arbitration, within 10 days of when the grievance was denied at the last grievance step or at management's top level. Grievances or demands for arbitration which are filed 30 days rather than 10 days later than the required date are patently not in conformity with the clear and unambiguous time limits of 10 days set forth above in the grievance and arbitration provisions of the contract. But if the parties have been uniformly lax in the past in applying the 10-day time limits, arbitrators will generally find this extenuating and will not hold the late filing of the grievance or the demand for arbitration to be a bar to the arbitration of the merits of the dispute. The positiveness toward arbitrability by the United States Supreme Court in its *Lincoln Mills* and *Trilogy* landmark decisions on arbitration has no doubt encouraged the adoption of this standard. Arbitrators, too, view this exception to the accepted rule that clear and unambiguous language prevails over past practice as a more than likely one-time "pass through" since notice has been served that the time requirements of the grievance procedure will henceforth be adhered to by the parties unelss they mutually agree otherwise.

Tenets in Disciplinary Action Disputes

Among the tenets of arbitration which frequently serve as guidelines or standards for arbitrators in addressing disciplinary questions are the following:

(1) An employee's responsibility is to obey a supervisor's order, and if the employee disagrees with it, to grieve later.

This is the basic tenet in the arbitration of disputes over disciplinary action. While there are, necessarily, reasonable and compelling exceptions, general adherence to the standard rule of "obey now, grieve later" is essential to the preservation of law and order at the workplace. Clearly management cannot permit, and arbitrators cannot condone, the actions of employees who "take matters into their own hands" rather than follow the prescribed steps of the grievance procedure. Even in so sensitive a matter as an order to perform what an employee strongly believes is not his work, the arbitrator will generally support management's insistence that it be obeyed and grieved later, and will find cause for disciplinary action if the employee refuses to do the work.

(2) A commonly accepted exception to the "obey now, grieve later" standard is work in which an employee's health and/or safety would be endangered, or an order that is demeaning or unlawful; and, here, it is the burden of the union to show this to be fact.

This standard sets forth the most widely accepted exceptions to the "obey now, grieve later" rule. Arbitrators will not hold as just cause for discipline an employee's refusal to comply with an order to perform work that endangers health and/or safety, or is demeaning or unlawful. However, the traditional burden of proof in disciplinary arbitrations shifts from management to the union when exceptions to the "obey now, grieve later" standard are being sought. In this sense, the "obey now, grieve later" standard is so widely held that, as in an interpretation dispute over a provision of the contract, the union is viewed as "the moving party" and the burden is its.

(3) An employee cannot be held to be insubordinate and to warrant discipline for failing to comply with an order unless supervision has met its responsibility; namely, the order given must be clear and meaningful and the consequences of failure to comply must be made known.

Arbitrators will generally hold as a mitigating circumstance (and hence will not find just cause to sustain management in its disciplinary action) a supervisor's order to an employee (grievant) that was not clear or meaningful or the failure of the supervisor to tell the employee the consequences of not complying with the order. While the latter is often held to be less extenuating than the former (the taking of disciplinary action can reasonably be implied in most refusals to obey a supervisor's order), there is a grievance that was sustained in arbitration on both grounds. The employee had been given a two-day suspension for refusing to "clean up the mess" around his machine and for having gone home before the end of the shift. The facts revealed, however, that although the supervisor had said, "This mess better be cleaned up," he had spoken in generalities and had never given the employee a direct order to clean up the debris. Further, when the supervisor checked back later and saw that the area around the machine had not been cleaned up, he turned to the employee and said, "For all the good you're doing around here, you might just as well go home." When the employee protested and the exchange became protracted, the supervisor ended it all by telling the employee, "Go home," and walked away. The employee then did what he had been told; he went home. In addition to not giving the employee a direct order to clean up, the supervisor never told the employee that he would be disciplined for going home. The suspension was not sustained.

(4) When management has been lax in enforcing a shop rule, the disciplining of an employee for violating the rule is subject to being set aside or modified on the grounds that discipline must be even-handed and uniformly applied.

Arbitrators invariably apply a "comparative standard" in adjudging disciplinary actions. Has the shop rule been made known to the employee or can he be reasonably held to have known it? Has management enforced the rule? Have violators been disciplined? Has the discipline been uniformly applied or, if not, have the disparities in the disciplinary action been for reasonable, understandable, and nondiscriminatory reasons? These are some of the questions that an arbitrator uses as guidelines when assessing and comparing the disciplinary actions taken by management in enforcing shop or employee rules of conduct.

(5) The acts of an employee away from the plant are generally not an acceptable basis for disciplinary action under a contract unless the employer can show a nexus between the employee's "off premises" act and his/her employment in the plant.

Consideration of an employee's right to privacy as well as concern for the application of due process in arbitration have led arbitrators to rely on the "nexus rule" in disciplinary disputes involving an employee's actions away from the plant. It is often contended in a grievant's behalf that what an employee does away from the shop and on his/her own time is his/her own business and, as frequently stated, "none of the employer's business." And normally this is so. But when it is shown that the employee's off-plant act impacts on the company and its standing in the community, or on the employee's job responsibilities, or on his/her ability to work with, and be accepted by, co-workers, and the like, the "nexus rule" may be invoked and just cause may be found for disciplining an employee for his/her deportment away from the plant. Management has been upheld on this ground in the discharge of a security guard who was convicted of the burglary of a private residence; in the discharge of a woman-molester and rapist who committed his acts "after dark" and far from the plant, but who was the subject of complaint to management by female co-workers protesting that they were afraid to work with him; and the disciplining of a utility worker whose arrest for "furiously and savagely" attacking the driver of the "other car" in an after-hours car accident was prominently featured in the local media, with the company's name being headlined and repeatedly referenced in the reports of the incident.

(6) Due process in disciplinary matters requires that supervision investigate the alleged offense and provide opportunity for the offending employee to have union representation and to give his/her version of the incident before final disciplinary action is taken.

Most arbitrators will apply this standard and not sustain disciplinary actions taken without prior investigation and/or without providing the employee with the opportunity to be represented by his/her union and to give "his/her side of the story." Arbitrators are especially alert to the need for compliance with this standard when the discipline involves a "one on one" situation. Most frequently, "one on ones" arise out of incidents between a foreman or operating supervisor and an employee. Management cannot expect that because the foreman "said it is so," it is fact. Certainly arbitrators will not accept this as just cause for disciplinary action and will insist on a showing that management had heard and evaluated the employee's version of the incident and had checked to ascertain whether there were others in the vicinity of the incident and, if so, what if anything they observed. Failure to permit an employee to have union representation often suffices in itself for a sustaining of the grievance on the ground that due process was denied. It is recognized, of course, that the nature of the act or the circumstances at the time may make if difficult, if not impossible, for management to follow any one or all of these expected procedures. When this is the case, it is generally acceptable for the employee to be suspended and sent home pending disciplinary investigation.

(7) Progressive or corrective discipline for minor offenses by an employee usually follows the disciplinary steps of oral warning, written warning, suspension, and discharge.

In assessing the quantum of discipline meted out by the employer for a minor offense such as lateness or absence, arbitrators will generally apply the standards of progressive discipline. Inasmuch as the basic purpose of discipline is, or should be, correction, the severity of discipline for minor offenses under the concept of progressive discipline is graduated. Initial offenses are met with oral warning or counseling, and repeat offenses are met with written warning. Arbitrators expect, too, for the union to be alerted to these disciplinary measures and, especially, for copies of the written warning to be sent to the union. This is not only essential for ensuring the employee proper representation but it additionally has the salutary effect on occasion of a union's being able "to straighten out" an employee before his/her infractions get too serious. Persistence in the wrong doing and failure of the employee to take corrective measures result in the more severe penalty of disciplinary suspension and, ultimately, discharge when it becomes clear that the employee is incorrigible and either unwilling or unable to mend his/her nonconforming ways. There is some disagreement over whether the precepts of progressive discipline are wholly applicable in the disciplining of excessive absenteeism caused by bonafide illness. It is largely held that even here suspensions serve to alert the employee to the seriousness of his/her situation. In contrast, it is argued, and frequently sustained by arbitrators, that suspensions serve little purpose as a curb or deterrent to absences when the nature of the illness is such that the employee has no control over his/her presence at the workplace. Under such circumstances, warnings are deemed sufficient to inform an employee that if the illness cannot be brought under control to permit sufficient regularity in attendance to fulfill the responsibilities of the job, it will be necessary to let the employee go. While there are differences as to precisely when this point of absenteeism is reached, it is generally recognized that management has the right to expect reasonable reliability and regularity of attendance from its employees.

(8) Although progressive discipline is generally viewed as a fair and equitable procedure, the increased severity of the disciplinary action taken is not likely to be upheld in arbitration if supervisory personnel apply the discipline automatically and fail to evaluate carefully the circumstances of each incident of offense.

In applying the standard of progressive discipline, arbitrators are generally insistent on evidence that it has not been followed by management in an automatic and slide-rule fashion. Every repetitive incident of a minor infraction is not in itself cause for discipline, let alone cause for a greater severity of discipline. An employee with a high frequency of lateness and absences and a prior suspension for excessive absenteeism and latenesses may well not warrant being discharged or even disciplined if extenuating circumstances are shown to have surrounded a subsequent lateness or absence. Circumstances that have been found to be mitigating in such cases include a breakdown in the transportation system on which the employee relies to go to and from work and an "involuntary" two-day absence by an employee who had been "sniffling and coughing" while on the job, was "sent to medical" by his supervisor, and after being given medication was told by the company doctor to go home, rest, and report back to work in two days.

(9) For the sustaining of disciplinary actions short of discharge, the preponderance of evidence generally suffices as acceptable proof, but in discharge cases the quantum of proof demanded is usually more stringent — namely, clear and convincing evidence for discharges generally, and for some arbitrators even proof beyond a reasonable doubt for offenses of criminal proportions or acts that are morally reprehensible.

There is, perhaps, no more variable standard in abitration than that used in assessing the quantum of proof provided in disciplinary actions generally and discharges in particular. Little distinction is made between the many variations in contract language which stipulate that employees may be disciplined for cause. Some contracts merely state "for cause"; others, "for just cause"; still others, "for reasonable cause," "sufficient cause," or "sufficient and reasonable cause." These and other variations of the requirement of "cause" in discipline lead, if not compel, arbitrators to insist on evidential proof and generally to vary the quantum of proof demanded with the nature and severity of the offense and the disciplinary action taken. For most offenses and discipline short of discharge, arbitrators are generally satisfied if the weight or preponderance of evidence shows cause for disciplinary action. The standard applied in discharges generally is more stringent, and here the arbitrator looks for clear and convincing proof. Because discharge is the "capital punishment" of industrial jurisprudence, some arbitrators lean toward a stringency of proof to justify discharge which is close to the requirement of proof beyond a reasonable doubt utilized in courts of law. Most arbitrators, however, either reject or use such a high standard of proof sparingly, and then only when the offense is shown to be of criminal proportions or morally reprehensible.

(10) For probationary employees, management's normal standard of burden of proof in discharge is generally set aside and the union is required to prove that management has acted improperly.

Unless the collective bargaining agreement expressly states otherwise, the standard usually applied by arbitrators in the adjudgment of the discharge of a probationary employee differs somewhat from that used generally. In the discharge of regular, as distinct from probationary, employees the burden of proof is management's. Not only is the employer generally required to put such evidence into the record first, but more importantly, as noted previously, the employer is required to show cause for having discharged the employee. In the discharge of a probationary employee, there must, of course, be acceptable and reasonable cause. But because of the contractually agreed upon tenuous nature of a probationary employee's entitlement to continued employment, the burden of proof is placed on the union to show that management's cause for terminating the probationary employee was improper, unreasonable, discriminatory, or the like. It is expected that probationary employees will be let go if their job performance is not acceptable. Indeed, in most instances management's reason for terminating the employment of a probationary employee is that his/her work was not satisfactory, and it is clearly not an easy task for a union to prove otherwise unless there was a blatant ignoring or distortion of the probationary employee's performance.

Bibliography

Glossaries and Dictionaries of Terms

Banki, Ivan Steven. *A Dictionary of Administration and Supervision.* Los Angeles, Calif.: Los Angeles Systems Research, 1971.

Benn, A. *The Management Dictionary: Standardization of Definitions and Concepts of the Terminology in the Field of Personnel Management.* New York: Exposition Press, 1952.

Casselman, Paul H. *Labor Dictionary: A Concise Encyclopaedia of Labor Information.* New York: 1949.

Doherty, Robert E. *Industrial and Labor Relations Terms: A Glossary.* 4th ed. ILR Bulletin No. 44. Ithaca: New York State School of Industrial and Labor Relations, Cornell University, 1979.

Marsh, Arthur. *Concise Encyclopaedia of Industrial Relations.* Aldershot, Hants.: Gower Press, 1979.

Midwest Center for Public Sector Labor Relations, School of Public and Environmental Affairs, Indiana University. *Terms in Public Sector Labor Relations: A Practioner's Guide.* Bloomington: MCPSLR, 1971.

National Federation of Federal Employees. "Glossary of Labor Relations Terms." Mimeographed. No. HO-11. Washington, D.C.: NFFE, May 1981.

Prentice-Hall Editorial Staff. *Manual for Drafting Union Contracts* [especially "Words and Phrases Used in Collective Bargaining"]. Englewood Cliffs, N.J.: Prentice-Hall, 1969.

Roberts, Harold Selig. *Robert's Dictionary of Industrial Relations.* Washington, D.C.: Bureau of National Affairs, 1971.

Shafritz, Jay M. *Dictionary of Personnel Management and Labor Relations.* Oak Park, Ill.: Moore Publishing Co., 1980.

U.S. Department of Labor. *Glossary of Current Industrial Relations and Wage Terms.* Bulletin No. 1438. Washington, D.C.: GPO, 1965.

Selected Texts

Allen, Robert E., and Timothy J. Keaveny. *Contemporary Labor Relations.* Reading, Mass.: Addison-Wesley, 1983.

Bok, Derek C., and John T. Dunlop. *Labor and the American Community.* New York: Simon and Schuster, 1970.

Bureau of National Affairs, Inc. *Basic Patterns in Union Contracts.* 11th ed. Washington, D.C.: BNA, 1986.

———. *Briefing Sessions on Employee Relations: Workbook and Outlines.* Washington, D.C.: BNA, 1985.

Chamberlain, Neil W. *The Labor Sector.* New York: McGraw-Hill, 1939.

Commons, John R., et al. *History of Labour in the United States.* Vols. 1 and 2. New York: Macmillan, 1918.

Cullen, Donald E. *National Emergency Strikes.* ILR Paperback No. 7. Ithaca: New York State School of Industrial and Labor Relations, Cornell University, 1968.

Davey, Harold W., Mario F. Bognanno, and David L. Estenson. *Contemporary Collective Bargaining.* 4th ed. Englewood Cliffs, N.J.: Prentice-Hall 1982.

Douglas, Ann. *Industrial Peacemaking.* New York: Columbia University Press, 1962.

Dunlop, John T., and Neil W. Chamberlain, eds. *Frontiers of Collective Bargaining.* New York: Harper and Row, 1967.

Elkouri, Frank, and Edna Asper Elkouri. *How Arbitration Works.* 4th ed. Washington, D.C.: Bureau of National Affairs, 1985.

Feldacker, Bruce S. *Labor Guide to Labor Law.* Reston, Va.: Reston Publishing Co., 1980.

Gregory, Charles O. *Labor and the Law.* 2nd ed. rev. New York: W. W. Norton, 1961.

Kochan, Thomas A. *Collective Bargaining and Industrial Relations: From Theory to Policy and Practice.* Homewood, Ill.: Richard D. Irwin, 1980.

Lester, Richard A. *Labor and Industrial Relations.* New York: Macmillan, 1951.

Lewin, David, Peter Feville, and Thomas A. Kochan. *Public Sector labor Relations: Analysis and Readings.* Glen Ridge, N.J.: Thomas Horton and Daughters, 1977.

Loughran, Charles S. *Negotiating a Labor Contract: A Management Handbook.* Washington, D.C.: Bureau of National Affairs, 1984.

McKelvey, Jean T., ed. *The Duty of Fair Representation.* Ithaca: New York State School of Industrial and Labor Relations, Cornell University, 1977.

Morris, Richard B., ed. *The U.S. Department of Labor Bicentennial History of the American Worker.* Washington, D.C.: GPO, 1976.

Perlman, Selig, and Philip Taft. *History of Labor in the United States, 1896–1932.* Vol. 4. New York: Macmillan, 1935.

Rayback, Joseph G. *A History of American Labor.* New York: Macmillan, 1978.

Richardson, Reed C. *Collective Bargaining by Objectives: A Positive Approach.* 2nd ed. Englewood Cliffs, N.J.: Prentice-Hall, 1985.

Ross, Philip. *The Government as a Source of Union Power: The Roll of Public Policy in Collective Bargaining.* Providence, R.I.: Brown University Press, 1965.

Schlossberg, Stephen L. *Organizing and the Law.* Washington, D.C.: Bureau of National Affairs, 1965.

Simkin, William E. *Mediation and the Dynamics of Collective Bargaining.* Washington, D.C.: Bureau of National Affairs, 1971.

Slichter, Sumner H., James J. Healy, and E. Robert Livernash. *The Impact of Collective Bargaining on Management.* Washington, D.C.: Brookings Institution, 1962.

Smith, Russell A., Harry T. Edwards, and Theodore R. Clark, Jr. *Labor Relations Law in the Public Sector: Cases and Materials.* Indianapolis: Bobbs-Merrill, 1974.

Taft, Philip. *Economics and Problems of Labor.* New York: Stackpole and Heck, 1949.

Ulman, Lloyd. *Challenges to Collective Bargaining.* Englewood Cliffs, N.J.: Prentice-Hall, 1967.

U.S. Department of Labor. *Growth of Labor Law in the United States.* Washington, D.C.: GPO, 1967.

―――. *Brief History of the American Labor Movement.* Bicentennial ed. Washington, D.C.: GPO, 1976.

Walton, Richard E., and Robert B. McKersie. *A Behavioral Theory of Labor Negotiations: An Analysis of a Social Interaction System.* New York: McGraw-Hill, 1965.

Webb, Sidney, and Beatrice Webb. *Industrial Democracy.* London: Longman, Green, 1914.

Weber, Arnold R., ed. *The Structure of Collective Bargaining.* New York: Free Press, 1961.

Wellington, Harry H. *Labor and the Legal Process.* New Haven, Conn.: Yale University Press, 1968.

Wolfbein, Seymour L., ed. *Emerging Sectors of Collective Bargaining.* Braintree, Mass.: D. H. Mark, 1970.

Zack, Arnold M., and Richard I. Bloch. *Labor Agreement in Negotiations and Arbitration.* Washington, D.C.: Bureau of National Affairs, 1983.

Zagoria, Sam. ed. *Public Workers and Public Unions.* Englewood Cliffs, N.J.: Prentice-Hall, 1972.

Index of Terms

AAA. *See* American Arbitration
  Association
Ad hoc arbitration, 3
Administrative organizer. *See* Labor
  organizer
Advisory arbitration, 3
Affidavit, 3
AFL–CIO. *See* American Federation of
  Labor and Congress of Industrial
  Organizations
Afternoon shift. *See* Shift differentials
Agency plan. *See* Agency shop
Agency shop, 4
American Arbitration Association, 4
American Federation of Labor. *See*
  American Federation of Labor and
  Congress of Industrial Organizations;
  Craft union; Federation of Organized
  Trade and Labor Unions of the United
  States and Canada
American Federation of Labor and
  Congress of Industrial Organizations,
  5
Annual bonus payments, 5
Apprentice, 6
Apprenticeship contract. *See* Apprentice
Arbitrability, 6
Arbitration, 6. *See also* Interest
  arbitration; Rights arbitration
Arbitration issue. *See* Submission
Arbitration panel list, 7
Arbitrator. *See* Arbitration; Permanent
  arbitrator
Arbitrator's award, 7

Arbitrator's fee, 8
Arbitrator's oath, 8
Area standards picketing. *See*
  Informational picketing
Area-wide bargaining, 8
Arsenal of weapons, 8
Assignability clause. *See* Successor
  clause
Assimilated craft union. *See* Craft union
Associated bargaining. *See*
  Multiemployer bargaining
Attitudinal structuring, 9
Automatic checkoff. *See* Checkoff
Automatic contract renewal clause, 9
Automation, 9

Back-loaded contract, 10
Back-to-work movement, 10
Bad faith bargaining. *See* Bargaining in
  good faith
Bargaining a benefit, 10
Bargaining a cost, 10
Bargaining agent, 10
Bargaining in good faith, 10
Bargaining pattern, 10
Bargaining ploy, 10
Bargaining scope. *See* Scope of
  bargaining
Bargaining structure, 11
Bargaining systems. *See* Bargaining
  structure
Bargaining unit, 11
Base contract hourly rate, 12
Base contract hours, 12

Index of Court Decisions

Matthew A. Kelly is a member of the National Academy of Arbitrators and serves as an arbitrator and mediator on many labor-management contract issues in both the public and private sectors. He is a professor emeritus of the New York State School of Industrial and Labor Relations at Cornell University. His publications include *New Applications of Collective Bargaining* (co-authored with Edward Levin) and *Technological Changes and Human Development* (co-edited with Wayne L. Hodges).

Labor and Industrial Relations

Designed by Chris L. Smith.
Composed by Capitol Communication Systems
  in Times Roman text and display.
Printed by the Maple Press Company on
  50-lb. Warren's Sebago Eggshell Cream Offset paper.

Lightning Source UK Ltd.
Milton Keynes UK
UKHW011049160123
415430UK00001B/14